STEP BY STEP
COOKBOOK
RECIPES FROM AROUND THE WORLD

Compiled by Judith Ferguson
Photographed by Peter Barry
Designed by Philip Clucas and Sara Cooper
Recipes Prepared for Photography by
Jacqueline Bellefontaine

3552
© 1993 Coombe Books
This edition published in 1993 by Coombe Books for
Parragon Book Service Ltd,
707 High Street, Finchley, London N12 0BT
Printed and bound in Singapore
ISBN 1-85813-425-0

STEP BY STEP
COOKBOOK

RECIPES FROM AROUND THE WORLD

PARRAGON

CONTENTS

ACKNOWLEDGMENT
The publishers wish to thank the following suppliers for their kind assistance: Corning Ltd for providing Pyrex and other cookware; Habasco International Ltd for the loan of basketware, and Stent (Pottery) Ltd for the loan of glazed pottery oven-to-table ware. Thanks also to Old El Paso for permission to feature their recipes for Leg of Lamb with Chilli Sauce, Spare Ribs in Chilli and Cream Sauce, Mexican Kebabs, Mexican Beef Patties and Minute Steaks with Taco Sauce.

INTRODUCTION

Outside our kitchen windows is a wide world full of culinary delights that are there for the tasting. If we were to travel to six different countries, what would we discover?

In France we find delicate crêpes with a multitude of interesting and delicious fillings. We can taste celebrated dishes like onion soup with a bubbling cheese topping, or rich beef stew aromatic with herbs and red wine.

A visit to Italy finds us developing a taste for fresh pasta, tender veal, an amazing selection of antipasti and vegetable dishes exciting enough to be a separate course.

Greek food offers a taste of Mediterranean holidays, when we can feast on aubergines, courgettes, artichokes, olives and succulent lamb, all flavoured with the characteristic combination of herbs and spices.

Spanish food is an unexpected delight, and dishes like Paella, with its golden saffron rice and mixture of chicken, seafood, and spicy sausage, are favourites far beyond the Spanish border, while combinations of fruit and meat in the same recipe challenge our usual ideas about main dishes.

The last two countries on our lightning tour are ones we may never visit – Mexico and China.

Mexican food is sunny and vibrant. As in most countries that enjoy a warm climate, the taste of the food is spicy hot, but that can easily be adjusted to suit individual palates. Its festive colours make Mexican food perfect for parties.

Chinese food is known mainly through restaurants, and Cantonese dishes are the most popular. There is more to Chinese food, though: Peking cuisine, using pancakes and noodles instead of rice; Shanghai cuisine, offering many fish and seafood dishes, and Szechuan cuisine, with its rich, fiery sauces, are worth discovering.

Foreign travel has introduced us to hundreds of new ideas about what other people of the world eat. But though travel may broaden our taste experience, we are frequently more adventurous on foreign soil than we are in our own kitchens. The thought of faithfully trying to reproduce some sauce or pastry we have only tasted once is daunting to say the least. We wonder, too, if those special ingredients will be available, and if not, whether they can successfully be substituted. Then there are the recipes; are we capable of tackling them without personal guidance? All these considerations can dampen creative and adventurous spirits, and send us back to those tired old recipes we are so familiar with.

This book can't offer you a world trip, but it can bring the cuisines of six different countries into your kitchen; it can't offer you private lessons with famous chefs, but it can help you to perfect your own skills. The recipes are broken down into numbered steps which will prove invaluable, however experienced the cook and complex or simple the recipe. Each recipe includes step-by-step photographs of some of the techniques and methods that make the preparation easier, while Cook's Notes offer information on cooking and preparation times, helpful hints on how to vary recipes to suit available ingredients, and how to prevent problems, or solve them. And to show you how your masterpiece will turn out, we have included a full-page colour photograph of each and every dish.

Bon Voyage!

FRENCH COOKING

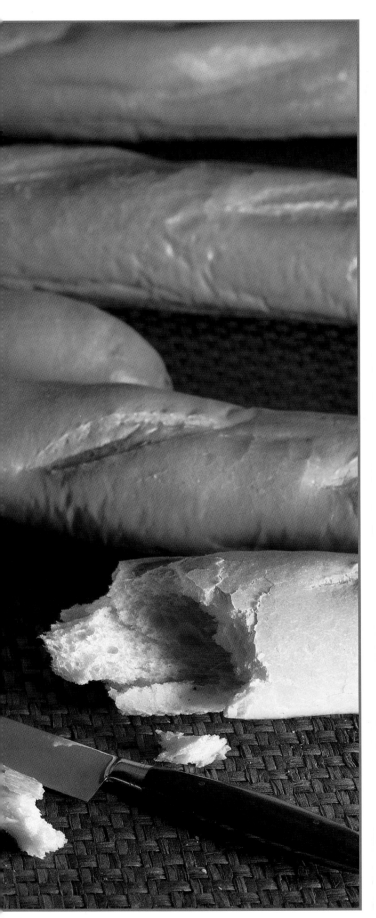

INTRODUCTION

The bureaucrats of France have divided the country, for offical purposes, into 95 départements, rather like counties. The cooks of France have a better way. They still rely on the old names of the regions, each with its own contribution to the country's legendary cuisine.

Brittany is the home of crêpes, thin French pancakes. Normandy is famous for its rich cream and apples. Cider comes from those apples and Calvados, an incendiary brandy, comes from the cider. And the seas around the coasts provide an abundance of seafood.

Champagne's main contribution is obvious, but there are also rich dishes of Flemish influence coming from this region on the Belgian border.

Touraine and the Loire are known as the garden of France, with the finest fruits and vegetables and some of the loveliest wines.

Ile de France has Paris at its centre, where hâute cuisine was born.

Alsace and Lorraine have been dominated by Germany more than once in their history and this is evident in many of their favourite dishes.

Burgundy and Bordeaux use their famous red and white wines to enhance their recipes, along with Dijon mustard from the former and truffles from the latter.

Franche Comté is a mountainous region that abounds with game and which produces robust dishes, many using its famous cheese.

Languedoc is on the Spanish border and its food shares many similarities with that of its neighbours, especially in the use of tomatoes, pepper and spicy sausage.

Provence is southern France, with all its colour and warmth reflected in food such as Salade Niçoise and Ratatouille.

With the whole history of French cuisine before us and with only limited space, we didn't know where to begin, or end! Then we thought of the many well-loved classics, the ones that conjure up the essence of the French gastronomic experience. With those, we felt, we couldn't go wrong.

SERVES 6

QUICHE LORRAINE

The history of this egg and bacon flan goes back
to the 16th century in the Lorraine region. Traditionally
it doesn't contain cheese, but it's a tasty addition.

Pâte Brisée

120g/4oz butter
180g/6oz plain flour, sifted
Pinch salt
1 egg
10ml/2 tsps ice water

Filling

6 strips smoked streaky bacon, cut into large dice
5ml/1 tsp butter or margarine
2 shallots, finely chopped
2 eggs plus 2 egg yolks
280ml/½ pint double cream
Salt, pepper and grated nutmeg
45g/3oz grated   Gruyère cheese (optional)

Step 2 Use rolling pin to lift pastry into dish.

1. Preheat the oven to 190°C/375°F/Gas Mark 5. To prepare the pastry, sift the flour and salt into a large bowl. Rub in the butter until the mixture looks like fine breadcrumbs - this may also be done in a food processor. Beat the egg lightly and mix into the flour by hand or with the machine. If the dough seems crumbly, add some of the water. Chill well before using.

2. Roll the pastry out to a circle about 5mm/¼ inch thick on a well-floured surface. Roll the pastry over a rolling pin and unroll it onto a 20-22.5cm/8-9 inch flan dish. Gently press the pastry into the bottom and up the sides of the dish, being careful not to stretch it. Trim off the excess pastry by running the rolling pin over the rim of the dish or using a sharp knife. Prick the bottom of the pastry lightly With a fork.

3. Place a circle of greaseproof paper on top of the pastry and fill with dry beans, or rice. Bake for about 10 minutes, remove the paper and filling. Prick base again lightly and return to the oven for another 3 minutes or until just beginning to brown. Allow the pastry to cool while preparing the filling.

4. Place the bacon in a small frying pan and fry over gentle heat until the fat begins to run. Raise the heat and cook until lightly browned and crisp. Place the bacon on paper towels to drain and add the butter to the pan if insufficient fat left. Add the chopped shallots and cook until just beginning to colour. Remove to the paper towel to drain with the bacon.

5. Beat the eggs and extra yolks, cream and seasonings together in a large bowl. Scatter the bacon and shallots over the bottom of the pastry case and ladle the custard filling on top of it. If using cheese, add with the custard.

6. Bake in the top half of the oven for about 25 minutes, or until the custard has puffed and browned and a knife inserted into the centre comes out clean. Allow to cool slightly and then remove from the dish, or serve directly from the dish.

Cook's Notes

Time
Preparation takes about 25 minutes, plus time for chilling the pastry. Cooking takes about 40 minutes.

Preparation

Baking a pastry case without a filling is called baking blind.
By pricking the bottom of the pastry, lining it with paper and filling with rice or beans you help the pastry hold its shape.

Variation
Use basic pastry and custard recipes, but substitute other ingredients such as ham, shellfish or vegetables for the bacon.

MAKES 1 OMELETTE

OMELETTE ROUSSILLON

Roussillon is on France's border with Spain.
The Spanish influence is evident in the use of
tomatoes and peppers combined with eggs.

3 eggs
Salt and pepper
15g/1 tbsp butter or margarine
¼ green pepper, cut into small dice
2 tomatoes, peeled, seeded and roughly chopped
60g/2oz ham, cut into small dice

1. Break the eggs into a bowl, season with salt and pepper and beat to mix thoroughly. Heat an omelette pan and drop in the butter, swirling it so that it coats the bottom and sides. When the butter stops foaming, add pepper and ham. Cook for 1-2 minutes to soften slightly, and add the tomatoes.

2. Pour in the eggs and, as they begin to cook, push the cooked portion with the flat of the fork to allow the uncooked portion underneath. Continue to lift the eggs and shake the pan to prevent them from sticking.

3. When the egg on top is still slightly creamy, fold ⅓ of the omelette to the centre and tip it out of the pan onto a warm serving dish, folded side down. Serve immediately.

Step 2 Push eggs with fork to let uncooked portion fall to the bottom of the pan.

Step 3 Fold ⅓ of the omelette to the middle.

Cook's Notes

Time
15 minutes preparation, 4-5 minutes cooking.

Preparation
To peel tomatoes, drop into boiling water for the count of 5 and remove to cold water. This loosens the peel.

Variations
Prepare the omelette in the same way, but use other ingredients such as mushrooms, chopped fresh herbs or spinach. If filling with cheese, sprinkle on before folding the omelette.

Serving Ideas
Accompany with French bread and a salad for a light lunch. May also be served as a first course.

SERVES 4-6

POTAGE À L'OIGNON GRATINÉ

Originally a Parisian speciality, every region in France now has a recipe for onion soup.

60g/2oz butter or margarine
900g/2lbs onions, peeled and thinly sliced
10ml/2 tsps sugar
Pinch salt and pepper
25g/1½ tbsps flour
5ml/1 tsp dried thyme
1.7 litres/3 pints brown stock
140ml/¼ pint dry white wine

Croûtes

12 2.5cm/1 inch slices French bread
15ml/1 tbsp olive oil
225g/8oz grated Gruyère cheese

1. Melt the butter in a large saucepan over a moderate heat. Stir in the onions and add the sugar. Cook, uncovered, over low heat, stirring occasionally, for 20-30 minutes or until the onions are golden brown.

2. Sprinkle the flour over the onions and cook for 2-3 minutes. Pour on the stock and stir to blend the flour. Add salt, pepper and thyme and return the soup to low heat. Simmer, partially covered, for another 30-40 minutes. Allow the soup to stand while preparing the croûtes.

3. Brush each side of the slices of bread lightly with olive oil and place them on a baking sheet. Bake in a preheated oven, 160°C/325°F/Gas Mark 3, for about 15 minutes. Turn the slices over and bake for a further 15 minutes, or until the bread is dry and lightly browned.

4. To serve, skim fat from the soup and ladle soup into a tureen or individual soup bowls. Place the croûtes on top of the soup and sprinkle over the grated cheese. Place the

Step 1 Brown the onions in a large saucepan with butter and sugar.

Step 3 Brush both sides of bread with olive oil and bake until lightly browned.

Step 4 Place the croûtes on soup and sprinkle with cheese.

soup in a hot oven and bake for 10-20 minutes, or until the cheese has melted. Brown under a preheated grill, if desired, before serving.

Cook's Notes

Time
Preparation takes about 20 minutes. Cooking takes about 50-60 minutes - 40 minutes for the soup, 30 minutes for the croûtes and 10-20 minutes to melt the cheese.

Cook's Tip
The addition of sugar helps the onions to brown.

SERVES 10

PÂTÉ DE CAMPAGNE

This is the pâté of French restaurants
known also as pâté maison or terrine
de chef. It should be coarse textured.

340g/¾lb pig liver, skinned and ducts removed
340g/¾lb pork, coarsely minced
120g/4oz veal, coarsely minced
225g/8oz pork fat, coarsely minced
1 clove garlic, crushed
2 shallots, finely chopped
225g/8oz streaky bacon, rind and bones removed
45ml/3 tbsps cognac
2.5ml/½ tsp ground allspice
Salt and freshly ground black pepper
5ml/1 tsp chopped fresh thyme or sage
120g/4oz smoked tongue or ham, cut into
    6mm/¼ inch cubes
30ml/2 tbsps double cream
1 large bay leaf

1.   Preheat the oven to 180°C/350°F/Gas Mark 4.

2.   Place the liver in a food processor and process once or twice to chop roughly. Add the minced meats and fat, shallots, garlic, Cognac, allspice, salt and pepper and thyme and process once or twice to mix. Do not over-work the mixture; it should be coarse.

3.   Stretch the strips of bacon with the back of a knife and line a terrine, metal baking pan or ovenproof glass dish. Stir the cream and the cubed tongue or ham into the meat mixture by hand and press it into the dish on top of the bacon.
Place the bay leaf on top and fold over any overlapping edges of bacon.

Step 3 Stretch the strips of bacon to line the terrine.

Step 5 Weight down the pâté with cans or scale weights.

4.   Cover the dish with a tight-fitting lid or two layers of foil and place the dish in a bain marie (dish of hand hot water) to come halfway up the sides of the terrine. Bake the pâté for 2 hours, or until the juices are clear. When it is done, remove it from the oven and remove the foil or lid.

5.   Cover with fresh foil and weight down the pâté with cans of food or balance scale weights. Allow to cool at room temperature and then refrigerate the pâté, still weighted, until completely chilled and firm.

6.   To serve, remove the weights and foil. Turn the pâté out and scrape off the fat. Slice through the bacon into thin slices.

Cook's Notes

Time
Preparation takes 25 minutes, plus refrigerating until firm.
Cooking takes about 2 hours.

Serving Ideas
The French often serve pâté with small pickled onions, and cornichons (small pickled gherkins). Serve as a first course with French bread or buttered toast, or with bread and salad for a light lunch.

Freezing
Cool and freeze in the dish. Pack well, label and store for up to 3 months. Allow to defrost in the refrigerator.

SERVES 4-6

GOUGÈRE AU JAMBON

This savoury pastry dish originated in Burgundy, but is also popular in the Champagne district and indeed in many other districts as well. Serve it as a starter or main course.

Choux Pastry

140ml/¼ pint water
60g/4 tbsps butter or margarine
60g/2oz plain flour, sifted
2 eggs, beaten
60g/2oz cheese, finely diced
Pinch salt, pepper and dry mustard

Ham Salpicon

15g/1 tbsp butter or margarine
15g/1 tbsp flour
140ml/¼ pint stock
60g/2oz mushrooms, sliced
10ml/2 tsps chopped fresh herbs
Salt and pepper
120g/4oz cooked ham, cut into julienne strips
30ml/2 tbsps grated cheese and dry breadcrumbs mixed

1. Preheat oven to 200°C/400°F/Gas Mark 6. Place the water for the pastry in a small saucepan. Cut the butter into small pieces and add to the water. Bring slowly to boil, making sure that the butter is completely melted before the water comes to a rapid boil. Turn up the heat and allow to boil rapidly for 30 seconds.

2. Sift the flour with a pinch of salt onto a sheet of paper. Take the pan off the heat and tip all the flour in at once. Stir quickly and vigorously until the mixture comes away from the sides of the pan. Spread onto a plate to cool.

3. Melt the butter in a small saucepan for the salpicon and add the flour. Cook for 1-2 minutes until pale straw coloured. Gradually whisk in the stock until smooth. Add a pinch of salt and pepper and the chopped herbs. Stir in the sliced mushrooms and ham and set aside.

Step 4 Beat in the egg gradually, but thoroughly.

Step 5 Spoon up the sides of the dish and fill the centre with the salpicon.

4. To continue with the pastry, add salt, pepper and dry mustard to the paste and return it to the saucepan. Gradually add the egg to the paste mixture, beating well between each addition – this may be done by hand, with an electric mixer or in a food processor. It may not be necessary to add all the egg. The mixture should be smooth and shiny and hold its shape when ready. If it is still too thick, beat in the remaining egg. Stir in the diced cheese by hand.

5. Spoon the mixture into a large ovenproof dish or 4 individual dishes, pushing the mixture slightly up the sides of the dish and leaving a well in the centre. Fill the centre with the ham salpicon and scatter over 30ml/2 tbsps grated cheese and dry breadcrumbs, mixed. Bake until the pastry is puffed and browned. Serve immediately.

Cook's Notes

 Serving Ideas
Cooked in individual dishes, this makes a nice first course for 6. Cooked in a large dish this makes a main course for 4 with a salad or vegetables.

 Time
Preparation takes about 30 minutes, cooking takes approximately 30-45 minutes if cooked in one large dish, 15-20 minutes for small individual dishes.

Variations
Vegetables, chicken, game or shellfish can be substituted for the ham.

SERVES 4

ARTICHAUTS AIOLI

Home-made mayonnaise is in a class by itself.
With the addition of garlic, it makes a perfect sauce
for artichokes – a typically Provencal starter.

4 medium-sized globe artichokes
1 slice lemon
1 bay leaf
Pinch salt

Sauce Aioli

2 egg yolks
280ml/½ pint olive oil
2 cloves garlic, peeled and crushed
Salt, pepper and lemon juice to taste
Chervil leaves to garnish

1. To prepare the artichokes, break off the stems and twist to remove any tough fibres. Trim the base so that the artichokes will stand upright. Trim the points from all the leaves and wash the artichokes well. Bring a large saucepan or stock pot full of water to the boil with the slice of lemon and bay leaf. Add a pinch of salt and, when the water is boiling, add the artichokes. Allow to cook for 25 minutes over a moderate heat. While the artichokes are cooking, prepare the sauce.

2. Whisk the egg yolks and garlic with a pinch of salt and pepper in a deep bowl or in a liquidiser or food processor. Add the olive oil a few drops at a time while whisking by hand, or in a thin, steady stream with the machine running. If preparing the sauce by hand, once half the oil is added, the remainder may be added in a thin steady stream. Add lemon juice once the sauce becomes very thick. When all the oil has been added, adjust the seasoning and add more lemon juice to taste.

Step 1 Trim the pointed ends from all the leaves of the artichoke.

Step 2 Add the oil to the egg yolks in a thin, steady stream to prevent curdling.

Step 3 Pull away one of the bottom leaves to see if the artichoke is cooked.

3. When the artichokes are cooked, the bottom leaves will pull away easily. Remove them from the water with a draining spoon and drain upside-down on paper towels or in a colander. Allow to cool and serve with the sauce aioli. Garnish with chervil.

Cook's Notes

Time
Preparation will take approximately 30 minutes and cooking approximately 25 minutes.

Cook's Tip
If this sauce or other mayonnaise needs to be thinned for coating, mix with a little hot water. A damp cloth under the mixing bowl will stop it spinning when making mayonnaise by hand.

Watchpoint
Sauce will curdle if oil is added too quickly. If it does, whisk another egg yolk and gradually beat curdled mixture into it. Sauce should come together again.

Serving Ideas
To eat, peel the leaves off one at a time and dip the fleshy part of the leaf into the sauce. Work down to the thistle or choke and remove with a teaspoon. Break artichoke bottom into pieces and dip into sauce.

SERVES 6-8

RATATOUILLE

This is probably one of the most familiar dishes from southern France. Either hot or cold, it's full of the warm sun of Provence.

2 aubergines, sliced and scored on both sides
4-6 courgettes, depending on size
45-90ml/3-6 tbsps olive oil
2 onions, peeled and thinly sliced
2 green peppers, seeded and cut into 2.5cm/1 inch
   pieces
10ml/2 tsps chopped fresh basil or 5ml/1 tsp dried basil
1 large clove garlic, crushed
900g/2lbs ripe tomatoes, peeled and quartered
Salt and pepper
140ml/¼ pint dry white wine

1. Lightly salt the aubergine slices and place on paper towels to drain for about 30 minutes. Rinse and pat dry. Slice the courgettes thickly and set them aside.

2. Pour 45ml/3 tbsps of the olive oil into a large frying pan and when hot, lightly brown the onions, green peppers and courgette slices. Remove the vegetables to a casserole and add the aubergine slices to the frying pan or saucepan. Cook to brown both sides lightly and place in the casserole with the other vegetables. Add extra oil while frying the vegetables as needed.

3. Add the garlic and tomatoes to the oil and cook for 1 minute. Add the garlic and tomatoes to the rest of the vegetables along with any remaining olive oil in the frying pan. Add basil, salt, pepper and wine and bring to the boil over moderate heat. Cover and reduce to simmering. If the vegetables need moisture during cooking, add a little white wine.

Step 1 Score and salt the aubergines and leave to drain.

Step 2 Brown all the vegetables lightly.

Step 3 Combine all the ingredients and simmer gently.

4. When the vegetables are tender, remove them from the casserole to a serving dish and boil any remaining liquid in the pan rapidly to reduce to about 30ml/2 tbsps. Pour over the ratatouille to serve.

Cook's Notes

Time
Leave aubergines to stand 30 minutes while preparing remaining vegetables. Cook combined ingredients for approximately 35 minutes.

Cook's Tip
Vegetables in this stew are traditionally served quite soft. If crisper vegetables are desired, shorten the cooking time but make sure the aubergine is thoroughly cooked.

SERVES 6

Fèves au Jambon

Touraine, where this dish comes from, is often
called the "Garden of France." Some of the finest
vegetables in the country are grown there.

900g/2lbs broad beans
140ml/¼ pint double cream
60g/2oz ham, cut into thin strips
15ml/1 tbsps chopped parsley or chervil

1. If using fresh beans, remove them from their pods. Cook
the beans in boiling salted water until tender, drain and
keep warm.

2. Combine the cream and ham in a small saucepan. Add
a pinch of salt and pepper and bring to the boil. Boil rapidly
for 5 minutes to thicken the cream.

Step 2 Reduce
the cream to
thicken by boiling.

Step 3 Peel off
outer skins of
beans before
adding to cream
and ham.

Step 1 Remove
fresh broad beans
from their pods.

3. If desired, peel the outer skins from the beans before
tossing with the cream and ham. Add parsley or chervil,
adjust the seasoning and reheat if necessary. Serve
immediately.

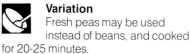

Cook's Notes

Time
Preparation takes 20-30
minutes, beans take
approximately 15 minutes to cook.

Variation
Fresh peas may be used
instead of beans, and cooked
for 20-25 minutes.

Cook's Tip
The finished dish has better
colour if the beans are peeled.

SERVES 4

TOMATES À LA LANGUEDOCIENNE

This dish from the Languedoc region of southern France
is similar to Provencal tomatoes, but is not as strong in flavour.

4 large ripe tomatoes
2 slices white bread, crusts removed
1 clove garlic, crushed
30ml/2 tbsps olive oil
15ml/1 tbsp chopped parsley
10ml/2 tsp chopped thyme or marjoram
Salt and pepper

1. Cut the tomatoes in half and score the cut surface. Sprinkle with salt and leave upside-down in a colander to drain. Allow the tomatoes to drain for 1-2 hours. Rinse the tomatoes and scoop out most of the juice and pulp.

2. Mix the olive oil and garlic together and brush both sides of the bread with the mixture, leaving it to soften. Chop the herbs and the bread together until well mixed.

Step 1 Scoop out seeds and juice to create space for the stuffing.

Step 2 Chop stuffing finely.

Step 3 Press in as much stuffing as possible.

3. Press the filling into the tomatoes and sprinkle with any remaining garlic and olive oil mixture.

4. Cook the tomatoes in an ovenproof dish under a pre-heated grill under low heat for the first 5 minutes. Then raise the dish or the heat to brown the tomatoes on top. Serve immediately.

Cook's Notes

Time
Preparation takes about 15 minutes, tomatoes need 1-2 hours to drain. Cooking takes approximately 5-8 minutes.

Preparation
Can be prepared up to grilling and finished off just before serving.

Serving Ideas
Serve as a first course or a side dish. Especially nice with lamb or beef.

SERVES 4-6

HARICOTS VERTS À L'OIGNON

These slender green beans are the classic French vegetable. Quickly blanched, then refreshed under cold water, they can be reheated and still stay beautifully green.

450g/1lb French beans
30g/1oz butter
1 medium onion
Salt and pepper

Step 1 Top and tail the beans, but leave them whole.

1. Top and tail the beans.

2. Cook the beans whole in boiling salted water for about 8-10 minutes. Meanwhile, finely chop the onion.

3. Melt the butter and fry the finely chopped onion until lightly brown. Drain the beans and toss them over heat to

Step 2 Finely chop the onion.

Step 3 Fry the onion in moderate heat until lightly browned.

dry. Pour the butter and onions over the beans and season with salt and pepper. Serve immediately.

Cook's Notes

 Watchpoint
Do not brown the onions too much as this will make them taste bitter.

Time
Preparation takes about 15 minutes, cooking takes 8-10 minutes.

 Preparation
Trim the beans with a sharp knife or kitchen scissors in large handfuls.

SERVES 6

POMMES DAUPHINÉ

The food from the mountainous province of Dauphiné is robust fare. Comté is the finest cheese of the area and like Gruyère it is creamy rather than stringy when melted.

1 clove garlic, peeled and crushed with the flat of a knife
30g/1oz butter
1kg/2¼lbs potatoes, peeled and thinly sliced
140ml/¼ pint single cream
Salt and pepper
180g/6oz grated Comté or Gruyère cheese
90g/3oz butter cut into very small dice

1. Preheat the oven to 200°C/400°F/Gas Mark 6. Rub the bottom and sides of a heavy baking dish with the crushed clove of garlic. Grease the bottom and sides liberally with the butter. Use a dish that can also be employed as a serving dish.

2. Spread half of the potato slices in the bottom of the dish, sprinkle with cheese, salt and pepper and dot with the butter dice. Top with the remaining slices of potato, neatly

Step 2 Layer the potatoes with cheese and seasonings.

Step 3 Pour cream into the side of the dish.

arranged. Sprinkle with the remaining cheese, salt, pepper and butter.

3. Pour the cream into the side of the dish around the potatoes.

4. Cook in the top part of the oven for 30-40 minutes, or until the potatoes are tender and the top is nicely browned. Serve immediately.

Step 1 Rub the dish with garlic and butter well.

Cook's Notes

Serving Ideas
A delicious side dish with poultry or roast meats, especially gammon.

Cook's Tip
Rubbing the dish with garlic gives just a hint of flavour.

Time
Preparation takes 25 minutes, cooking takes 30-40 minutes.

SERVES 4

POULET GRILLÉ AU LIMON

Crisp chicken with a tang of limes makes an elegant
yet quickly-made entrée. From the warm regions of
southern France, it is perfect for a summer meal.

2 900g/2lb chickens
4 limes
5ml/1 tsp basil
90ml/6 tbsps olive oil
Salt, pepper and sugar

1. Remove the leg ends, neck and wing tips from the chicken and discard them.

2. Split the chicken in half, cutting away the backbone completely and discarding it.

3. Loosen the ball and socket joint in the leg and flatten each half of the chicken by hitting it with the flat side of a cleaver.

4. Season the chicken on both sides with salt and pepper and sprinkle over the basil. Place the chicken in a shallow dish and pour over 30ml/2 tbsps of olive oil. Squeeze the juice from 2 of the limes over the chicken. Cover and leave to marinate in the refrigerator for 4 hours.

5. Heat the grill to its highest setting and preheat the oven to 190°C/375°F/Gas Mark 5. Remove the chicken from the marinade and place in the grill pan. Cook one side until golden brown and turn the pieces over. Sprinkle with 15ml/1 tbsp olive oil and brown the other side.

6. Place the chicken in a roasting dish, sprinkle with the

Step 2 Split the chicken in half and cut out the backbone.

Step 3 Bend chicken leg back to loosen ball and socket joint.

remaining oil and roast in the oven for about 25 minutes. Peel the remaining limes and slice them thinly. When the chicken is cooked, place the lime slices on top and sprinkle lightly with sugar. Place under the grill for a few minutes to caramelise the sugar and cook the limes. Place in a serving dish and spoon over any remaining marinade and the cooking juices. Serve immediately.

Cook's Notes

Time
Preparation takes about 25 minutes, plus 4 hours marinating, cooking takes about 35 minutes.

Variation
If limes are too expensive, use lemons instead. Vary the choice of herb.

Preparation
Chicken can be prepared and marinated overnight in the refrigerator.

Watchpoint
Sugar will burn and turn bitter quickly, so watch carefully while grilling.

Serving Ideas
Tomato salad makes a good accompaniment.

Cook's Tip
Marinating the chicken adds moisture as well as flavour.

SERVES 4

POULET SAUTÉ VALLÉE D'AUGE

This dish contains all the ingredients that Normandy is famous for - butter, cream, apples and Calvados.

60g/2oz butter or margarine
30ml/2 tbsps oil
1.5kg/3lbs chicken, cut into eight pieces
60ml/4 tbsps Calvados
90ml/6 tbsps chicken stock
2 apples, peeled, cored and coarsely chopped
2 sticks celery, finely chopped
1 shallot, finely chopped
2.5ml/½ tsp dried thyme, crumbled
90ml/6 tbsps double cream
2 egg yolks, lightly beaten
Salt and white pepper

Garnish

1 bunch watercress or small parsley sprigs
2 apples, quartered, cored and cut into cubes
30g/2 tbsps butter
Sugar

1. Melt half the butter and all of the oil in a large sauté pan over moderate heat. When the foam begins to subside, brown the chicken, a few pieces at a time, skin side down first. When all the chicken is browned, pour off most of the fat from the pan and return the chicken to the pan.

2. Pour the Calvados into a ladle or small saucepan and warm over gentle heat. Ignite with a match and pour, while still flaming, over the chicken. Shake the sauté pan gently until the flames subside. If the Calvados should flare up, cover the pan immediately with the lid.

3. Pour over the stock and scrape any browned chicken juices from the bottom of the pan. Set the chicken aside. Melt the remaining butter in a small saucepan or frying pan. Cook the chopped apples, shallot and celery and the thyme for about 10 minutes or until soft but not brown.

Step 1 Brown the chicken a few pieces at a time, skin side down first.

Step 4 Cook diced apple until it begins to caramelise.

Spoon over the chicken and return the pan to the high heat. Bring to the boil, then reduce heat, cover the pan and simmer 50 minutes. When the chicken is cooked, beat the eggs and cream. With a whisk, gradually beat in some of the hot sauce. Pour the mixture back into a saucepan and cook over a low heat for 2-3 minutes, stirring constantly until the sauce thickens and coats the back of a spoon. Season the sauce with salt and white pepper and set aside while preparing the garnish.

4. Put the butter in a small frying pan and when foaming, add the apple. Toss over a high heat until beginning to soften. Sprinkle with sugar and cook until the apple begins to caramelise. To serve, coat the chicken with the sauce and decorate with watercress or parsley. Spoon the caramelised apples over the chicken.

Cook's Notes

Time
Preparation takes 25-30 minutes, cooking takes 55-60 minutes.

Watchpoint
Do not allow the sauce to boil once the egg and cream is added or it will curdle.

Serving Ideas
Serve with sauté potatoes and fresh young peas.

SERVES 4

COQ AU VIN

Originating from the Burgundy region, this dish is
probably the most famous chicken recipe in all of France.
It is very rich, definitely a cold weather meal.

225g/8oz thick cut streaky bacon
430ml/¾ pint water
30g/1oz butter or margarine
12-16 button onions or shallots
225g/8oz mushrooms, left whole if small, quartered if
　　large
430ml/¾ pint dry red wine
1.5kg/3lb chicken, cut into eight pieces
45ml/3 tbsps brandy
1 bouquet garni
1 clove garlic, crushed
45g/3 tbsps flour
430ml/¾ pint chicken stock
30ml/2 tbsps chopped parsley
4 slices bread, crusts removed
Oil for frying
Salt and pepper

1. Preheat oven to 180°C/350°F/Gas Mark 4. Cut the
bacon into strips about 5mm/¼ inch thick. Bring water the
boil and blanch the bacon by simmering for 5 minutes.
Remove the bacon with a draining spoon and dry on paper
towels. Re-boil the water and drop in the onions. Allow them
to boil rapidly for 2-3 minutes and then plunge into cold
water and peel. Set the onions aside with the bacon.

2. Melt half the butter in a large frying pan over moderate
heat and add the bacon and onions. Fry over high heat,
stirring frequently and shaking the pan, until the bacon and
onions are golden brown. Remove them with a draining
spoon and leave on paper towels. Add the remaining butter
to the saucepan and cook the mushrooms for 1-2 minutes.
Remove them and set them aside with the onions and
bacon.

3. Reheat the frying pan and brown the chicken, a few
pieces at a time. When all the chicken is browned, transfer
it to a large ovenproof casserole.

Step 1 Cut the
bacon into small
strips and blanch
to remove excess
salt.

4. Pour the wine into a small saucepan and boil it to reduce
to about 280ml/½ pint. Pour the brandy into a small
saucepan or ladle and warm over low heat. Ignite with a
match and pour the brandy (while still flaming) over the
chicken. Shake the casserole carefully until the flames die
down. If the brandy should flare up, cover quickly with the
casserole lid. Add the bouquet garni and garlic to the
casserole.

5. Pour off all but 15ml/1 tbsp of fat from the frying pan and
stir in the flour. Cook over gentle heat, scraping any of the
browned chicken juices from the bottom of the pan. Pour in
the reduced wine and add the stock. Bring the sauce to the
boil over high heat, stirring constantly until thickened. Strain
over the chicken in the casserole and cover tightly.

6. Place in the oven and cook for 20 minutes. After that
time, add the bacon, onions and mushrooms and continue
cooking for a further 15-20 minutes, or until the chicken is
tender. Remove the bouquet garni and season with salt
and pepper.

7. Cut each of the bread slices into 4 triangles. Heat
enough oil in a large frying pan to cover the triangles of
bread. When the oil is very hot, add the bread triangles two
at a time and fry until golden brown and crisp. Drain on
paper towels. To serve, arrange the chicken in a deep dish,
pour over the sauce and vegetables and arrange the fried
bread croûtes around the outside of the dish. Sprinkle with
chopped parsley.

Cook's Notes

! Watchpoint
Make sure the oil for frying the
croûtes is hot enough when
the bread is added, otherwise croûtes
can be very oily.

Cook's Tip
Blanching the bacon in
boiling water removes excess
saltiness. Boiling the onions makes
them easier to peel.

Time
Preparation takes 30-40
minutes, cooking takes about
50 minutes.

SERVES 4

POULET FRICASSÉE

This is a white stew, enriched and thickened with an egg and cream mixture which is called a liaison in French cooking.

1.5kg/3lb chicken, quartered and skinned
60g/2oz butter or margarine
30g/1oz flour
570ml/1 pint chicken stock
1 bouquet garni
12-16 small onions, peeled
340g/12oz button mushrooms, whole if small, quartered if large
Juice and grated rind of ½ lemon
2 egg yolks
90ml/6 tbsps double cream
30ml/2 tbsps chopped parsley and thyme
Salt and pepper
45ml/3 tbsps milk (optional)
Garnish with lemon slices

1. Melt 45g/3 tbsps of the butter in a large sauté pan or frying pan. Place in the chicken in 1 layer and cook over gentle heat for about 5 minutes, or until the chicken is no longer pink. Do not allow the chicken to brown. If necessary, cook the chicken in two batches. When the chicken is sufficiently cooked, remove it from the pan and set aside.

2. Stir the flour into the butter remaining in the pan and cook over very low heat, stirring continuously for about 1 minute, or until a pale straw colour. Remove the pan from the heat and gradually beat in the chicken stock. When blended smoothly, add lemon juice and rind, return the pan to the heat and bring to the boil, whisking constantly. Reduce the heat and allow the sauce to simmer for 1 minute.

3. Return the chicken to the pan with any juices that have

Step 3 Tie a bay leaf, sprig of thyme and parsley stalks together to make a bouquet garni.

accumulated and add the bouquet garni. The sauce should almost cover the chicken. If it does not, add more stock or water. Bring to the boil, cover the pan and reduce the heat. Allow the chicken to simmer gently for 30 minutes.

4. Meanwhile, melt the remaining butter in a small frying pan, add the onions, cover and cook very gently for 10 minutes. Do not allow the onions to brown. Remove the onions from the pan with a draining spoon and add to the chicken. Cook the mushrooms in the remaining butter for 2 minutes. Set the mushrooms aside and add them to the chicken 10 minutes before the end of cooking.

5. Test the chicken by piercing a thigh portion with a sharp knife. If the juices run clear, the chicken is cooked. Transfer chicken and vegetables to a serving plate and discard the bouquet garni. Skim the sauce of any fat and boil it rapidly to reduce by almost half.

6. Blend the egg yolks and cream together and whisk-in several spoonfuls of the hot sauce. Return the egg yolk and cream mixture to the remaining sauce and cook gently for 2-3 minutes. Stir the sauce constantly and do not allow it to boil. If very thick, add milk. Adjust the seasoning, stir in the parsley and spoon over the chicken in a serving dish. Garnish with lemon slices.

Cook's Notes

Time
Preparation takes about 30 minutes, cooking takes about 30-40 minutes.

Serving Idea
Serve with boiled potatoes or rice.

Cook's Tip
Pour boiling water over the onions and leave to soak 10 minutes to make them easier to peel. Alternatively, prepare as for Coq au Vin.

Watchpoint
A fricassée is a white stew. Cook gently to avoid browning the ingredients.

SERVES 4-6

SALADE NIÇOISE

Almost everyone knows what Salade Niçoise is, but there are so many variations that it need never be ordinary.

1 head cos lettuce
2 hard-boiled eggs, quartered
2 large tomatoes, quartered
6 anchovy fillets
10 pitted black olives
15g/1 tbsp capers
¼ cucumber, diced but not peeled
1 can tuna fish, drained
4 large artichoke hearts, quartered

Dressing

90ml/6 tbsps olive oil
30ml/2 tbsps white or red wine vinegar
½ clove garlic, crushed
5ml/1 tsp mustard
Salt, pepper and lemon juice

Step 2 If anchovy fillets are thick, cut in half. Eggs, tomatoes, and artichoke hearts may be cut into smaller pieces if desired.

Step 2 Whisk the dressing ingredients well to blend thoroughly.

1. Wash the lettuce well, pat dry and break into bite-size pieces.

2. Prepare the remaining ingredients and toss with the lettuce in a large bowl, taking care not to break up the eggs. Mix the dressing ingredients together and whisk until well emulsified. Pour the dressing over the salad just before serving.

Step 1 Break well washed lettuce into bite-sized pieces.

Cook's Notes

Serving Ideas
Makes a light lunch with French bread or a first course.

Time
Preparation takes about 20 minutes, cooking approximately 9-10 minutes to hard-boil the eggs.

Variations
Add cubed new potatoes or lightly cooked French beans or broad beans. Substitute prawns for tuna, if desired.

Preparation
If cooking eggs in advance, leave them in cold water to prevent a grey ring forming around the yolks.

SERVES 4

MOULES MARINIÈRE

Brittany and Normandy are famous for mussels and for cream
and so cooks combined the two in one perfect seafood dish.

1.5kg/3lbs mussels
430ml/¾ pint dry cider or white wine
4 shallots, finely chopped
1 clove garlic, crushed
1 bouquet garni
140ml/¼ pint double cream
45g/3 tbsps butter, cut into small pieces
30ml/2 tbsps finely chopped parsley

1. Scrub the mussels well and remove the beards and any barnacles from the shells. Discard any mussels that have cracked shells and do not open when lightly tapped. Put the mussels into a large bowl and soak in cold water for at least 1 hour. Meanwhile, chop the parsley very finely.

2. Bring the cider or wine to the boil in a large stock pot and add the shallots, garlic and bouquet garni. Add the mussels, cover the pan and cook for 5 minutes. Shake the pan or stir the mussels around frequently until the shells open. Lift out the mussels into a large soup tureen or individual serving bowls. Discard any mussels that have not opened.

3. Reduce the cooking liquid by about half and strain into another saucepan. Add the cream and bring to the boil to thicken slightly. Beat in the butter, a few pieces at a time. Adjust the seasoning, add the parsley and pour the sauce over the mussels to serve.

Step 1 Break off thick stems from parsley and chop leaves very finely.

Step 2 Whilst cooking the mussels, stir or shake them frequently until the shells open.

Step 3 Beat the butter into the thickened cream and cooking liquid, a few pieces at a time.

Cook's Notes

Preparation
Soak mussels with a handful of flour or cornmeal in the water. They will then expel sand and take up the flour or cornmeal, which plumps them up.

Serving Ideas
Serve as a first course with French bread, or double the quantity of mussels to serve for a light main course.

Time
Preparation takes about 30 minutes, cooking takes about 15 minutes.

SERVES 4

RAIE AU BEURRE NOIR

It is amazing how the addition of simple ingredients
like browned butter, vinegar, capers and parsley can
turn an ordinary fish into a French masterpiece.

4 wings of skate
1 slice onion
2 parsley stalks
Pinch salt
6 black peppercorns

Beurre Noir

60g/4 tbsps butter
30ml/2 tbsps white wine vinegar
15ml/1 tbsp capers
15ml/1 tbsp chopped parsley (optional)

1. Place the skate in one layer in a large, deep pan.
Completely cover with water and add the onion, parsley
stalks, salt and peppercorns. Bring gently to the boil with
pan uncovered. Allow to simmer 15-20 minutes, or until the
skate is done.

2. Lift the fish out onto a serving dish and remove the skin
and any large pieces of bone. Take care not to break up the
fish.

3. Place the butter in a small pan and cook over high heat
until it begins to brown. Add the capers and immediately
remove the butter from the heat. Add the vinegar, which will
cause the butter to bubble. Add parsley, if using, and pour
immediately over the fish to serve.

Step 1 Place the skate in a pan with the poaching liquid and flavouring ingredients.

Step 2 Carefully remove any skin or large bones from the cooked fish, with a small knife.

Step 3 Pour sizzling butter over the fish to serve.

Cook's Notes

Variations
Chopped black olives, shallots or mushrooms may be used instead of or in addition to the capers. Add lemon juice instead of vinegar, if desired.

Cook's Tip
When the skate is done, it will pull away from the bones in long strips.

Time
Preparation takes about 20 minutes, cooking takes 15-20 minutes for the fish and about 5 minutes to brown the butter.

SERVES 4

ROUGETS À LA PROVENÇALE

Red Mullet is a very attractive fish, with a flavour quite
like prawns. It is also known as "woodcock of the sea"
because it is often served with the liver left inside.

30ml/2 tbsps olive oil
1 clove garlic, crushed
2 shallots, finely chopped
450g/1lb ripe tomatoes, peeled, seeded and sliced
10ml/2 tsps chopped marjoram and parsley mixed
90ml/3 fl oz dry white wine
Salt, pepper and pinch saffron
Oil for frying
2 small bulbs fennel, quartered and cored
4 red mullet, about 180g/6oz each
Flour mixed with salt and pepper

1. Heat 30ml/2 tbsps olive oil in a deep saucepan and add
the garlic and shallots. Cook 1-2 minutes to soften slightly,
then add tomatoes, herbs, wine, salt, pepper and saffron.
Allow to simmer, uncovered, for 30 minutes and set aside
while preparing the fennel and fish.

2. Pour about 60ml/4 tbsps oil into a large frying pan or
sauté pan. Place over moderate heat and add the fennel.
Cook quickly until the fennel is slightly browned. Lower the
heat and cook a further 5-10 minutes to soften the fennel.

3. Scale the fish, remove the gills and clean, leaving in the
liver if desired. Wash the fish and dry thoroughly. Trim the
fins and roll the fish in seasoned flour, shaking off the
excess.

4. When the fennel is tender, remove it from the pan and
set it aside. Fry the fish until golden brown on both sides,
about 2-3 minutes per side. Arrange the fish in a warm

Step 3 To scale
fish, run the blunt
end of a knife
from the tail to the
head.

Step 3 Remove
the fins with
kitchen scissors.

Step 3 Gut the
fish, cut along the
stomach and
remove insides,
leaving liver if
desired.

serving dish and surround with the fennel. Reheat the
sauce and spoon over the fish. Serve remaining sauce
separately.

Cook's Notes

Time
Preparation takes about 30
minutes unless the fish are
already cleaned. Cooking takes
approximately 40 minutes.

Watchpoint
Red mullet spoils quickly, so
use on day of purchase.

Cook's Tip
Saffron is expensive, so use a
pinch of turmeric as a
substitute for colour.

SERVES 4

TRUITE MEUNIÈRE AUX HERBES

The miller (meunier) caught trout fresh from the mill stream and his wife used the flour which was on hand to dredge them with, or so the story goes.

4 even-sized trout, cleaned and trimmed
Flour
Salt and pepper
120g/4oz butter
Juice of 1 lemon
30ml/2 tbsps chopped fresh herbs such as parsley, chervil, tarragon, thyme or marjoram
Lemon wedges to garnish

1. Trim the trout tails to make them more pointed. Rinse the trout well.

2. Dredge the trout with flour and shake off the excess. Season with salt and pepper. Heat half the butter in a very large sauté pan and, when foaming, place in the trout. It may be necessary to cook the trout in two batches to avoid overcrowding the pan.

3. Cook over fairly high heat on both sides to brown evenly. Depending on size, the trout should take 5-8 minutes per side to cook. The dorsal fin will pull out easily when the trout are cooked. Remove the trout to a serving dish and keep them warm.

4. Wipe out the pan and add the remaining butter. Cook over moderate heat until beginning to brown, then add the lemon juice and herbs. When the lemon juice is added, the butter will bubble up and sizzle. Pour immediately over the fish and serve with lemon wedges.

Step 1 Trim the trout tails with scissors to make them neater.

Step 2 Coat trout in flour, shaking off excess.

Step 3 Brown the trout on both sides. Dorsal fin will pull out easily when done.

Cook's Notes

Time
Preparation takes 15-20 minutes, cooking takes 5-8 minutes per side for the fish and about 5 minutes to brown the butter.

Preparation
If trout is coated in flour too soon before cooking it will become soggy.

Serving Ideas
Serve with new potatoes and peeled, cubed cucumber quickly sautéed in butter and chopped dill.

SERVES 6

ROGNONS À LA DIJONNAISE

Veal kidneys are lighter in colour and milder in flavour than lamb's kidneys. Since they must be quickly cooked, kidneys make an ideal sauté dish.

60g/2oz unsalted butter
3-4 whole veal kidneys
1-2 shallots, finely chopped
280ml/½ pint dry white wine
90g/3oz butter, softened
45ml/3 tbsps Dijon mustard
Salt, pepper and lemon juice to taste
30ml/2 tbsps chopped parsley

1. Melt the unsalted butter in a large sauté pan. Cut the kidneys into 2.5cm/1 inch pieces and remove any fat or core. When the butter stops foaming, add the kidneys and sauté them, uncovered, until they are light brown on all sides, about 10 minutes. Remove the kidneys from the pan and keep them warm.

2. Add the shallots to the pan and cook for about 1 minute, stirring frequently. Add the wine and bring to the boil, stirring constantly and scraping the pan to remove any browned juices. Allow to boil rapidly for 3-4 minutes until the wine is reduced to about 45ml/3 tbsps. Remove the pan from the heat.

3. Mix the remaining butter with the mustard, add salt and pepper and whisk the mixture into the reduced sauce. Return the kidneys to the pan, add the lemon juice and parsley and cook over low heat for 1-2 minutes to heat through. Serve immediately.

Step 1 Slice the kidneys and remove any fat or core.

Step 2 Add wine to the pan and scrape to remove browned juices (deglaze).

Step 3 Whisk the butter and mustard mixture gradually into the reduced sauce.

Cook's Notes

Variations
If veal kidneys are not available, use lamb kidneys instead.

Time
Preparation takes about 25 minutes, cooking 15-17 minutes.

Cook's Tip
Use unsalted butter for sautéeing or shallow frying because it does not burn as quickly as salted butter.

Watchpoint
Kidneys and all offal need careful, quick cooking or they will toughen.

SERVES 6

CARBONNADE À LA FLAMANDE

This carbonnade is a rich stew cooked in the
Flemish style with dark beer.

30ml/2 tbsps oil
675g/1½lbs braising steak
1 large onion, thinly sliced
30g/1oz flour
1 clove garlic, crushed
280ml/½ pint brown ale
280ml/½ pint hot water
Bouquet garni, salt and pepper
Pinch sugar and nutmeg
Dash red wine vinegar
6 slices French bread cut about 1.25cm/½ inch thick
French or Dijon mustard

1. Preheat the oven to 160°C/325°F/Gas Mark 3. Place the oil in a large, heavy-based frying pan. Cut the meat into 5cm/2 inch pieces and brown quickly on both sides in the oil. Brown the meat 5-6 pieces at a time to avoid crowding the pan.

2. Remove the meat when browned, lower the heat and add the onion. Cook until the onion is beginning to soften and colour. Stir in the flour and add the garlic. Add the hot water and ale.

3. Add the bouquet garni, season with salt and pepper, add the sugar, nutmeg and vinegar. Bring to the boil on top of the stove. Transfer to an ovenproof casserole with the meat, cover and cook in the oven for 2-2½ hours.

4. Fifteen minutes before serving, skim off any fat from the surface and reserve it. Spread the mustard on the bread and spoon some of the fat over each slice.

Step 1 Cut the meat into 5cm/2 inch pieces and brown in the oil.

Step 4 Spread the bread with mustard and spoon reserved fat over each slice.

Step 5 Place bread on top of casserole and push down slightly.

5. Place the bread on top of the casserole, pushing it down slightly. Cook a further 15-20 minutes, uncovered, or until the bread is browned and crisp.

Cook's Notes

Time
Preparation takes about 30 minutes, cooking takes 2-2¾ hours.

Watchpoint
Add the ale gradually to the hot casserole as it may foam up and boil over.

Preparation
The casserole may be prepared in advance and the bread added just before reheating to serve.

Variations
Add carrots or mushrooms, if desired.

Freezing
Prepare the casserole in advance without the bread topping. Cool it completely, pour into a freezer container, cover, label and freeze for up to 3 months.

SERVES 4-6

FILET DE PORC AUX PRUNEAUX

Tours, situated on the River Loire, is where this dish originated.
It is a rich dish with its creamy sauce and wine-soaked prunes.

2-3 small pork fillets
450g/1lb pitted prunes
570ml/1 pint white wine
45g/1½oz butter or margarine
15-30g/1-2 tbsps flour
Salt and pepper
15ml/1 tbsp redcurrant jelly
280ml/½ pint double cream

1. Soak the prunes in the white wine for about 1 hour and then put them into a very low oven to soften further. If the prunes are the ready-softened variety, soak for 20 minutes and omit the oven cooking.

2. Slice the pork fillet on the diagonal into 2.5cm/1-inch-thick pieces. Flatten them slightly with the palm of the hand. Dredge them with the flour, and melt the butter in a heavy pan. When the butter is foaming, put in the pork and cook until lightly browned on both sides. It may be necessary to cook the pork fillet in several batches.

3. Add half the soaking liquid from the prunes, cover the pan and cook very gently on moderate heat for about 45 minutes. If necessary, add more wine from the prunes while the pork is cooking.

4. When the pork is tender, pour liquid into a small saucepan and bring to the boil. Reduce by about ¼ and add the redcurrant jelly. Stir until dissolved and then add the cream. Bring the sauce back to the boil and allow to boil rapidly, stirring frequently. When the sauce is reduced and

Step 1 Cook the prunes in wine until softened.

Step 2 Slice the pork fillet and flatten the slices with the palm of the hand.

Step 4 Whisk the redcurrant jelly into the boiling sauce.

thickened slightly, pour over the meat and reheat. Add the prunes and transfer to a serving dish. Sprinkle with chopped parsley if desired.

Cook's Notes

Variation
Substitute water or stock for half of the wine measurement.

Time
Preparation about 25 minutes, cooking about 45 minutes.

Watchpoint
Pork fillet is very lean meat and can easily dry out. Be careful not to over-cook and make sure to use enough liquid.

Cook's Tip
Pork fillet may be cooked in a moderate oven for the same length of time.

SERVES 6

RAGOÛT DE VEAU MARENGO

There is an Italian influence evident in this stew recipe.
Pie veal is relatively inexpensive, thus making this
recipe easier on the budget than most veal dishes.

1.5kg/3lbs lean pie veal
60g/4 tbsps flour, mixed with salt and pepper
60ml/4 tbsps olive oil
2 shallots, finely chopped
½ clove garlic, crushed
90ml/6 tbsps dry white wine
280ml/½ pint brown stock
225g/8oz canned tomatoes, drained and crushed
1 bouquet garni
2 strips lemon peel
120g/4oz mushrooms, whole if small, quartered if large
45g/1½oz butter or margarine
30ml/2 tbsps chopped parsley (optional)

1. Preheat oven to 160°C/325°F/Gas Mark 3. Dredge the pieces of veal with the seasoned flour.

2. Pour the oil into a large sauté pan or heatproof casserole and place over a moderate heat. When the oil is hot, cook the veal 5-10 pieces at a time, depending upon the size of the pan. Brown the veal well on all sides, remove from the pan and set aside.

3. Add the shallots and garlic to the pan, lower the heat and cook until softened, but not coloured. Return the veal to the pan, add the wine, stock, tomatoes, bouquet garni and lemon peel. Bring to the boil on top of the stove, cover and cook in the oven for 1¼ hours, or until the veal is tender.

4. Meanwhile, melt the remaining butter in a frying pan and add the mushrooms and toss over a moderate heat for 2-3 minutes, stirring occasionally. When the veal is cooked, skim the surface of the sauce to remove excess fat and add the mushrooms with their cooking liquid to the veal. Cook for a further 10-15 minutes then remove the bouquet garni and the lemon peel.

Step 2 Brown the veal well on all sides.

Step 3 Cook the shallots and garlic gently until softened but not coloured.

Step 4 Tilt the pan to make it easier to skim off excess fat.

5. Transfer the veal and mushrooms to a serving dish and reduce the sauce to about 430ml/¾ pint by boiling rapidly. Adjust the seasoning and pour the sauce over the veal and mushrooms before serving. Reheat if necessary and garnish with chopped parsley, if desired.

Cook's Notes

Time
Preparation takes about 30 minutes, cooking approximately 1/1½ hours.

Serving Ideas
Serve with plain boiled potatoes, pasta or rice.

Watchpoint
Do not allow garlic to brown as it will turn bitter.

SERVES 6

NAVARIN PRINTANIER

This is a ragôut or brown stew traditionally made with
mutton chops. Substitute lamb for a milder taste.
Printanier means that a selection of vegetables is added.

90ml/6 tbsps vegetable oil
12 even-sized lamb cutlets
Flour mixed with salt, pepper and a pinch dried thyme
2 shallots, finely chopped
1 clove garlic, crushed
570ml/1 pint brown stock
140ml/¼ pint dry white wine
5 tomatoes, peeled, seeded and coarsely chopped
1 bouquet garni

Spring Vegetables

12 new potatoes, scrubbed but not peeled
8 baby carrots, scraped (if green tops are in good
    condition, leave on)
6 small turnips, peeled and left whole
340g/12oz frozen petits pois
225g/8oz French beans cut into 2.5cm/1 inch lengths on
    the diagonal
12 spring onions, roots ends trimmed and green tops
    trimmed about 7.5cm/3 inches from the ends
15ml/1 tbsps chopped parsley (optional)

Remove the cores from the tomatoes.

Plunge into boiling water for a few seconds.

Refresh in cold water them peel off skins.

1. Preheat the oven to 180°C/350°F/Gas Mark 4. Heat about half the oil in a large, heavy-based frying pan. Dredge the lamb cutlets with the flour mixture, shaking off the excess. Brown the lamb cutlets 4 at a time, adding more oil if necessary. When the cutlets are brown on all sides, remove them to a heavy casserole.

2. Remove most of the oil from the pan and cook the shallots and garlic over moderate heat, stirring constantly. Add the stock and bring to the boil, scraping the bottom of the pan to remove the browned meat juices. Allow to boil rapidly to reduce slightly, then add the tomatoes.

3. Pour the sauce over the lamb, turning the cutlets to coat all of them with the sauce. Add the bouquet garni, cover tightly and cook in the oven for about 30 minutes, or until the lamb is tender.

4. After about 10 minutes, add the potatoes and carrots to the lamb.

5. Add the turnips, French beans, peas and spring onions 15 minutes before the end of cooking time.

6. After 30 minutes, remove the lamb and any vegetables that are tender. Boil the sauce rapidly to reduce it and cook any vegetables that need extra time. Pour the sauce over the lamb and vegetables to serve and sprinkle with chopped parsley, if desired.

Cook's Notes

 Variations
Substitute other vegetables as desired, but always cook root vegetables first. Canned tomatoes may be substituted for fresh ones.

 Time
Preparation takes 30-40 minutes, cooking about 30-35 minutes.

SERVES 6

Poires au Vin Rouge

A marvellous recipe for using firm cooking pears to their best advantage. They look beautiful served in a glass bowl.

570ml/1 pint dry red wine
Juice of half lemon
1 strip lemon peel
225g/8oz sugar
1 small piece stick cinnamon
6 small ripe but firm pears, peeled, but with the stalks left on

1. Bring the wine, lemon juice and peel, sugar and cinnamon to the boil in a deep saucepan or ovenproof casserole that will accommodate 6 pears snugly. Stir until the sugar dissolves and then allow to boil rapidly for 1 minute.

2. Peel the pears lengthwise and remove the small eye from the bottom of each pear. Place the pears upright in the simmering wine. Allow to cook slowly for 20 minutes, or until they are soft but not mushy. If the syrup does not completely cover the pears, allow the pears to cook on their sides and turn and baste them frequently. Cool the pears in the syrup until lukewarm and then remove them. Remove the cinnamon stick and the lemon peel and discard.

3. If the syrup is still very thin, remove pears, boil to reduce slightly or mix 15ml/1 tbsp arrowroot with a little cold water, add some of the warm syrup and return the arrowroot to the rest of the syrup. Bring to the boil, stirring constantly until thickened and cleared. Spoon the syrup over the pears and refrigerate or serve warm. Pears may be decorated with flaked toasted almonds and served with lightly whipped cream if desired.

Step 2 Peel the pears lengthwise and remove the eye from the bottom.

Step 2 Place the pears in the simmering wine, upright or on their sides.

Step 3 Spoon the syrup over the pears and decorate with almonds.

Cook's Notes

Variations
Pears may be cooked au Vin Blanc with a dry white wine or in fruit juice.

Cook's Tip
Add a few drops of red food colouring to the syrup if the pears appear too pale when cooked.

Time
Preparation takes about 25 minutes, cooking 20 minutes.

SERVES 6

MOUSSE AU CHOCOLAT BASQUE

This mousse is a dark chocolate mixture which
sets to a rich cream in the refrigerator.

180g/6oz plain chocolate
75ml/2½ fl oz water
15g/1 tbsp butter
3 eggs, separated
30ml/2 tbsps rum

1. Chop the chocolate into small pieces and combine with
the water in a heavy-based saucepan. Cook over very
gentle heat so that the chocolate and water form a thick
cream. Remove from the heat, allow to cool slightly and
then beat in the butter.

2. Add the rum and beat in the egg yolks one at a time.

Step 1 Melt chopped chocolate in water over gentle heat.

Step 2 Beat in egg yolks one at a time.

Step 3 Fold lightly whipped egg whites into the chocolate mixture.

3. Whip the egg whites until stiff but not dry and fold
thoroughly into the chocolate mixture. Pour into small pots
or ramekins and chill overnight. Finish with whipped cream
and chocolate curls to serve, if desired.

Cook's Notes

Watchpoint
Never melt chocolate over
direct heat without using
some liquid. Do not over-whip egg
whites; this will make the mousse
grainy in texture.

Variations
Add strong coffee in place of
water, or flavour with grated
orange rind. Use juice instead of the
water and add Grand Marnier instead
of rum.

Time
Preparation takes 20 minutes,
cooking takes approximately
10 minutes to melt the chocolate.

SERVES 6

SOUFFLÉ AU CITRON FROID

A cold soufflé is really a mousse in disguise. It doesn't
"rise" in the refrigerator, but is set above the rim of
its dish with the help of a paper collar and gelatine.

3 eggs, separated
180g/6oz sugar
Grated rind and juice of 2 small lemons
15g/1 tbsp gelatine dissolved in 45-60ml/3-4 tbsps water
180ml/6 fl oz cream, lightly whipped

Decoration

140ml/¼ pint cream, whipped
Thin strips lemon rind or lemon twists
Finely chopped almonds or pistachios

1. Tie a double thickness of greaseproof paper around a
soufflé dish to stand about 7.5cm/3 inches above the rim of
the dish.

2. Beat the egg yolks in a large bowl until thick and lemon
coloured. Add the sugar gradually and then the lemon rind
and juice. Set the bowl over a pan of hot water and whisk
until the mixture is thick and leaves a ribbon trail. Remove
the bowl from the heat and whisk a few minutes longer.

3. Melt the gelatine and the water until clear, pour into the
lemon mixture and stir thoroughly. Set the bowl over ice and
stir until beginning to thicken.

4. Whip the egg whites until stiff but not dry and fold into
the lemon mixture along with the lightly whipped cream.
Pour into the prepared soufflé dish and chill in the
refrigerator until the gelatine sets completely. To serve, peel
off the paper carefully and spread some of the cream on the
sides of the mixture. Press finely chopped nuts into the
cream. Pipe the remaining cream into rosettes on top of the
soufflé and decorate with strips of rind or lemon twists.

Step 2 When
thick enough,
mixture will leave
a ribbon trail.

Step 4 Fold the
egg whites and
cream into the
mixture and pour
into the prepared
dish.

Step 4 Peel off
the paper
carefully.

Cook's Notes

 Time
Preparation takes about 25-30
minutes.

 Watchpoint
Do not allow gelatine to boil; it
will loose its setting qualities.

 Cook's Tip
If gelatine sets before cream
and egg whites are added,
gently reheat the lemon mixture,
stirring constantly until soft again.

 Preparation
Do not fill the dish more than
3cm/1½ inches above the rim
of the dish or, once decorated, the
mixture will collapse.

SERVES 6

CRÊPES AU CHOCOLAT ET FRAMBOISES

Crêpes Suzette may be more famous, but these,
filled with chocolate and raspberry, are incredibly delicious.

Crêpe Batter

430ml/¾ pint milk and water mixed
4 eggs
Pinch salt
225g/8oz plain flour, sifted
15ml/1 tbsp sugar
60ml/4 tbsps melted butter or oil

Filling

225g/8oz plain dessert chocolate, grated
120g/4oz seedless raspberry jam
Whipped cream and chopped, browned hazelnuts

Step 1 Cook until edges are brown then turn over.

Step 1 When underside is lightly speckled with brown, slide onto a plate.

1. Put all the ingredients for the crêpes into a food processor or blender and process for about 1 minute, pushing down the sides occasionally. Process a few seconds more to blend thoroughly. Leave, covered, in a cool place for 30 minutes to 1 hour. The consistency of the batter should be that of thin cream. Add more milk if necessary. Brush a crêpe pan or small frying pan lightly with oil and place over high heat. When a slight haze forms, pour a large spoonful of the batter into the pan and swirl the pan to cover the base. Pour out any excess into a separate bowl. Cook on one side until just beginning to brown around the edges. Turn over and cook on the other side until lightly speckled with brown. Slide each crêpe onto a plate and repeat using the remaining batter. Reheat the pan occasionally in between cooking each crêpe. The amount of batter should make 12 crêpes.

2. As the crêpes are cooked, sprinkle them evenly with grated chocolate and divide the raspberry jam among all the crêpes. Roll them up so that the jam shows at the ends, or fold into triangles.

3. Reheat in a moderate oven for about 10 minutes before serving. Top with whipped cream and a sprinkling of browned nuts.

Cook's Notes

 Time
Preparation takes about 30 minutes, cooking takes about 30 minutes.

 Variation
To make savoury crêpes, leave out the sugar but prepare them in the same way.

 Watchpoint
Batter works best when only one quarter water to three quarters milk used in the mixture. The batter must stand for at least 30 minutes before use to allow it too thicken properly.

 Freezing
Allow crêpes to cool completely and stack between sheets of nonstick or wax paper. Place in a plastic bag and freeze for up to 3 months. Defrost completely but separate and reheat as needed.

MAKES 12

ECLAIRS

Think of French pastry and eclairs immediately spring
to mind. French patisseries - pastry shops - sell
them filled and iced in many different flavours.

Choux Pastry

200ml/7 fl oz water
90g/3oz butter or margarine
90g/3oz plain flour, sifted
3 eggs

Crème Patissière

1 whole egg
1 egg yolk
60g/2oz sugar
15g/1 tbsp cornflour
25g/1½ tbsps flour
280ml/½ pint milk
Few drops vanilla essence

Glacé Icing

450g/1lb icing sugar
Hot water
Few drops vanilla essence

1. Preheat the oven to 180°C/350°F/Gas Mark 4.

2. Combine the water and butter for the pastry in a deep saucepan and bring to the boil. Once boiling rapidly, take the pan off the heat. Stir in the flour all at once and beat just until the mixture leaves the sides of the pan. Spread out onto a plate to cool. When cool, return to the saucepan and gradually add the beaten egg. Beat in well in between each addition of egg until the paste is smooth and shiny – should be of soft dropping consistency, but holding its shape well. It may not be necessary to add all the egg. Pipe or spoon into strips of about 7.5cm/3 inches long, spaced well apart on lightly-greased baking sheets.

3. Sprinkle the sheets lightly with water and place in the oven. Immediately increase oven temperature to

Step 6 Cut the eclairs almost in half. Pipe or spoon in the crème patissière.

190°C/375°F/Gas Mark 5. Make sure the pastry is very crisp before removing it from the oven, this will take about 20-30 minutes cooking time. If the pastry is not crisp, return to the oven for a further 5 minutes.

4. To prepare the Crème Patissière, separate the whole egg and reserve the white. Mix the egg yolks and sugar together, sift in the flours and add about half the milk, stirring well. Bring the remainder of the milk to the boil and pour onto the yolk mixture, stirring constantly. Return the mixture to the pan and stir over heat until boiling point is reached. Take off the heat and whip the egg white until stiff but not dry. Fold the egg white into the mixture and return to the heat. Cook gently for about 1 minute, stirring occasionally. Add the vanilla essence at this point. Pour the mixture into a bowl and press a sheet of greaseproof paper directly onto the surface of the crème and leave it to cool.

5. Sift the icing sugar into a bowl and add hot water, stirring constantly until the mixture is of thick coating consistency. The icing should cover the back of a wooden spoon but run off slowly. Add the vanilla essence.

6. To assemble the eclairs, cut the choux pastry almost in half lengthways and either pipe or spoon in the Crème Patissière. Using a large spoon, coat the top of each eclair with a smooth layer of glacé icing. Allow the icing to set before serving.

Cook's Notes

Time
Preparation takes about 40 minutes, cooking takes about 30-40 minutes.

Cook's Tip
Water sprinkled on the baking sheet creates steam to help pastry rise.

Preparation
5-10ml/1-2 tsps oil added to the icing will keep it shiny when set.

ITALIAN COOKING

INTRODUCTION

The food of Italy is among the best-loved in the world. The ingredients reflect all the warmth, colour and variety that the country has to offer. There are beautiful lemons, limes and oranges in the orchards up and down the peninsula. Miles and miles of coastline mean a plentiful supply of fish and seafood. Tomatoes, peppers and most other vegetables flourish in the sun throughout spring and summer. Herbs, garlic and the fragrant bouquet of olive oil all provide taste interest. Cheeses and cured meats are superb in quality and selection.

When putting together a traditional Italian meal, begin with an antipasto, which means 'before the pasta'. Follow with a pasta dish or soup, but not both. Then choose a main course of fish, meat or poultry accompanied by polenta, risotto or potatoes and a salad. A sweet is served next, and this can be as rich as Zuppa Inglese or as simple as fresh fruit. Cheese is considered an antipasto and not the final course.

Vegetables are highly prized in Italy and often appear as a separate course before the main dish. Sicilian Caponata is a perfect choice, hot or cold.

If all that food seems too much, turn to Italy's best-known contributions, pizza and pasta. Once you make your own pizza dough, you won't go back to frozen pizzas again! Home-made pasta is also a wonderful thing and easy to make, too, but if you can't find time, try to buy fresh pasta, which is readily available these days.

There is room for endless creativity with sauces for pastas and toppings for pizzas so boredom need never set in. Just add a salad and perhaps a glorious pudding like cassata for an authentic taste of Italy that is as close as your kitchen.

SERVES 6-8

BRUSCHETTA WITH TOMATOES

Cooked over a wood fire in the traditional way, or more
conveniently in the oven, tomatoes, basil and crisp bread
make an unusual and informal starter.

18 slices of crusty Italian bread, cut 2.5cm/1 inch thick
2 cloves garlic, crushed
140ml/¼ pint olive oil
Salt and pepper
18 large fresh basil leaves
4-5 ripe tomatoes, depending on size

Step 3 Warm the oil in a small saucepan and pour over the bread.

Step 1 Toast the bread in the oven until golden brown on both sides and spread each side with some of the garlic.

Step 4 Slice the tomatoes with a serrated knife and arrange on top of the bread with the basil leaves.

1. Place the bread slices on a baking sheet and toast for about 10 minutes on each side at 190°C/375°F/Gas Mark 5.

2. Spread some of the garlic on both sides of each slice.

3. Heat the oil gently in a small saucepan. Arrange the bread on a serving plate and immediately pour over the warm oil. Sprinkle with salt and pepper.

4. Slice the tomatoes in 1.25cm/½ inch rounds. Place one basil leaf and one slice of tomato on each slice of bread and serve immediately.

Cook's Notes

 Time
Preparation takes about 15 minutes, cooking time about 25 minutes.

 Variations
French bread may be used if Italian bread is not available, but the taste will be different. White or brown bread may be used.

 Serving Ideas
May be served as a first course or as cocktail savouries.

SERVES 4

MELON AND PROSCIUTTO

This is one of the best-loved Italian starters. It deserves
to be, because the flavour of a ripe melon and the richness
of Italian ham complement one another perfectly.

1 large ripe melon
16 thin slices prosciutto ham

Step 1 Cut the melon in half and scoop out the seeds.

Step 2 Cut the melon in quarters and carefully remove the rind. Cut into thin slices.

Step 3 Roll up the melon in the prosciutto to serve.

1. Cut the melon in half lengthways, scoop out the seeds and discard them.

2. Cut the melon into quarters and carefully pare off the rind. Cut each quarter into four slices.

3. Wrap each slice of melon in a slice of prosciutto and place on a serving dish. Alternatively, place the melon slices on the dish and cover with the slices of prosciutto, leaving the ends of the melon showing. Serve immediately.

Cook's Notes

Time
Preparation takes about 20 minutes.

Variations
Place the slices of prosciutto flat on serving plates or roll them up into cigar shapes. Serve with quartered fresh figs instead of melon.

SERVES 6-8

SEAFOOD TORTA

A very stylish version of a fish flan, this makes
a perfect accompaniment to an Italian aperitif or
serves as a light supper dish with salad.

Pastry

225g/8oz plain flour, sifted
120g/4oz unsalted butter
Pinch salt
60ml/4 tbsps cold milk

Filling

120g/4oz whitefish fillets (plaice, sole or cod)
225g/8oz cooked prawns
120g/4oz dressed crab
140ml/¼ pint white wine
140ml/¼ pint water
Large pinch hot pepper flakes
Salt and pepper
30g/2 tbsps butter
30g/2 tbsps flour
1 clove garlic, crushed
2 egg yolks
140ml/¼ pint double cream
Chopped fresh parsley

1. To prepare the pastry, sift the flour into a bowl or onto a work surface. Cut the butter into small pieces and begin mixing them into the flour. Mix until the mixture resembles fine breadcrumbs - this may also be done in a food processor. Make a well in the flour, pour in the milk and add the pinch of salt. Mix with a fork, gradually incorporating the butter and flour mixture from the sides until all the ingredients are mixed. This may also be done in a food processor.

2. Form the dough into a ball and knead for about 1 minute. Leave the dough in the refrigerator for about 1 hour.

3. To prepare the filling, cook whitefish fillets in the water and wine with the red pepper flakes for about 10 minutes or

Step 5 Press a sheet of grease-proof paper on the pastry and fill with beans, rice or baking beans to weight down.

until just firm to the touch. When the fish is cooked, remove it from the liquid and flake it into a bowl with the prawns and the crab meat. Reserve the cooking liquid.

4. Melt the butter in a small saucepan and stir in the flour. Gradually strain on the cooking liquid from the fish, stirring constantly until smooth. Add garlic, place over high heat and bring to the boil. Lower the heat and allow to cook for 1 minute. Add to the fish in the bowl and set aside to cool.

5. On a well-floured surface, roll out the pastry and transfer it with a rolling pin to a tart pan with a removable base. Press the dough into the pan and cut off any excess. Prick the pastry base lightly with a fork and place a sheet of greaseproof paper inside. Fill with rice, dried beans or baking beans and chill for 30 minutes. Bake the pastry shell blind for 15 minutes in a 190°C/375°F/Gas Mark 5 oven.

6. While the pastry is baking, combine the egg yolks, cream and parsley and stir into the fish filling. Adjust the seasoning with salt and pepper. When the pastry is ready, remove the paper and beans and pour in the filling.

7. Return the tart to the oven and bake for a further 25 minutes. Allow to cool slightly and then remove from the pan. Transfer to a serving dish and slice before serving.

Cook's Notes

Time
Filling takes about 15-20 minutes to prepare. Pastry takes about 20 minutes to prepare plus 1 hour refrigeration. Tart takes about 40 minutes to cook.

Variation
Substitute lobster for the whitefish for a special occasion or dinner party first course.

Freezing
Make the pastry in advance and wrap it very well. Label and freeze for up to 3 months. Defrost at room temperature before using. Also freeze uncooked in the flan dish.

SERVES 8-10

MINESTRONE

Everyone's favourite Italian soup doesn't always have to contain pasta. Our's substitutes potatoes and is hearty enough to serve as a meal.

225g/8oz dried white cannellini beans
30ml/2 tbsps olive oil
1 large ham bone, preferably prosciutto
1 onion, chopped
2 cloves garlic, crushed
4 sticks celery, sliced
2 carrots, diced
1 small head Savoy cabbage or 450g/1lb fresh spinach, well washed
120g/4oz French beans, cut into 2.5cm/1 inch lengths
225g/8oz tomatoes, peeled, seeded and diced
1 dried red chilli pepper
2.5 litres/5 pints water (or half beef stock)
Salt and pepper
1 sprig fresh rosemary
1 bay leaf
3 potatoes, peeled and cut into small dice
3 courgettes, trimmed and cut into small dice
15ml/1 tbsp chopped fresh basil
15ml/1 tbsp chopped fresh parsley
Grated Parmesan cheese
Salt and pepper

1. Place the beans in a large bowl, cover with cold water and leave to soak overnight.

2. Heat the oil in a large stock pot and add ham bone, onion and garlic. Cook until onion has softened but not coloured. Add the celery, carrots, cabbage and green beans. If using spinach, reserve until later.

3. Drain the beans and add them to the pot with the tomatoes and the chilli pepper. Add the water and bring to the boil, skimming the surface as necessary. Add the rosemary and bay leaf and simmer, uncovered, until the beans are tender, about 1¼ hours.

4. Add the potatoes and cook for the further 20 minutes.

5. Add the courgettes and spinach and cook, skimming the surface, about 20 minutes longer. Remove the ham bone, rosemary and bay leaf and add basil and parsley. Serve with Parmesan cheese.

Step 1 Soak beans overnight in enough water to cover. They will swell in size.

Step 3 Using a metal spoon, skim any fat from the surface of the soup as it cooks.

Cook's Notes

Time
Preparation takes about 20 minutes plus overnight soaking for the beans. Cooking takes about 2 hours.

Watchpoint
The beans must be thoroughly cooked - it can be dangerous to eat them insufficiently cooked.

Serving Ideas
If desired, cooked pasta may be substituted for the potatoes and added at the end of cooking time.

Variation
Other varieties of white beans may be used and canned beans may also be used. If using canned beans, add them with courgettes and spinach. Other vegetables such as broccoli, turnips, leeks or quartered Brussels sprouts, may be substituted.

SERVES 4-6

Spinach Gnocchi

Gnocchi are dumplings that are served like pasta. A dish of gnocchi can be served as a first course or as a light main course, sprinkled with cheese or accompanied by a sauce.

120g/4oz chopped, frozen spinach
225g/8oz ricotta cheese
90g/3oz Parmesan cheese
Salt and pepper
Freshly grated nutmeg
1 egg, slightly beaten
45g/3 tbsps butter

Step 3 Shape the gnocchi mixture with well-floured hands into ovals or balls.

Step 1 Press the spinach between two plates to remove excess moisture.

Step 5 Gnocchi will float to the surface of the water when cooked. Remove with a draining spoon.

1. Defrost the spinach and press it between two plates to extract all the moisture.

2. Mix the spinach with the ricotta cheese, half the Parmesan cheese, salt, pepper and nutmeg. Gradually add the egg, beating well until the mixture holds together when shaped.

3. With floured hands, shape the mixture into oval shapes. Use about 15ml/1 tbsp mixture for each gnocchi.

4. Lower into simmering water, 3 or 4 at a time, and allow to

cook gently until the gnocchi float to the surface, about 1-2 minutes.

5. Remove with a draining spoon and place in a well buttered ovenproof dish.

6. When all the gnocchi are cooked, sprinkle on the remaining Parmesan cheese and dot with the remaining butter.

7. Reheat 10 minutes in a hot oven and brown under a pre-heated grill before serving.

Cook's Notes

Time
Preparation takes about 15 minutes, cooking takes about 20 minutes.

Serving Ideas
Accompany with a tomato or cheese sauce for a light meal with a salad and hot bread.

Cook's Tip
Gnocchi are best served soon after they are cooked. If allowed to stand overnight they become very heavy.

SERVES 4

TOMATO SALAD RUSTICA

An informal salad with a country flavour, this is
perfect with barbecued meat, poultry or fish.

450g/1lb tomatoes
1 onion
4-6 anchovies
Milk
2 tbsps capers
1 tsp chopped fresh oregano or basil
90ml/6 tbsps olive oil
15ml/1 tbsp lemon juice

Step 1 Remove the cores from the quartered tomatoes and slice again if large.

Step 1 Soak the anchovies in milk, rinse well and dry before using.

Step 2 Hold the onion with a fork to steady it while slicing into rings.

1. Soak the anchovies in a little milk before using, rinse, pat dry and chop. Cut the tomatoes into quarters and remove the cores. Slice each quarter in half again and place them in a serving bowl.

2. Slice the onion into rounds and then separate into rings. Scatter over the tomatoes. Cut the anchovies into small pieces and add to the tomatoes and onions along with the capers.

3. Mix the herbs, salt, pepper, oil and lemon juice together until well emulsified and pour over the salad. Mix all the ingredients gently and leave to stand for about 30 minutes before serving.

Cook's Notes

Cook's Tip
Soaking the anchovies in milk removes some of the strong taste and saltiness of the fish.

Time
Preparation takes about 20 minutes. Salad must stand for 30 minutes before serving.

Serving Ideas
Serve as a side dish with grilled meat, poultry or fish, or with a combination of other salads in an antipasti selection.

Variations
Use red onions or spring onions for a change. Add sliced black olives if desired.

SERVES 4-6

PEPPER SALAD WITH CAPERS

Capers, the flower buds of a plant that flourishes in the warm
Italian climate, are a favourite ingredient in Italian cooking.

3 large peppers, red, green and yellow
90ml/6 tbsps olive oil
1 clove garlic, peeled and finely chopped
Basil leaves, roughly chopped
Fresh marjoram roughly chopped
30ml/2 tbsps capers
15ml/1 tbsp white wine vinegar

1. Cut the peppers in half and remove the core and seeds. Press with the palm of the hand or the back of a knife to flatten. Brush the skin side with oil and place the peppers under a preheated grill.

2. Grill the peppers until the skins are well charred. Wrap in a towel and leave for 15 minutes. Unwrap and peel off the charred skin.

3. Cut the peppers into thick strips and arrange on a serving dish. Scatter over the chopped garlic, basil leaves, marjoram and capers.

4. Mix together the remaining olive oil with the vinegar and salt and pepper and pour over the salad. Refrigerate for 1 hour before serving.

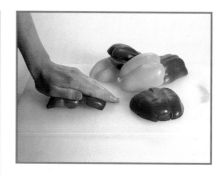

Step 1 Flatten the pepper halves with the palm of the hand or a large knife.

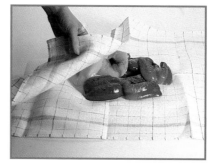

Step 2 Brush lightly with oil and grill until the skins are charred. Wrap in towels and leave for 15 minutes.

Cook's Notes

Time
Preparation takes about 30 minutes plus 1 hour refrigeration.

Preparation
The peppers may also be roasted in a hot oven for about 30 minutes. Alternatively, pierce whole peppers with a fork and hold them over a gas flame to char the skin.

Watchpoint
The peppers must become very charred on the outside before the skin will peel well.

Cook's Tip
Instead of chopping them, the basil leaves may be rolled up and cut into strips with kitchen scissors.

Variation
The salad may be prepared with all red or all yellow peppers instead of the combination of the three colours. If using only red peppers, substitute red wine vinegar.

SERVES 6

SICILIAN CAPONATA

Vegetables, so important in Italian cuisine, are
often served separately. This combination makes an
excellent starter, vegetable course or accompaniment.

1 aubergine
Salt
140ml/¼ pint olive oil
1 onion, sliced
2 sweet red peppers, cored, seeded and cut into
   2.5cm/1 inch pieces
2 sticks celery, sliced thickly
450g/1lb canned plum tomatoes
30ml/2 tbsps red wine vinegar
15ml/1 tbsp sugar
1 clove garlic, crushed
12 black olives, pitted
15ml/1 tbsp capers
Salt and pepper

1. Cut the aubergine in half and score the cut surface.
Sprinkle with salt and leave to drain in a colander or on
paper towels for 30 minutes. Rinse, pat dry and cut into
2.5cm/1 inch cubes.

2. Heat the oil in a large sauté pan and add the onion,
peppers and celery. Lower the heat and cook for about 5
minutes, stirring occasionally. Add the aubergine and cook
a further 5 minutes.

3. Sieve the tomatoes to remove the seeds and add the
pulp and liquid to the vegetables in the sauté pan. Add the
remaining ingredients except the olives and capers and
cook for a further 2 minutes.

4. To remove the stones from the olives, roll them on a flat
surface to loosen the stones and then remove them with a
swivel vegetable peeler. Alternatively, use a cherry pitter.
Slice the olives in quarters and add to the vegetables with
the capers.

5. Simmer, uncovered, over moderate heat for 15 minutes
to evaporate most of the liquid. Adjust the seasoning and
serve hot or cold.

Step 1 Halve
aubergines and
score cut surface.
Sprinkle with salt
and leave to
drain.

Step 4 Roll black
olives on a flat
surface to loosen
stones.

Cook's Notes

Preparation
Scoring and salting the
aubergine helps remove any
bitter taste. Be sure to rinse all the salt
off before cooking.

Cook's Tip
When serving cold, caponata
may be prepared two days
in advance.

Serving Ideas
Caponata may be served as a
first course or in an antipasti
selection. Also serve as a side dish.

SERVES 6-8

FLAGEOLET, TUNA AND TOMATO SALAD

Tuna and tomatoes are two popular ingredients in Italian antipasto dishes.
Add beans, with their pale green colour, for an attractive and easy first course or salad.

450g/1lb canned flageolet beans (substitute white haricot beans or butter beans)
180g/6oz canned tuna in oil
Juice of 1 lemon
Chopped fresh herbs (parsley, oregano, basil or marjoram)
120ml/8 tbsps olive oil
Salt and pepper
6-8 tomatoes, sliced

1. Drain the beans, rinse and leave in a colander to dry. Drain the tuna and flake it into a bowl.

2. Chop the herbs finely and mix with lemon juice, oil, salt and pepper. Add the beans to the tuna fish in the bowl and pour over the dressing, tossing carefully. Do not allow the tuna to break up too much.

3. Adjust the seasoning and pile the salad into a mound in a shallow serving dish. Cut the tomatoes into rounds about 5mm/¼ inch thick and place against the mound of salad. Serve immediately.

Step 2 Chop the herbs finely with a large knife using a mixture of different herbs, if desired.

Step 3 Mound the salad in the serving dish and place the tomatoes around it.

Cook's Notes

Time
Preparation takes about 15 minutes.

Serving Ideas
If desired, serve the salad on individual plates lined with radicchio or curly endive.

Variations
Add chopped spring onions or red onions to the salad or add finely chopped garlic.

SERVES 4

SPIRALI WITH SPINACH AND BACON

Pasta doesn't have to have a sauce that cooks for hours.
This whole dish takes about 15 minutes. True Italian "fast food"!

340g/12oz pasta spirals
225g/8oz fresh spinach
90g/3oz bacon
1 clove garlic, crushed
1 small red or green chilli pepper
1 small red sweet pepper
1 small onion
45ml/3 tbsps olive oil
Salt and pepper

1. Cook the pasta in boiling salted water about 10-12 minutes or until just tender. Drain the pasta in a colander and rinse it under hot water. Keep the pasta in a bowl of water until ready to use.

2. Tear the stalks off the spinach and wash the leaves well, changing the water several times. Set aside to drain.

3. Remove the rind and bones from the bacon, if necessary, and dice the bacon finely. Cut the chilli and the red pepper in half, remove the stems, core and seed and slice finely. Slice the onion thinly.

4. Roll up several of the spinach leaves into a cigar shape and then shred them finely. Repeat until all the spinach is shredded.

5. Heat the oil in a sauté pan and add garlic, onion, peppers and bacon. Fry for 2 minutes, add the spinach and fry for a further 2 minutes, stirring continuously. Season with salt and pepper.

6. Drain the pasta spirals and toss them in a colander to remove excess water. Mix with the spinach sauce and serve immediately.

Step 2 Tear stalks off the spinach and wash the leaves well.

Step 3 Slice red pepper and chilli pepper in half, remove seeds and core and shred finely with a large, sharp knife.

Step 4 Roll up the leaves in several layers to shred them faster.

Cook's Notes

Time
Pasta takes about 10-12 minutes to cook. Sauce takes about 4 minutes to cook. Preparation takes about 20 minutes.

Preparation
Wash spinach leaves in cold water to keep them crisp and change the water about three times to make sure all the grit is washed away.

Watchpoint
Handle chillis with care and wash hands well after chopping chillis as the juice tends to stick to the skin.

SERVES 6

LASAGNE NAPOLETANA

This is lasagne as it is cooked and eaten in Naples.
With its layers of red, green and white it looks as delicious
as it tastes and is very easy to prepare and assemble.

9 sheets spinach lasagne pasta

Tomato Sauce

45ml/3 tbsps olive oil
2 cloves garlic, crushed
900g/2lbs fresh tomatoes, peeled, or canned tomatoes, drained
2 tbsps chopped fresh basil, six whole leaves reserved
Salt and pepper
Pinch sugar

Cheese Filling

450g/1lb ricotta cheese
60g/4 tbsps unsalted butter
225g/8oz Mozzarella cheese, grated
Salt and pepper
Pinch nutmeg

1. Cook the pasta for 8 minutes in boiling salted water with 15ml/1 tbsp oil. Drain and rinse under hot water and place in a single layer on a damp cloth. Cover with another damp cloth and set aside.

2. To prepare the sauce, cook the garlic in remaining oil for about 1 minute in a large saucepan. When pale brown, add the tomatoes, basil, salt, pepper and sugar. If using fresh tomatoes, drop into boiling water for 6-8 seconds. Transfer to cold water and leave to cool completely. This will make the peels easier to remove.

3. Lower the heat under the saucepan and simmer the sauce for 35 minutes. Add more seasoning or sugar to taste.

4. Beat the ricotta cheese and butter together until creamy and stir into the remaining ingredients.

5. To assemble the lasagne, oil a rectangular baking dish and place 3 sheets of lasagne on the base. Cover with one third of the sauce and carefully spread on a layer of cheese. Place another 3 layers of pasta over the cheese and cover with another third of the sauce. Add the remaining cheese filling and cover with the remaining pasta. Spoon the remaining sauce on top.

6. Cover with foil and bake for 20 minutes at 190°C/375°F/ Gas Mark 5. Uncover and cook for 10 minutes longer. Garnish with the reserved leaves and leave to stand 10-15 minutes before serving.

Step 5 Place pasta on the base of an oiled baking dish. Spread tomato sauce over.

Step 5 Carefully spread the softened cheese mixture on top of the tomato sauce.

Cook's Notes

 Cook's Tip
Lasagne can be assembled the day before and refrigerated. Allow 5-10 minutes more cooking time in the oven if not at room temperature.

 Time
Preparation takes about 25 minutes, cooking takes about 1-1¼ hours.

 Variations
Use plain pasta instead, if desired. If using pre-cooked lasagne pasta, follow the baking times in the package directions.

SERVES 4

PENNE WITH HAM AND ASPARAGUS

The Italian word penne means quills,
due to the diagonal cut on both ends.

225g/8oz penne
430g/12oz fresh asparagus
120g/4oz cooked ham
30g/2 tbsps butter or margarine
280ml/½ pint double cream

Step 1 Peel the asparagus stalks with a swivel vegetable peeler.

1. Using a swivel vegetable peeler, scrape the sides of the asparagus spears starting about 5cm/2 inches from the top. Cut off the ends of the spears about 2.5cm/1 inch from the bottom.

2. Cut the ham into strips about 1.25cm/½ inch thick.

3. Bring a sauté pan of water to the boil, adding a pinch of salt. Move the pan so it is half on and half off direct heat. Place in the asparagus spears so that the tips are off the heat. Cover the pan and bring back to the boil. Cook the asparagus spears for about 2 minutes. Drain and allow to cool.

4. Cut the asparagus into 5cm/1 inch lengths, leaving the tips whole.

5. Melt the butter in the sauté pan and add the asparagus and ham. Cook briefly to evaporate the liquid, and add the cream. Bring to the boil and cook for about 5 minutes to thicken the cream.

6. Meanwhile, cook the pasta in boiling salted water with 15ml/1 tbsp oil for about 10-12 minutes.

7. Drain the pasta and rinse under hot water. Toss in a colander to drain and mix with the sauce. Serve with grated Parmesan cheese, if desired.

Step 4 Cut ham and cooked asparagus into 2.5cm/1 inch lengths. Leave the asparagus tips whole.

Step 5 Boil the cream with the asparagus and ham for about 5 minutes to thicken.

Cook's Notes

Time
Pasta takes 10-12 minutes to cook. Sauce takes about 8 minutes to cook. Preparation takes about 20 minutes.

Variations
If using frozen instead of fresh asparagus, do not peel or pre-cook. Substitute broccoli spears for the asparagus and prepare in the same way. If using peas instead of asparagus, cook them in the butter with the ham, add the cream and cook 5 minutes.

Serving Ideas
May be served as a first course in smaller amounts.

SERVES 4

SPAGHETTI AMATRICIANA

This is another quickly cooked sauce with a rich spicy taste.
Use less of the chilli pepper for a less fiery flavour.

1 onion
6 strips smoked back bacon
450g/1lb ripe tomatoes
1 red chilli pepper
25ml/1½ tbsps oil
340g/12oz spaghetti

1. Slice the onion thinly. Remove rind from the bacon and cut into thin strips.

2. Drop the tomatoes into boiling water for 6-8 seconds. Remove with a draining spoon and place in cold water, and leave to cool completely. This will make the peels easier to remove.

3. When the tomatoes are peeled, cut them in half and remove the seeds and pulp with a teaspoon. Rub the seeds and pulp through a strainer and retain juice to use in the sauce if desired. Chop the tomato flesh roughly and set it aside.

4. Cut the stem off the chilli pepper and cut the pepper in half lengthways. Remove the seeds and core and cut the pepper into thin strips. Cut the strips into small dice.

5. Heat the oil in a sauté pan and add the onion and bacon. Stir over medium heat for about 5 minutes, until the onion is transparent. Drain off excess fat and add the tomatoes and chilli and mix well. Simmer the sauce gently, uncovered, for about 5 minutes, stirring occasionally.

6. Meanwhile, cook the spaghetti in boiling salted water with 15ml/1 tbsp oil for about 10-12 minutes. Drain and rinse in hot water and toss in a colander to dry. To serve, spoon the sauce on top of the spaghetti and sprinkle with freshly grated Parmesan cheese, if desired.

Step 2 Placing tomatoes in boiling water and then in cold water makes the skins easier to remove.

Step 3 Cut the peeled tomatoes in half and remove the seeds and pulp with a teaspoon. Cut the flesh roughly.

Step 4 Remove the stems, seeds and cores from the chilli pepper, cut into thin strips and then chop into fine dice.

Cook's Notes

Time
Spaghetti takes about 10-12 minutes to cook, sauce takes about 8 minutes to cook, preparation takes about 20-25 minutes.

Cook's Tip
It is not necessary to use the whole chilli pepper; use as much as desired.

Watchpoint
Wash hands very well after handling chilli peppers or use rubber gloves while chopping them.

SERVES 4

Home-made Tagliatelle with Summer Sauce

Pasta making is not as difficult as you might think.
It is well worth it, too, because home-made pasta is in a class by itself.

Pasta Dough

120g/4oz plain flour
120g/4oz fine semolina
2 large eggs
10ml/2 tsps olive oil
Pinch salt

Sauce

450g/1lb unpeeled tomatoes, seeded and cut into small
   dice
1 large green pepper, cored, seeded and cut in small
   dice
1 onion, cut in small dice
15ml/1 tbsps chopped fresh basil
15ml/1 tbsp chopped fresh parsley
2 cloves garlic, crushed
140ml/¼ pint olive oil and vegetable oil mixed

1. Place the flours in a mound on a work surface and make a well in the centre. Place the eggs, oil and salt in the centre of the well.

2. Using a fork, beat the ingredients in the centre to blend them and gradually incorporate the flour from the outside edge. The dough may also be mixed in a food processor.

3. When half the flour is incorporated, start kneading using the palms of the hands and not the fingers. This may also be done in a food processor. Cover the dough and leave it to rest for 15 minutes.

4. Divide the dough in quarters and roll out thinly with a rolling pin on a floured surface or use a pasta machine, dusting dough lightly with flour before rolling. If using a machine, follow the manufacturer's directions. Allow the sheets of pasta to dry for about 10 minutes on a floured surface or tea towels. Cut the sheets into strips about 5mm/¼ inch wide by hand or machine, dusting lightly with flour while cutting. Leave the cut pasta to dry while preparing the sauce.

5. Combine all the sauce ingredients, mixing well. Cover and refrigerate overnight.

6. Cook the pasta for 5-6 minutes in boiling salted water with a spoonful of oil. Drain the pasta and rinse under very hot water. Toss in a colander to drain excess water. Place the hot pasta in serving dish. Pour the cold sauce over and toss.

Step 3 Knead with palms of hands to bring dough together until smooth.

Step 4 Roll the dough out thinly and cut into thin strips.

Cook's Notes

Time
Preparation time takes about 30 minutes, cooking takes about 5-6 minutes.

Watchpoint
Pasta must remain very hot to balance the cold sauce.

Serving Ideas
This basic pasta recipe can be used with other shapes of pasta such as lasagne, cannelloni, ravioli, farfalle (butterflies or bows) or cut into very fine noodles.

SERVES 4

PIZZA WITH PEPPERS, OLIVES & ANCHOVIES

Pizza really needs no introduction. It originated in Naples
and has been adopted everywhere. Change the toppings to suit your taste.

Pizza Dough

15g/½oz fresh yeast
2.5ml/½ tsp sugar
180ml/6 fl oz lukewarm water
225g/8oz plain flour
Pinch salt
30ml/2 tbsps oil

Topping

10ml/2 tsps olive oil
1 onion, finely chopped
1 clove garlic, crushed
450g/1lb canned tomatoes
15ml/1 tbsp tomato purée
2.5ml/½ tsp each oregano and basil
5ml/1 tsp sugar
Salt and pepper
½ red pepper
½ green pepper
60g/2oz black olives, pitted
60g/2oz canned anchovies, drained
120g/4oz Mozzarella cheese, grated
30g/2 tbsp grated Parmesan cheese

1. Cream the yeast with the sugar in a small bowl, add the lukewarm water and leave to stand for 10 minutes to prove. Bubbles will appear on the surface when ready.

2. Sift flour and salt into a bowl, make a well in the centre, add the oil and the yeast mixture. Using a wooden spoon, beat the liquid in the centre of the well, gradually incorporating the flour from the outside until it forms a firm dough.

3. Turn the dough out onto a floured surface and knead for 10 minutes or until the dough is smooth and elastic. Place in a lightly oiled bowl or in a large plastic bag, cover or tie the bag and leave to stand in a warm place for 30 minutes, or until the dough has doubled in bulk.

4. Knock the dough back and knead it into a smooth ball. Flatten the dough and roll out into a circle on a floured surface. The circle should be about 25cm/10 inches in diameter.

5. To prepare the topping, heat the oil in a heavy-based saucepan and add the onion and the garlic. Cook until the onion and garlic have softened but not coloured. Add the tomatoes and their juice, tomato purée, herbs, sugar, salt and pepper. Bring the sauce to the boil and then allow to simmer, uncovered, to reduce. Stir the sauce occasionally to prevent sticking. When the sauce is thick and smooth, leave it to cool. Spread the cooled sauce over the pizza dough. Sprinkle half the cheese on top of the tomato sauce and then arrange the topping ingredients. Sprinkle with remaining cheese and bake in a 200°C/400°F/Gas Mark 6 oven for 15-20 minutes or until the cheese is melted and bubbling and the crust is brown.

Step 4 When the dough has doubled in bulk, knock back before kneading again lightly.

Cook's Notes

Time
Dough takes about 40 minutes to make, including the rising. The tomato sauce needs to cook for 10-15 minutes. Pizza takes 15-20 minutes to bake.

Variations
Other ingredients, such as Italian hams and sausages, fish and shellfish, capers, green olives, or courgettes, may be used as toppings.

SERVES 4-6

PIZZA RUSTICA

This farmhouse pie is really a cross between quiche
and pizza. Whichever you think it resembles most,
there is no question that it is delicious.

Pizza Dough

(see recipe for Pizza with Peppers, Olives and Anchovies)

Filling

Grated Parmesan cheese
120g/4oz prosciutto or Parma ham, sliced
2 tomatoes, peeled, seeded and roughly chopped
60g/2oz Mozzarella cheese, diced
15ml/1 tbsp chopped fresh parsley
15ml/1 tbsp chopped fresh basil
2 eggs, lightly beaten
75ml/5 tbsps double cream
60g/2oz Fontina cheese, finely grated
Pinch nutmeg
Salt and pepper

Step 2 Roll out the dough, place in a dish and press up the sides to form an edge.

1. Prepare the dough as for the Pizza with Peppers, Olives
and Anchovies. When the dough has doubled in bulk,
knock it back and knead lightly. Flatten the dough into a
circle or rectangle and roll out. Roll to a circle about
25cm/10 inches in diameter or a rectangle about
28x18cm/11x7 inches.

2. Lightly oil the baking dish, place in the dough and press
out with floured fingertips to form a raised edge on the sides
of the dish.

3. Sprinkle the base of the dough with some of the
Parmesan cheese and place on a layer of ham. Cover the
ham with the chopped tomato. Mix the remaining
ingredients together and pour over the tomato and ham.

4. Bake on the lowest shelf of the oven for about 35
minutes at 190°C/375°F/Gas Mark 5. The top of the pizza
should be nicely browned and the edge of the dough
should be golden when the pizza is ready. Serve hot.

Step 3 Fill with Parmesan, ham and tomatoes.

Step 3 Mix cream, cheese and eggs together and pour onto the pizza.

Cook's Notes

Time
Pizza dough takes 40 minutes
to make, including rising time.
Bake pizza for 35 minutes.

Freezing
Pizzas can be prepared and
frozen in their unbaked form.
When cooking from frozen, allow an
extra 10 minutes. Pizza dough bases
may also be frozen unfilled. Allow to
defrost before topping.

Variations
If Fontina cheese is not
available, substitute Gruyère
or Emmental. Vary the filling
ingredients using different vegetables
and meats as desired.

SERVES 4-6

LIVER VENEZIANA

As the name indicates, this recipe originated
in Venice. The lemon juice offsets the rich
taste of liver in this very famous Italian dish.

Risotto

300g/9oz Italian rice
45g/3 tbsps butter or margarine
1 large onion, chopped
60ml/4 tbsps dry white wine
570ml/1 pint chicken stock
1.25ml/¼ tsp saffron
30g/2 tbsps grated fresh Parmesan cheese
Salt and pepper

Liver

450g/1lb calves' or lambs' liver
Flour for dredging
3 onions, thinly sliced
30g/2 tbsps butter or margarine
45ml/3 tbsps oil
Salt and pepper
Juice of ½ a lemon
15ml/1 tbsp chopped parsley

1. Melt the butter for the risotto in a large sauté pan, add the onion and cook until soft but not coloured, over gentle heat.

2. Add the rice and cook for about a minute until the rice looks clear.

3. Add the wine, stock, saffron and seasoning. Stir well and bring to the boil. Lower the heat and cook gently, stirring frequently until the liquid has evaporated. This will take about 20 minutes.

4. Meanwhile, skin the liver and cut out any large tubes.

5. Cut the liver into strips and toss in a sieve with the flour to coat.

6. Heat the butter or margarine and 15ml/1 tbsp oil in a large sauté or frying pan. Cook the onions until golden. Remove the onions from the pan to a plate. Add more oil if necessary, raise the heat under the pan and add the liver. Cook, stirring constantly, for about 2 minutes. Return the onions and add the lemon juice and parsley. Cook a further 2 minutes or until the liver is done. Season with salt and pepper and serve with the risotto.

7. To finish the risotto, add the cheese and salt and pepper to taste when the liquid has evaporated and toss to melt the cheese.

Step 3 Lower the heat and cook gently, stirring frequently until the liquid has evaporated.

Step 5 Cut the liver into strips and toss with flour in a sieve to coat each piece evenly.

Cook's Notes

Time
Risotto takes about 30 minutes to prepare and cook. Liver takes about 4 minutes to cook.

Watchpoint
Liver and all offal needs quick cooking or it will toughen.

Preparation
Tossing the liver and flour together in a sieve coats each piece of meat more evenly than can be done by hand.

Cook's Tip
If desired, add 60ml/4 tbsps stock to the recipe for a little more sauce.

SERVES 4

VEAL SCALOPPINE WITH PROSCIUTTO AND CHEESE

Veal is the meat used most often in Italian cooking. Good veal is tender and quick cooking, but expensive. Save this recipe for your next dinner party!

8 veal escalopes
30ml/2 tbsps butter or margarine
1 clove garlic, crushed
1 sprig rosemary
8 slices prosciutto ham
8 slices Mozzarella cheese
45ml/3 tbsps sherry
140ml/¼ pint beef stock
Salt and pepper

Step 3 Place a slice of ham on top of each slice of veal and pour over the sherry and stock and add the rosemary.

Step 2 Cook the veal on both sides until lightly browned.

Step 6 Place the meat under a preheated grill and cook to melt the cheese and lightly brown the top.

1. Pound the veal escalopes out thinly between two pieces of greaseproof paper with a meat mallet or a rolling pin.

2. Melt the butter or margarine in a sauté pan and add the veal and garlic. Cook until the veal is lightly browned on both sides.

3. Place a piece of prosciutto on top of each piece of veal and add the sherry, stock and sprig of rosemary to the pan. Cover the pan and cook the veal for about 10 minutes over

gentle heat or until done.

4. Remove the meat to a heatproof serving dish and top each piece of veal with a slice of cheese.

5. Bring the cooking liquid from the veal to the boil and allow to boil rapidly to reduce slightly.

6. Meanwhile, grill the veal to melt and brown the cheese. Remove the sprig of rosemary from the sauce and pour the sauce around the meat to serve.

Cook's Notes

Time
Preparation takes about 15 minutes, cooking takes 15-20 minutes.

Variations
White wine may be substituted for the sherry, if desired. 5ml/1 tsp of tomato purée may be added to the sauce. Use chicken, turkey or pork instead of the veal.

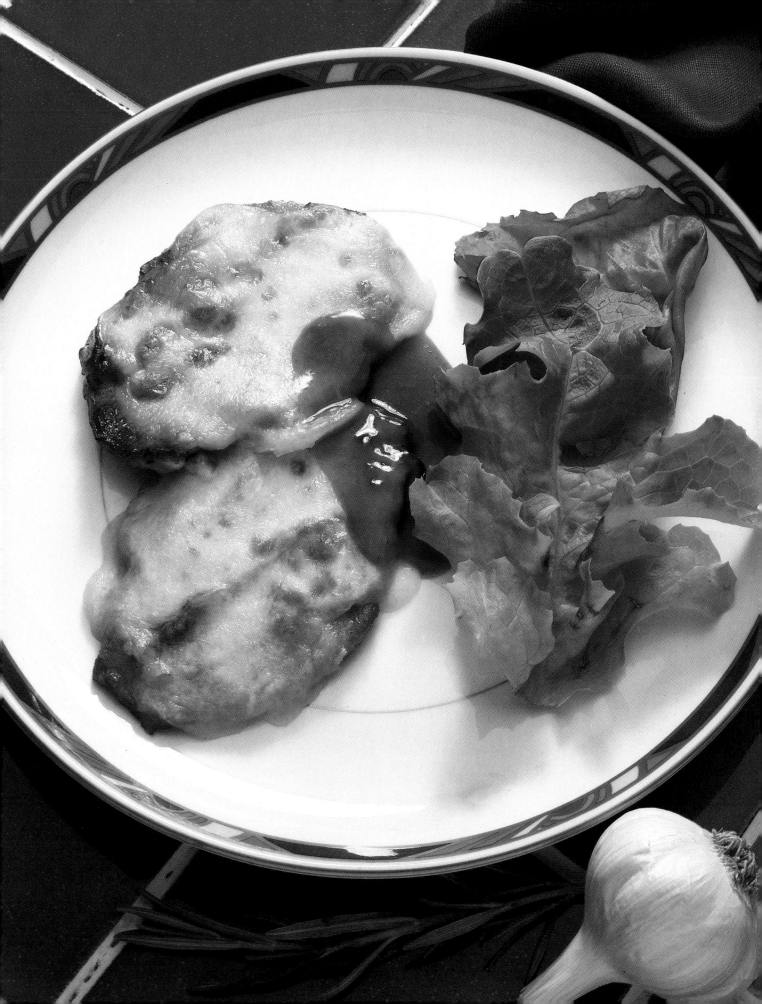

SERVES 4-8

PORK ROULADES WITH POLENTA

Polenta, either boiled or fried, is a staple dish in
Italy as potatoes are elsewhere in the world.

225g/8oz coarse yellow cornmeal
1.5 litres/3 pints chicken stock
Salt and white pepper

Roulades

8 pork escalopes or steaks
8 slices Parma ham
4 large cup mushrooms
60g/4 tbsps grated Parmesan cheese
15ml/1 tbsp chopped fresh sage
Seasoned flour for dredging
60ml/4 tbsps olive oil
1 small onion, finely chopped
2 sticks celery, finely chopped
1 clove garlic, crushed
90ml/6 tbsps brown stock
140ml/¼ pint dry white wine
120g/4oz canned plum tomatoes, drained and juice
   reserved
5ml/1 tsp tomato purée
Salt and pepper
90ml/6 tbsps dry Marsala
Fresh sage leaves for garnish

---

1. Bring the chicken stock for the polenta to the boil in a
large stock pot and start adding the cornmeal in a very slow,
steady stream, stirring continuously. Add salt and pepper
and continue cooking over very low heat, stirring frequently
for about 55 minutes.

2. Flatten the pork escalopes or steaks and place a slice of
Parma ham on top of each. Chop the mushrooms and
divide among the pork escalopes, spooning on top of the
ham slices. Sprinkle over the Parmesan cheese and the
fresh sage.

3. Fold the sides of the pork escalopes into the centre to

seal them, and roll up the pork like a Swiss roll. Secure each
roll with a cocktail stick. Dredge each roulade in flour,
shaking off the excess.

4. Heat the olive oil in a large sauté pan or frying pan and
add the pork roulades, seam side down first. Cook on all
sides until nicely browned. Remove the roulades and keep
them warm.

5. Add the onion and celery to the oil in the pan and cook
until lightly browned. Add the garlic and all the remaining
ingredients except the Marsala. Reserve the juice from the
tomatoes for later use if necessary. Bring the sauce to the
boil, breaking up the tomatoes. Return the roulades to the
pan, cover and cook over moderate heat for about 15-20
minutes or until the pork is completely cooked. Add
reserved tomato juice, as necessary, if liquid is drying out.

6. When the pork is cooked, remove to a dish and keep it
warm. Add the Marsala to the sauce and bring to the boil.
Allow to boil 5-10 minutes. The sauce may be puréed in a
food processor and also sieved if desired.

7. To assemble the dish, spoon the polenta on a serving
plate. Remove the cocktail sticks from the roulades and
place on top of the polenta. Spoon the sauce over the meat
and garnish the dish with fresh sage leaves.

Step 2 Place all
the filling
ingredients on top
of the pork
scallops, fold in
the sides and roll
up. Secure with
cocktail sticks.

Cook's Notes

Time
Polenta takes almost 1 hour to
cook. Roulades will take about
20 minutes to prepare and 20 minutes
to cook.

Watchpoint
Be sure to stir the polenta
often and add more liquid if it
begins to dry out as it can easily stick to
the pan.

Variations
Double the quantity of
cornmeal and cut the cooking
time down to 30-35 minutes. Spoon
into a lightly oiled pan and allow to
cool. This version of polenta can be cut
into squares and fried in hot oil. Serve
as an accompaniment to any meat.

SERVES 6-8

CRESPELLE ALLA BOLOGNESE

Almost all countries in the world have a kind of
pancake and crespelle are the Italian version. Use
other fillings and sauces for lots of variety.

Bolognese Filling

30g/2 tbsps butter or margarine
15ml/1 tbsp olive oil
2 onions, finely chopped
225g/8oz minced beef
1 small green pepper, seeded, cored and finely chopped
120g/4oz canned plum tomatoes
15ml/1 tbsp tomato purée
140ml/¼ pint beef stock
1 bay leaf
10ml/2 tsps chopped basil
5ml/1 tsp chopped oregano
30ml/2 tbsps sherry
Salt and pepper

Crespelle Batter

3 eggs
120g/4oz plain flour
Pinch salt
200ml/8 fl oz water
10ml/2 tsps olive oil
Melted butter

Tomato sauce

15g/1 tbsp butter or margarine
1 clove garlic, crushed
1 onion, finely chopped
450g/1lb canned plum tomatoes
Salt, pepper and a pinch of sugar
Fresh basil leaves

1. Heat the butter and oil in a deep saucepan for the Bolognese filling. Put in the onion and cook slowly until soft but not coloured. Increase the heat and add the beef. Stir the beef while cooking until all the meat is brown. Add chopped pepper, tomatoes and their juice, tomato purée, stock, herbs, salt and pepper to taste and simmer gently for about 45 minutes or until the mixture thickens, stirring occasionally. Add the sherry and cook for a further 5 minutes and set aside.

2. Sift the flour for the crespelle with a pinch of salt. Break the eggs into a bowl and beat to mix thoroughly. Mix the flour into the eggs gradually, beating all the time until the mixture is smooth. Add water and the oil and stir in well. Cover the bowl with a damp cloth and leave in a cool place for 30 minutes.

3. Heat the crêpe pan or a 19cm/7 inch frying pan. Lightly grease with the melted butter and pour a large spoonful of the batter into the centre of the pan. Swirl the pan to coat the base evenly. Fry until the crespelle is brown on the underside, loosen the edge with a pallete knife, and turn over and brown the other side. Stack and wrap in a clean towel until needed.

4. To make the tomato sauce, melt the butter in a small saucepan and cook garlic and onion slowly for about 5 minutes, or until softened but not coloured. Reserve whole basil leaves for garnish and chop 10ml/2 tsps. Add the tomatoes to the onions and garlic along with the basil, salt, pepper and a pinch of sugar. Cook for about 10-15 minutes or until the onions are completely soft. Drain to remove the seeds, pressing the pulp against the strainer to extract as much liquid as possible.

5. To assemble, lay the crespelle out on a large, clean work surface and put 2 heaped spoonfuls of Bolognese filling into each. Roll up and place in an ovenproof dish. Repeat until all the crespelle have been filled.

6. Put into a 200°C/400°F/Gas Mark 6 oven and heat for about 8 minutes. Heat the tomato sauce and spoon over the crespelle before serving. Garnish with basil leaves and serve immediately.

Cook's Notes

Time
Preparation takes about 45 minutes, cooking takes about 1 hour 15 minutes.

Preparation
The crespelle batter must stand for 30 minutes to allow the starch to swell for the batter to thicken properly.

Variations
Crespelle can be used with a variety of fillings and toppings, both sweet and savoury.

SERVES 4-6

CHICKEN CACCIATORE

The name means Chicken the Hunter's Way, and that
means the addition of mushrooms. Though not
traditional, pasta is a good accompaniment.

45ml/3 tbsps oil
120g/4oz mushrooms, quartered, if large
1.5kg/3lb chicken, skinned if desired and cut into pieces
1 onion
2 cloves garlic
140ml/¼ pint vermouth
15ml/1 tbsp white wine vinegar
140ml/¼ pint chicken stock
5ml/1 tsp oregano
1 sprig fresh rosemary
450g/1lb canned tomatoes
60g/2oz black olives, pitted
30g/2 tbsps chopped parsley
Salt and pepper

1. Heat the oil in a heavy-based frying pan and cook the
mushrooms for about 1-2 minutes. Remove them and set
aside. Brown the chicken in the oil and transfer the browned
pieces to an ovenproof casserole.

2. Chop the onion and garlic finely. Pour off all but 15ml/1
tbsp of the oil in the frying pan and reheat the pan. Cook the
onion and garlic until softened but not coloured. Add the
vermouth and vinegar and boil to reduce by half. Add the
chicken stock, tomatoes, oregano, rosemary, salt and
pepper. Break up the tomatoes and bring the sauce to the
boil. Allow to cook for 2 minutes.

3. Pour the sauce over the chicken in the casserole, cover
and cook at 180°C/350°F/Gas Mark 4 for about 1 hour.

4. To remove the stones from the olives, roll them on a flat
surface to loosen the stones and then use a swivel
vegetable peeler to extract them. Alternatively use a cherry
pitter.

5. Add mushrooms and olives during the last 5 minutes of
cooking.

Step 2 Cut onion
in half lengthways
leaving the root
end intact.
Holding the knife
parallel to the
chopping board,
cut the onion in
thin horizontal
slices, but not
through to the
root end.

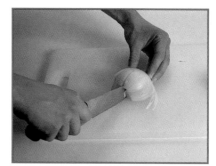

Step 2 Cut the
onion lengthwise
in thin strips,
leaving the onion
attached at the
root end.

Step 2 Cut cross-
wise through the
onion; the onion
will fall apart into
small dice.

6. Remove the rosemary before serving and sprinkle with
chopped parsley.

Cook's Notes

 Time
Cooking takes approximately
1 hour 15 minutes,
preparation takes about 25-30 minutes.

Cook's Tip
Pitted black olives are
available in some
delicatessens.

 Serving Idea
Serve with spaghetti or pasta
shapes and sprinkle with
grated Parmesan cheese.

SERVES 4

TURKEY MARSALA

Marsala is a dessert wine from Sicily which also complements chicken, veal or turkey surprisingly well. It is traditional, but sherry will serve as a substitute if Marsala is unavailable.

4 turkey breast fillets or escalopes
60g/4 tbsps butter or margarine
1 clove garlic
4 anchovy fillets, soaked in milk
Capers
4 slices Mozzarella cheese
10ml/2 tsps chopped marjoram
15ml/1 tbsp chopped parsley
45ml/3 tbsps Marsala
140ml/¼ pint double cream
Salt and pepper

1. Flatten the turkey breasts between two sheets of greaseproof paper with a meat mallet or rolling pin if necessary.

2. Melt butter in a sauté pan and, when foaming, add the garlic and the turkey. Cook for a few minutes on each side until lightly browned. Remove them from the pan.

3. Drain the anchovy fillets and rinse them well. Dry on paper towels. Put a slice of cheese on top of each turkey fillet and arrange the anchovies and capers on top of each. Sprinkle with the chopped herbs and return the turkey to the pan.

4. Cook the turkey a further 5 minutes over moderate heat, until the turkey is done and the cheese has melted. Remove to a serving dish and keep warm. Return the pan to the heat and add the Marsala. Scrape the browned pan juices off the bottom and reduce the heat. Add the cream and whisk in well. Lower the heat and simmer gently, uncovered, for a few minutes to thicken the sauce. Season the sauce with salt and pepper and spoon over the turkey fillets to serve.

Step 1 Flatten the turkey breasts between two sheets of paper with a rolling pin or meat mallet.

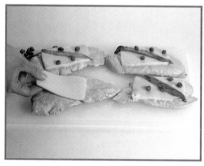

Step 3 Place a slice of cheese on top of each turkey breast and top with anchovies, capers and herbs.

Step 4 Cook until turkey is done and the cheese has melted.

Cook's Notes

Time
Preparation takes about 25 minutes and cooking about 15 minutes.

Watchpoint
Turkey breast fillets are very lean so can dry out easily if over-cooked.

Serving Suggestions
Accompany the Turkey Marsala with new potatoes and lightly cooked courgettes.

SERVES 6

TURKEY KEBABS

You don't have to buy a whole turkey for these! Small portions are now readily available at supermarkets and butchers.

1.5kg/3lbs turkey meat
10ml/2 tsps chopped sage
1 sprig rosemary
Juice of 1 lemon
30ml/2 tbsps olive oil
Salt and pepper
120g/4oz streaky bacon, rinds and bones removed
Whole sage leaves

Step 2 Stretch the bacon by scraping it with the blunt side of a knife.

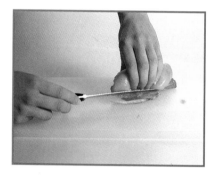

Step 1 Remove the turkey bones and cut the meat into small, even-sized pieces.

Step 3 Cut the bacon into halves and wrap around a piece of turkey. Thread the ingredients onto skewers.

1. Remove any bones from the turkey and cut the meat into even-sized pieces. Combine the chopped sage, rosemary, lemon juice, oil, salt and pepper in a large bowl and add the turkey meat. Stir once or twice to coat evenly, cover and leave in the refrigerator overnight.

2. Cut the bacon in half and wrap around some of the pieces of turkey. Leave other pieces of turkey unwrapped.

3. Thread the bacon, wrapped turkey, plain turkey and whole sage leaves onto skewers, alternating the ingredients.

4. Cook in a preheated 200°C/400°F/Gas Mark 6 oven for about 40 minutes. Alternatively, cook for 30 minutes and place the kebabs under a preheated grill for 10 minutes to crisp the bacon. Baste frequently with the marinade while cooking. Pour any remaining marinade and pan juices over the kebabs to serve.

Cook's Notes

Time
Kebabs take about 20 minutes to assemble and need to marinate overnight. Cooking takes about 40 minutes.

Serving Ideas
Serve with a green salad, fried polenta or risotto.

Variation
Use chicken, if desired.

SERVES 4-6

SWORDFISH KEBABS

Swordfish is one of the most commonly caught fish
in Southern Italy and Sicily. It won't fall apart
during cooking — a bonus when making kebabs.

1kg/2¼lbs swordfish steaks
90ml/6 tbsps olive oil
5ml/1 tsp chopped oregano
5ml/1 tsp chopped marjoram
Juice and rind of ½ a lemon
4 tomatoes, cut in thick slices
2 lemons, cut in thin slices
Salt and freshly ground pepper
Lemon slices and Italian parsley for garnish

1. Cut the swordfish steaks into 5cm/2 inch pieces.

2. Mix the olive oil, herbs, lemon juice and rind together
and set it aside. Thread the swordfish, tomato slices and
lemon slices on skewers, alternating the ingredients. Brush
the skewers with the oil and lemon juice mixture and cook
under a preheated grill for about 10 minutes, basting
frequently with the lemon and oil. Serve garnished with
lemons and parsley.

Step 1 Cut the swordfish steaks into even-sized pieces.

Step 2 Thread the ingredients onto the skewers, alternating the colours.

Cook's Notes

Time
Preparation takes about 15
minutes, cooking takes about
10 minutes.

Variations
Fresh tuna may be used
instead of swordfish. Use
cherry tomatoes instead of sliced
tomatoes, if available.

Serving Ideas
Accompany the kebabs with
risotto and a green salad.

SERVES 4

RED MULLET WITH HERB & MUSHROOM SAUCE

This is a Mediterranean fish with a slight taste of prawns.
It is often cooked with the liver left in — a delicacy.

450g/1lb small mushrooms, left whole
1 clove garlic, finely chopped
45ml/3 tbsps olive oil
Juice of 1 lemon
15ml/1 tbsp finely chopped parsley
10ml/2 tsps finely chopped basil
5ml/1 tsp finely chopped marjoram or sage
60ml/4 tbsps dry white wine mixed with 2.5ml/½ tsp
  cornflour
Few drops anchovy essence
4 red mullet, each weighing about 225g/8oz
10ml/2 tsps white breadcrumbs
10ml/2 tsps freshly grated Parmesan cheese

1. Combine the mushrooms, garlic and olive oil in a small frying pan. Cook over moderate heat for about 1 minute, until the garlic and mushrooms are slightly softened. Add all the herbs, lemon juice and white wine and cornflour mixture. Bring to the boil and cook until thickened. Add anchovy essence to taste. Set aside while preparing the fish.

2. To clean the fish, cut along the stomach from the gills to the vent, the small hole near the tail. Clean out the cavity of the fish, leaving the liver, if desired.

3. To remove the gills, lift the flap and snip them out with a sharp pair of scissors. Rinse the fish well and pat dry.

4. Place the fish head to tail in a shallow ovenproof dish that can be used for serving. The fish should fit snugly into the dish.

5. Pour the prepared sauce over the fish and sprinkle with the breadcrumbs and Parmesan cheese.

6. Cover the dish loosely with foil and cook in the preheated oven 190°C/375°F/Gas Mark 5, for about 20 minutes. Uncover for the last 5 minutes, if desired, and raise the oven temperature slightly. This will lightly brown the fish.

Step 3 Lift the flap over the gills and use kitchen scissors to snip the gills away.

Step 4 Place the fish head to tail in a shallow baking dish just large enough to accommodate them.

Cook's Notes

Time
Preparation takes about 30 minutes, cooking takes about 5 minutes for the sauce and 20 minutes for the fish.

Preparation
If the fish need to be scaled, use the blunt edge of a knife and scrape from the tail to the head. Rinse well and remove any loose scales. The fishmonger will gut the fish, scale them and remove the gills if desired.

Variations
Use other fish such as bream or sardines.

SERVES 4

FISH MILANESE

These fish, cooked in the style of
Milan, have a crispy crumb coating
and the fresh tang of lemon juice.

8 sole or plaice fillets
30ml/2 tbsps dry vermouth
1 bay leaf
90ml/6 tbsps olive oil
Salt and pepper
Seasoned flour for dredging
2 eggs, lightly beaten
Dry breadcrumbs
Oil for shallow frying
90g/6 tbsps butter
1 clove garlic, crushed
10ml/2 tsps chopped parsley
30ml/2 tbsps capers
5ml/1 tsp chopped fresh oregano
Juice of 1 lemon
Salt and pepper
Lemon wedges and parsley to garnish

1. Skin the fillets with a sharp filleting knife. Remove any small bones and place the fillets in a large, shallow dish. Combine the vermouth, oil and bay leaf in a small saucepan and heat gently. Allow to cool completely and pour over the fish. Leave the fish to marinate for about 1 hour, turning them occasionally.

2. Remove the fish from the marinade and dredge lightly with the seasoned flour.

3. Dip the fillets into the beaten eggs to coat, or use a pastry brush to brush the eggs onto the fillets. Dip the egg-coated fillet into the breadcrumbs, pressing the crumbs on firmly.

4. Heat the oil in a large frying pan. Add the fillets and cook slowly on both sides until golden brown. Cook for about 3 minutes on each side, remove and drain on paper towels.

5. Pour the oil out of the frying pan and wipe it clean. Add the butter and the garlic and cook until both turn a light brown. Add the herbs, capers and lemon juice and pour immediately over the fish. Garnish with lemon wedges and sprigs of parsley.

Step 1 Hold each fillet firmly by the tail end and work a sharp filleting knife down the length of the fillet, holding the knife at a slight angle. Keep the blade as close as possible to the fish.

Step 3 Dip or brush the fillets with the beaten egg and press on the breadcrumb coating firmly.

Cook's Notes

Time
Preparation takes 1 hour for the fish to marinate, cooking takes about 6 minutes. It may be necessary to cook the fish in several batches, depending upon the size of the frying pan.

Cook's Tip
If necessary, keep the fish fillets warm by placing on a wire cooling rack covered with paper towels and place in a warm oven, leaving the door slightly ajar. Sprinkling the fish fillets lightly with salt as they drain on paper towels helps remove some of the oil.

Variations
Other whitefish fillets may be prepared in the same way. Choose fillets that are of even size so that they cook in the same length of time. Chopped onion may be substituted for the garlic, if desired.

SERVES 4

CARAMEL ORANGES

This is one of the classic Italian sweets.
Vary the darkness of the caramel to suit
your taste, but watch it carefully!

4 large oranges
300g/10oz sugar
340ml/12 fl oz water
60ml/2 fl oz extra water
30ml/2 tbsps brandy or orange liqueur

1. Use a swivel vegetable peeler to peel thin strips from two of the oranges. Take off any white pith and cut the strips into very thin julienne strips with a sharp knife.

2. Place the julienne strips in a small saucepan, cover with water and bring to the boil.

3. Peel all the oranges with a serrated-edged knife. Cut the ends off first and then take the peel and pith off in very thin strips using a sawing motion. Cut the oranges horizontally into slices about 5mm/¼ inch thick. Drain the orange peel strips and leave to dry. Combine sugar and water in a heavy-based pan. Reserve 60ml/2 fl oz water for later use. Place the mixture over medium heat until the sugar has dissolved. Add the drained orange peel strips to the pan.

4. Boil the syrup gently, uncovered, for about 10 minutes or until the orange strips are glazed. Remove the strips from the pan and place on a lightly oiled plate.

5. Return the pan to high heat and allow the syrup to boil, uncovered, until it turns a pale golden brown. Remove from the heat immediately and quickly add the extra water. Return to gentle heat and cook for a few minutes to dissolve hardened sugar. Remove the pan from the heat and allow to cool completely. Stir in the brandy.

6. Arrange the orange slices in a serving dish and pour over the cooled syrup. Pile the glazed orange strips on top and refrigerate for several hours, or overnight, before serving.

Step 1 Peel the oranges into thin strips with a vegetable peeler. Remove any white pith and cut into thin julienne strips.

Step 3 Use a serrated knife to take off orange peel in thin strips.

Step 5 Cook the sugar and water to a pale golden brown syrup.

Cook's Notes

Time
Preparation takes about 25 minutes, cooking takes about 10 minutes to parboil the orange strips and about 10-15 minutes to caramelize the syrup.

Watchpoint
Keep a close eye on the syrup as it is caramelizing. It can burn very quickly.

Cook's Tip
All the white pith must be removed from the oranges and the orange strips or the whole dish will taste bitter.

SERVES 4-8

CHESTNUT & ALMOND STUFFED PEACHES

A favourite sweet in Milan during the peach season.

4 large freestone peaches
280ml/½ pint dry white wine
30ml/2 tbsps brandy

Filling

60g/2oz plain chocolate
7-8g/2¾oz chestnut spread
1 egg yolk
15g/1 tbsp ground almonds
15ml/1 tbsp peach liqueur or brandy
140ml/¼ pint double cream
4 amaretti or ratafia biscuits

Step 4 Fold whipped cream into the chocolate-chestnut mixture along with the almonds.

Step 6 Pipe the filling into the hollow in each peach half.

Step 1 Remove the peach stones using a small knife or swivel vegetable peeler.

1. Wash the peaches, peel them and cut them in half. Carefully remove the stones and place the peaches in a large bowl with the wine, brandy and enough water to cover them completely. Marinate for 1 hour.

2. Cut the chocolate into small pieces and melt in the top of a double boiler. Stir in the chestnut spread. Remove the chocolate from the heat and leave to cool for about 2 minutes, stirring frequently.

3. Beat in the egg yolk until well incorporated. Add the

peach liqueur or brandy and stir well. Allow to cool.

4. Whip the cream and fold into the chocolate-chestnut mixture with the ground almonds. Allow to cool completely before using.

5. Remove the peaches from the marinade with a draining spoon and place them in serving dishes. Fill a piping bag fitted with a large rosette nozzle with the chocolate chestnut mixture.

6. Pipe out a large rosette of chocolate-chestnut mixture into the hollow of each peach half. Place a biscuit on top of each peach and serve chilled, with cream if desired.

Cook's Notes

 Time
Peaches take 1 hour to marinate, preparation takes about 40 minutes.

 Variations
Nectarine halves may be used instead of peaches.

 Preparation
Fresh peaches or nectarines must be placed in the wine and brandy mixture as soon as they are peeled or they will darken.

Serving Ideas
Peach liqueur or brandy may be poured over each peach before filling, if desired.

SERVES 6-8

CASSATA

No sweet selection is complete without ice cream.
The Italian kind is rich, creamy and justly famous.

Almond Layer
2 eggs, separated
60g/2oz icing sugar
140ml/¼ pint double cream
2.5ml/½ tsp almond essence

Chocolate Layer
2 eggs, separated
60g/2oz icing sugar
140ml/¼ pint double cream
60g/2oz plain chocolate
30g/2 tbsps cocoa
25ml/1/1½ tbsps water

Fruit Layer
280ml/½ pint double cream
30ml/2 tbsps maraschino or light rum
1 egg white
60g/2oz icing sugar
60g/2oz mixed glacé fruit
30g/1oz shelled chopped pistachios

1. To prepare the almond layer, beat egg whites until stiff peaks form, gradually beating in the icing sugar, a spoonful at a time. Lightly beat the egg yolks and fold in the whites.

Whip the cream with the almond essence until soft peaks form and fold into the egg mixture. Lightly oil a 20cm/8 inch round cake pan. Pour in the almond layer mixture and smooth over the top. Cover with clingfilm and freeze until firm.

2. To prepare the chocolate layer, beat the egg whites until stiff but not dry and gradually beat in the icing sugar. Whip the cream until soft and fold into the egg white mixture. Put the chocolate in the top of a double boiler over simmering water. Remove it from the heat and stir in the egg yolks. Combine cocoa and water and add to the chocolate mixture. Allow to cool and then fold into the egg white mixture. Spoon the chocolate layer over the almond layer and return, covered, to the freezer.

3. To make the rum fruit layer, whip the cream until soft peaks form. Whip the egg white until about the same consistency as cream. Gradually add the icing sugar, beating well after each addition. Combine the two mixtures, fold in the rum, fruit and nuts. Spread this mixture on top of the chocolate layer, cover and freeze until firm.

4. To serve, loosen the cassata from around the edges of the pan with a small knife. Place a hot cloth around the pan for a few seconds to help loosen. Turn out onto a serving plate and cut into wedges to serve.

Step 2 Fold the chocolate mixture into the egg white and cream mixture with a rubber spatula or large spoon, taking care not to over fold.

Step 3 Pour the prepared rum fruit layer over the top of the firmly frozen chocolate layer.

Cook's Notes

Time
Preparation can take several hours, so that one ice cream layer can freeze before another is added.

Preparation
Whisk the cream softly; over-whisking will cause it to separate. Whisk the egg whites in between each addition of sugar. If sugar is added too quickly, egg whites will not stiffen sufficiently.

Serving Ideas
Sprinkle the top layer of the cassata with more chopped pistachios and chocolate curls. Decorate with rosettes of whipped cream, if desired. Can be served with a fruit or chocolate sauce or with maraschino poured over the top.

SERVES 6-8

ZUPPA INGLESE

This is Italy's tribute to trifle. The name means
English soup, but the custard is rich and thick.

30g/2 tbsps cornflour
570ml/1 pint milk
2 eggs, lightly beaten
30g/2 tbsps sugar
Grated rind of ½ a lemon
Pinch nutmeg
1 punnet ripe strawberries
16 sponge fingers
Amaretto
140ml/¼ pint double cream

1. Mix the cornflour with some of the milk. Beat the eggs, sugar lemon rind and nutmeg together and pour in the remaining milk. Mix with the cornflour mixture in a heavy-based pan and stir over gentle heat until the mixture thickens and comes to the boil.

2. Allow to boil for 1 minute or until the mixture coats the back of a spoon. Place a sheet of greaseproof paper directly on top of the custard and allow it to cool slightly.

3. Save 8 even-sized strawberries for garnish and hull the remaining ones. Place half of the sponge fingers in the bottom of a glass bowl and sprinkle with some of the amaretto. Cut the strawberries in half and place a layer on top of the sponge fingers. Pour a layer of custard on top and repeat with the remaining sliced strawberries and sponge fingers. Top with another layer of custard and allow to cool completely.

4. Whip the cream and spread a thin layer over the top of the set custard. Pipe the remaining cream around the edge of the dish and decorate with the reserved strawberries. Serve chilled.

Step 1 Combine the custard ingredients in a heavy-based saucepan and cook until the mixture thickens and coats the back of a spoon.

Step 3 Place a layer of sponge fingers and strawberries in a serving dish and coat with a layer of custard. Repeat with remaining ingredients.

Step 4 Decorate the top using a piping bag fitted with a rosette nozzle.

Cook's Notes

Time
Preparation takes about 20 minutes, custard takes about 5 minutes to cook.

Variations
Decorate the top of the dessert with grated chocolate, toasted almonds or shelled pistachios in addition to, or instead of, the strawberries. Other fruit may be used, if desired.

GREEK COOKING

INTRODUCTION

Greek cookery has much in common with that of other countries which share the Mediterranean climate, and yet, it is different.

Herbs are used liberally – oregano and basil being the favourites – but the resulting taste is not Italian. Spices, such as cinnamon and coriander, figure prominently, but the taste is not Middle Eastern. Olives and olive oil are essential ingredients, but the taste is not Provencal. The taste is undeniably Greek and reflects all the vitality of the country and the belief that food is part of life and to be enjoyed without pretensions.

Greek recipes rely on the freshest possible ingredients prepared to let the natural flavours shine through. Aubergines, courgettes and artichokes all speak of the warmth of the country and are used in many delicious ways. Olive oil is an essential ingredient and lends its fragrant bouquet to all food, even sweets. Vegetables are usually cooked in it in preference to water. Lots of herbs and lemon juice offset any oiliness, and olive oil is both a health and flavour bonus since it is less fattening and more nourishing than most other cooking fats.

Walnuts, almonds, fresh figs and feta cheese – the list of ingredients that make Greek food special could go on and on. They all add up, though, to a cuisine as vibrant and colourful as the country itself.

SERVES 6-8

SALTED ALMONDS AND CRACKED OLIVES

Olives take on a special flavour when prepared in this way.
Served with crisp toasted almonds, they make a perfect snack.

450g/1lb almonds, unskinned
15g/1 tbsp citric acid
60ml/4 tbsps cold water
15g/1 tbsp salt
450g/1lb green olives
60g/2oz coarse salt
1 clove garlic, peeled and left whole
2 sprigs of fresh dill
1 bay leaf
1 sprig thyme
15ml/1 tbsp chopped oregano
Vine leaves

1. Spread the almonds in a large roasting pan. Mix the citric acid with the water and sprinkle over the almonds. Stir them around to coat evenly and leave for 10 minutes. Remove them, rinse out the pan and dry it.

2. Place the almonds back into the pan, spread them out and sprinkle with the salt. Shake the pan to coat evenly in salt and then spread the almonds out in an even layer.

3. Cook in a preheated 180°C/350°F/Gas Mark 4 oven for about 30 minutes, stirring frequently until brown and crisp. Allow them to cool completely before sealing tightly in jars for storage.

4. Hit the green olives gently with a meat mallet or rolling pin to crack the flesh. Alternatively, cut a cross in one side of each olive with a small, sharp knife. Rinse the olives and place them in storage jars. Cover with water and divide the

Step 1 Put the almonds into a large roasting pan and spread into an even layer. Pour the citric acid mixture over the top and stir them to coat evenly.

Step 4 Crack the skin on the olives by gently hitting with a meat mallet or rolling pin.

Step 4 Alternatively, make a small cross on the side of each olive with a sharp knife.

ingredients between the jars. Cover the surface of the olives with the vine leaves.

5. Seal the jars to keep in a cool, dark place for 3-4 weeks. To serve, remove the olives and sprinkle with chopped oregano, if desired. Serve with the salted almonds.

Cook's Notes

Preparation
When cracking the olives, take care not to crack the stones. Taste the olives after about 2 weeks; if they have absorbed enough flavour from the various ingredients, they are ready to use.

Cook's Tip
In Greece raw olives are used. If using olives that have already been preserved in brine, they will not need to be stored as long. Use half the quantity of coarse salt.

Time
Preparation takes about 20 minutes, with 3-4 weeks storage time for the olives. Cooking time for the almonds is about 30 minutes.

SERVES 4

FRIED SQUID

Serve this sweet and delicious seafood
as a starter or main course. It's
easier to prepare than you think!

675g/1½lb fresh squid
60g/2oz plain flour
Salt and pepper
Oil for deep-frying
Lemon wedges and parsley for garnishing

1. Hold the body of the squid with one hand and the head with the other and pull gently to separate. Remove the intestines and the quill, which is clear and plastic-like. Rinse the body of the squid inside and outside under cold running water.

2. Cut the tentacles from the head, just above the eye. Separate into individual tentacles.

3. Remove the brownish or purplish outer skin from the body of the squid and cut the flesh into 5mm/¼ inch rings.

4. Mix the flour, salt and pepper together on a sheet of paper or in a shallow dish. Toss the rings of squid and the tentacles in the flour mixture to coat. Heat the oil to 180°C/350°F and fry the squid, about 6 pieces at a time, saving the tentacles until last. Remove them from the oil when brown and crisp with a draining spoon and place on

Step 2 Cut the tentacles from the head just below the eye and separate them into individual pieces.

Step 3 Remove the outer skin from the body of the squid and cut the body into thin rings.

paper towels. Sprinkle lightly with salt and continue with the remaining squid. The pieces will take about 3 minutes to cook. Place on serving dishes and garnish each dish with a wedge of lemon and some parsley.

Cook's Notes

 Time
Preparation takes about 25 minutes, cooking takes 3 minutes per batch of 6 pieces.

 Serving Ideas
Sprinkle the squid with chopped fresh oregano just before serving.

 Preparation
Do not coat the pieces of squid too soon before frying or they will become soggy.

 Watchpoint
Once the squid is added to the hot oil, cover the fryer as the oil will tend to spatter.

 Cook's Tip
If the squid must be re-heated, spread the pieces on wire cooling racks covered with paper towels and place in a slow oven for about 10 minutes. Do not re-fry, as this toughens the squid.

SERVES 4

FRIED AUBERGINE WITH TZATZIKI

The fresh taste of cucumber, mint and yogurt is the perfect complement to rich, fried aubergine slices.

4 small or 2 medium sized aubergines
60g/2oz plain flour
Salt and pepper
Vegetable oil for frying

Tzatziki

¼ cucumber, finely chopped or grated
Salt and pepper
15ml/1 tbsp olive oil
5ml/1 tsp white wine vinegar
1 clove garlic, crushed
140ml/¼ pint natural yogurt
10ml/2 tsps chopped fresh mint
Whole mint leaves for garnishing

1. Wash the aubergines and dry them. Cut into 5mm/¼ inch rounds and lightly score the sides with a sharp knife. Sprinkle both sides with salt and leave to drain in a colander or on paper towels for 30 minutes before using.

2. Sprinkle the cucumber lightly with salt and leave in a colander, slightly weighted down, to drain.

3. Rinse both the aubergine slices and cucumber to remove the salt, pat the aubergine slices dry on paper towels and squeeze excess moisture from the cucumber.

4. Mix the salt and pepper together with the flour and coat the aubergine slices well. Heat the oil to 180°C/350°F and fry the aubergine slices a few at a time. Remove them with a draining spoon to paper towels and sprinkle lightly with salt. Continue with the remaining slices.

5. Meanwhile, mix the oil and vinegar until well blended and add the crushed garlic. Mix in the yogurt and add the

Step 1 Score the aubergine slices on both sides, sprinkle lightly with salt and leave to drain in a colander or on paper towels.

Step 3 Rinse the cucumber and squeeze, or press between two plates to remove excess moisture.

Step 4 Coat the aubergine slices in seasoned flour and fry them, a few at a time, in hot oil until they turn golden brown. Remove with a draining spoon.

drained cucumber. To serve, arrange the aubergine slices on individual plates or one large plate and add the Tzatziki. Garnish with mint leaves.

Cook's Notes

Cook's Tip
Sprinkling aubergine and cucumber with salt before using draws out excess moisture and bitter juices. Sprinkling deep-fried food lightly with salt while it stands helps to draw out excess fat.

Variation
Courgettes may be used instead of aubergines. Top and tail the courgettes and slice them into 3-4 lengthwise slices. Courgettes do not have to be sprinkled with salt and left to stand.

Time
Preparation takes about 30 minutes, cooking time takes about 2-3 minutes per batch of aubergine slices.

SERVES 6

EGG AND LEMON SOUP

This is one of the best known of all
Greek soups. Diced chicken can be
added to make a more filling soup.

1.5 litres/2½ pints chicken stock
2 eggs, separated
2 lemons
60g/2oz rice, rinsed

1. Bring the stock to the boil in a large saucepan. When boiling, add the rice and cook for about 10 minutes. Meanwhile, beat the eggs with 15ml/1 tbsp cold water for about 3 minutes, or until lightly frothy. Squeeze the lemons for juice and add to the eggs, straining out any seeds. Beat for about 1 minute to blend well.

2. Beat a few spoonfuls of the hot stock into the egg mixture.

Step 1 Squeeze the lemons for juice and add to the egg yolks, straining out any seeds. Beat for about a minute to blend well.

Step 2 Beat a few spoonfuls of the hot stock into the egg mixture.

Step 3 Pour the egg mixture back into the stock in a thin, steady stream, stirring continuously. Do not allow to boil.

3. Gradually add that back to the stock, stirring continuously. Put the soup back over very low heat for about 1-2 minutes, stirring constantly. Do not allow the soup to boil. Serve immediately.

Cook's Notes

Variation
The soup may be served without rice, if desired.

Watchpoint
If the stock boils once the egg is added, it will curdle and the soup will be spoiled.

Time
Preparation takes about 15 minutes, longer if making stock from scratch. Cooking takes about 12-13 minutes. Home made stock will take about 1-1½ hours to make.

Serving Ideas
Sprinkle the soup with chopped fresh oregano or parsley. Also, slice a lemon thinly and float one slice on the top of each serving bowl.

MAKES 1 OMELETTE

FRESH TOMATO OMELETTE

For a summer starter or lunch, don't forget
about omelettes. This one is especially
summery with its ripe tomatoes and fresh herbs.

450g/1lb tomatoes
2.5ml/½ tsp chopped fresh oregano or basil
Salt and pepper
4 eggs, lightly beaten
45ml/3 tbsps oil

1. To make the tomatoes easier to peel, drop them into boiling water and leave them for about 5 seconds. Remove them with a draining spoon and put immediately into ice cold water. Peel with a sharp knife.

2. Cut the tomatoes in half and remove the seeds and juice with a teaspoon. Cut the tomato halves into thin strips.

3. Beat the eggs with the herbs, salt and pepper and heat

Step 1 Dropping tomatoes in boiling water for about 5 seconds will make them easier to peel.

Step 1 Put the tomatoes immediately into cold water to stop the cooking, and loosen the peels with a small, sharp knife.

Step 2 Remove the seeds and juice from the tomatoes by cutting them in half and scooping the flesh out with a small teaspoon.

the oil in a large frying pan. When the oil is hot, pour in the eggs and stir with a spatula for about 2-3 minutes, or until the eggs are cooked but not completely set. Sprinkle over the tomato strips and cook until just heated through. Sprinkle with chopped parsley, if desired, before serving.

Cook's Notes

Time
Preparation takes about 25 minutes, cooking about 2-3 minutes.

Preparation
Tomatoes may be prepared well in advance and kept in the refrigerator, tightly covered.

Serving Ideas
This omelette is usually served in the frying pan it was cooked in. Alternatively, cut into wedges to serve.

Variation
One clove of garlic, crushed, may be added to the egg mixture if desired.

SERVES 4

TARAMASALATA

This is a classic Greek starter, luxurious
in taste and texture. It is also a
delicious dip for vegetable crudités.

60g/2oz smoked cod's roe
6 slices white bread, crusts removed
1 small onion, finely chopped
1 lemon
90ml/6 tbsps olive oil
Black olives and chopped parsley for garnishing

1. Cut the cod's roe in half and scrape the centre into a bowl, food processor or blender. Discard the skin. Soak the bread in a bowl of water to soften.

2. Squeeze most of the water from the bread and add it to the roe. Squeeze the lemon and add the juice to the roe and bread, straining to remove the seeds. Add the onion and process until the ingredients form a smooth paste, or beat very well with a wooden spoon.

3. Gradually beat in the oil a drop at a time as if making mayonnaise. If using a blender, it is best to make the Taramasalata in two batches.

4. When all the oil has been added, spoon the Taramasalata into a bowl and chill slightly before serving. Sprinkle with chopped parsley and garnish with black olives.

Step 1 Remove the soft insides of the smoked cod's roe by cutting it in half and scraping with a spoon. Discard the skin.

Step 2 Squeeze the bread to remove excess moisture.

Step 3 Add the oil gradually, drop by drop, beating well continuously, or with the blender or food processor running.

Cook's Notes

 Time
Preparation takes about 15 minutes using a blender or food processor and about 25 minutes if beating by hand.

 Preparation
If prepared in advance, remove from the refrigerator about 20 minutes before serving.

 Watchpoint
Do not add the oil too quickly or the mixture will curdle. If it does, add a bit more soaked bread and it should come together.

 Cook's Tip
Home-made taramasalata is not as pink as that bought commercially.

Variation
If desired, substitute garlic for the onion.

 Serving Ideas
Warm pitta bread or toast makes a good accompaniment.

SERVES 6-12

SPINACH AND CHEESE PIE

Traditionally made at Easter, this classic
Greek pie is now enjoyed all year round.
Packaged pastry makes it simplicity itself.

450g/1lb package fyllo pastry
120g/4oz butter, melted
900g/2lbs fresh spinach
45ml/3 tbsps olive oil
2 onions, finely chopped
45ml/3 tbsps chopped fresh dill
Salt and pepper
3 eggs, slightly beaten
225g/8oz feta cheese, crumbled

1. Preheat the oven to 190°C/375°F/Gas Mark 5. Unfold the pastry on a flat surface and cut it to fit the size of the baking dish to be used. Keep the pastry covered.

2. Tear the stalks off the spinach and wash the leaves well. Shred the leaves with a sharp knife.

3. Heat the oil in a large sauté pan and cook the onions until soft. Add the spinach and stir over a medium heat for about 5 minutes. Turn up the heat to evaporate any moisture.

4. Allow the spinach and onions to cool. Mix in the dill, eggs, salt, pepper, and cheese.

5. Melt the butter and brush the baking dish on the bottom and sides. Brush top sheet of fyllo pastry and place it in the dish. Brush another sheet and place that on top of the first. Repeat to make 8 layers of pastry.

6. Spread on the filling and cover the top with 6 or 7 layers

Step 2 Before washing the spinach, cut off the stalks by holding the leaves firmly and pulling the stems backwards.

Step 5 To assemble the pie, butter the base and sides of the dish and then brush each layer of pastry before stacking them up in the dish.

of pastry, brushing each layer with melted butter. Brush the top layer well and score the pastry in square or diamond shapes. Do not cut through to the bottom layer.

7. Sprinkle with water and bake for 40 minutes or until crisp and golden.

8. Leave the pie to stand for about 10 minutes and then cut through the scoring completely to the bottom layer. Lift out the pieces to a serving dish.

Cook's Notes

Serving Ideas
Serve hot or cold. If serving cold, use olive oil to brush the pastry instead of butter. Serves 6 as a main course, 12 as first course.

Buying Guide
Pastry is available fresh or frozen in large supermarkets or speciality shops.

Time
Preparation takes about 25 minutes, cooking about 40 minutes.

Preparation
The pie can be cooked in advance and reheated for 10 minutes to serve hot.

Cook's Tip
Pastry will go a little soggy when prepared more than a day in advance.

SERVES 6

SAVOURY FILLED PIES

Packaged pastry makes these pies very
easy. They make excellent starters,
snacks or light meals with a salad.

225g/8oz package fyllo pastry
90g/3oz butter, melted
225g/8oz sprue (thin asparagus)
120g/4oz feta cheese
140g/¼ pint plain yogurt
2 eggs, beaten
3 spring onions, finely chopped
15ml/1 tbsp chopped mint
Salt and pepper

1. Use a patty tin with 12 spaces or use 12 ramekin dishes.
Cut the pastry in squares large enough to fill the pans or
dishes, with enough to overlap the tops by about 2.5cm/1
inch.

2. Layer 3 sheets of pastry, each brushed with melted
butter. Cut into 7.5cm/3 inch squares and stack 3 squares,
turning each slightly to make a frilled edge. Carefully push
the pastry into buttered patty tins or ramekins and keep
covered while preparing the filling.

3. Cut the sprue into 2.5cm/1 inch pieces, leaving the tips
whole. Cook in boiling salted water until just tender. Rinse
under cold water and allow to drain completely. Mix
together thoroughly the cheese, yogurt, eggs, onions,
mint, salt and pepper. Stir in the drained sprue and fill the
pastry to within 1.25cm/½ inch of the top.

4. Bake in a preheated 190°C/375°F/Gas Mark 5 oven for
about 25 minutes or until the pastry is crisp and golden and
the filling is set and risen. Allow to cool for about 10 minutes
and then remove to a serving dish.

To chop spring
onions quickly, cut
several into
quarters
lengthways and
then cut crosswise
into small pieces
using a very
sharp knife.

Step 2 Fill patty
tins or ramekin
dishes with the
prepared pastry
to form tartlet
cases.

Step 3 The
cheese should still
be fairly chunky
when all the filling
ingredients are
mixed.

Cook's Notes

Variation
Use spinach instead of
asparagus. Cook the spinach
briefly and drain it well before
combining with the filling ingredients.
Substitute other herbs for mint, if
desired.

Time
Preparation takes about 30
minutes, cooking takes about
25 minutes.

Cook's Tip
If prepared in advance, reheat
for about 5 minutes to serve.
The pies can also be served cold.

SERVES 6-8

DOLMADES

In Greece, stuffed vine leaves are not
served with a tomato sauce. Try a light
egg-lemon sauce or plain yogurt instead.

225g/8oz fresh vine leaves or leaves packed in brine
180g/6oz long-grain rice, cooked
8 spring onions, finely chopped
25ml/1½ tbsps chopped fresh dill
45ml/3 tbsps chopped fresh mint
15ml/1 tbsp chopped fresh parsley
60g/2oz pine nuts
60g/2oz currants
Salt and pepper
140ml/¼ pint olive oil
Juice of 1 lemon

1. If using fresh vine leaves, put them into boiling water for about 1 minute. Remove them and drain. If using preserved vine leaves, rinse them and then place in a bowl of hot water for 5 minutes to soak. Strain and pat dry.

2. Mix together all the remaining ingredients except the olive oil and lemon juice. Taste the filling and adjust the seasoning if necessary.

3. Spread the vine leaves out on a flat surface, vein side upwards. Cut off the stems and place about 10ml/2 tsps of filling on each leaf, pressing it into a sausage shape.

4. Fold the sides of the leaves over to partially cover the stuffing and roll up as for a Swiss roll. Place the rolls seam side down in a large saucepan. Pour over the olive oil and lemon juice.

Step 3 Spread the leaves out on a flat surface. Place spoonfuls of stuffing on the leaves and make into a sausage shape.

Step 4 Fold the sides over the filling and roll up the leaves.

5. Pour hot water over the rolls until it comes about halfway up their sides. Place a plate on top of the rolls to keep them in place, cover the pan and cook slowly for about 40 minutes.

6. Remove the Dolmades to a serving plate and accompany with lemon wedges, black olives and plain yogurt if desired.

 Cook's Notes

 Time
Preparation takes about 30 minutes, cooking takes about 40 minutes.

 Serving Ideas
Dolmades may be served either hot or cold, and are ideal for picnics.

 Variation
Other ingredients may be used in the filling. Substitute chopped olives, almonds or chopped cooked lamb.

 Preparation
Dolmades may be prepared a day before serving. Leave in their liquid in the refrigerator and reheat just before serving.

SERVES 4

GREEK COUNTRY SALAD

Lettuce is cut finely for salads
in Greece. In fact, the finer the shreds of lettuce
the better the salad is considered to be.

30ml/2 tbsps olive oil
15ml/1 tbsp lemon juice
Salt and ground black pepper
1 clove garlic, crushed
1 cos lettuce, well washed
3 tomatoes, sliced
90g/3oz black olives
120g/4oz feta cheese, diced
½ red pepper, seeded, cored, and sliced
6 peperonata
Fresh or dried oregano

Step 2 To shred the lettuce leaves faster, stack them up and use a sharp knife to shred 5 or 6 leaves at a time.

Step 3 Use a serrated fruit knife or a bread knife to make the tomatoes easier to slice and the slices neater looking.

Step 1 If a thick dressing is desired, first whisk the lemon juice, salt, pepper and garlic together in a small bowl and then add the oil gradually, whisking constantly.

1. Whisk the oil, lemon juice, salt, pepper and garlic together until well emulsified. A blender or food processor may be used for this.

2. Stack up 5 or 6 lettuce leaves and shred them finely with a sharp knife.

3. Place the lettuce in the bottom of a serving dish and arrange the other ingredients on top. Spoon over the dressing and sprinkle on the oregano.

Cook's Notes

 Buying Guide
Peperonata are small whole peppers preserved in brine. They can be bought bottled in delicatessens and some supermarkets.

 Variation
Substitute green pepper for red pepper if desired. Other varieties of lettuce may also be used.

 Time
Preparation takes about 10-15 minutes.

SERVES 4

STUFFED TOMATOES

In Greece, stuffed vegetables are
often cooked in olive oil and no
other liquid except the natural juices

4 large beefsteak tomatoes
180g/6oz cooked rice
10ml/2 tsps chopped oregano
1 clove garlic, crushed
2 hard-boiled eggs
60g/4 tbsps feta cheese, grated
30g/1oz black olives, chopped
Salt and pepper
Olive oil

1. Preheat the oven to 190°C/375°F/Gas Mark 5. Choose tomatoes with nice looking stems and leaves. Cut about 2.5cm/1 inch off the top of each tomato on the stem end. Reserve the tops. Scoop out the pulp and seeds with a small teaspoon into a strainer. Sieve and reserve the juice and pulp.

2. Chop the egg using an egg slicer or a food processor. Mix all the stuffing ingredients together and add some of the reserved tomato pulp and juice.

3. Stuff the tomatoes and place on the caps, leaving some stuffing showing around the edges. Place the tomatoes in a baking dish.

4. Drizzle olive oil over the tops of the tomatoes and bake for about 20 minutes, depending on the ripeness of the tomatoes. Transfer to a serving dish and serve hot or cold.

Step 1 Cut the top off of each tomato on the stem end. Scoop out the pulp and seeds with a small teaspoon or use a serrated grapefruit knife.

Step 2 To chop an egg using an egg slicer, place the egg in the slicer and cut down into rounds.

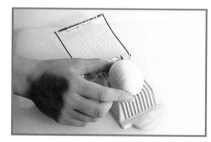

Step 2 Carefully remove the egg, replace it in the slicer and cut down lengthways.

Cook's Notes

Variation
Mix the filling ingredients with oil and lemon juice. Stuff the tomatoes and serve them cold.

Time
Preparation takes about 30 minutes, cooking takes about 20 minutes.

Watchpoint
The 20 minute cooking time is just a guide. Watch the tomatoes carefully – they will fall apart easily if overcooked.

Cook's Tip
Keep the hard-boiled eggs in cold water until ready to use. This prevents a grey ring from forming around the yolk.

SERVES 4

STUFFED COURGETTES

When stuffed vegetables are served with a sauce
in Greece, it is usually a lemon-egg mixture.
Try the sauce with peppers or vine leaves, too.

4 medium-sized courgettes
30g/2 tbsps butter or margarine
1 small onion, finely chopped
120g/4oz minced lamb or beef
5ml/1 tsp ground cumin
5ml/1 tsp chopped oregano
10ml/2 tsps chopped fresh parsley
10ml/2 tsps chopped fresh fennel
60g/2oz cooked long-grain rice
30g/2 tbsps grated cheese
Salt and pepper

Egg and Lemon Sauce

2 egg yolks
1 lemon
Salt and pepper

Step 1 Once the courgettes are washed, topped and tailed, cut off a thin strip of skin lengthwise, then hollow out courgettes using a swivel vegetable peeler.

Step 4 Pile the stuffing into the hollowed-out courgette using a teaspoon.

1. Wash the courgettes well and top and tail them. Using a swivel vegetable peeler, apple corer or a small baller, scoop the middle out of the courgettes, being careful not to damage the outer skins. Leave a thin margin of flesh on the inside for support. Alternatively, slice lengthwise and scoop out the middle.

2. Place the courgettes in boiling salted water and parboil for about 2 minutes. Rinse immediately in cold water and leave to drain. Meanwhile, chop parsley using a large, sharp knife.

3. Prepare the stuffing by softening the onions in half of the butter until they are just transparent. Add the meat and cook until just beginning to brown. Chop up reserved courgette flesh and add it to the meat. Mix with the remaining stuffing ingredients.

4. Mix the stuffing well and fill the hollow in each courgette using a small teaspoon.

5. Melt the remaining butter in a large frying pan or sauté pan and, when foaming, place in the courgettes in a single layer. Add water to the pan to come halfway up the sides of the vegetables and cover the pan. Cook over gentle heat for about 20 minutes, basting the courgettes occasionally. Add more water during cooking as necessary.

6. When the courgettes are tender, remove them to a serving dish and keep them warm. Reserve about 60-90ml/4-6 tbsps of the liquid in the pan.

7. To prepare the sauce, beat the egg yolks and the lemon juice together until slightly thickened. Add some of the hot cooking liquid to the eggs and lemon juice and then return the mixture to a small saucepan. Cook over gentle heat, whisking constantly until slightly thickened. Strain over the courgettes before serving. Garnish with sprigs of fresh herbs if desired.

Cook's Notes

 Serving Ideas
Stuffed vegetables may be served as a first dish or side dish. The courgettes may be served cold without the sauce.

Watchpoint
Do not allow the sauce to boil once the eggs have been added; it will curdle.

 Time
Preparation takes about 30 minutes, cooking takes about 20 minutes.

SERVES 4

STUFFED AUBERGINE

In Greece aubergines are hollowed out from one end and stuffed. Our recipe employs the easy method of cutting them in half.

2 small aubergines
30g/2 tbsps butter or margarine
1 small onion, finely chopped
1 clove garlic, crushed
150g/5oz long-grain rice, cooked
10ml/2 tsps oregano
Pinch cinnamon
Salt and pepper
120g/4oz tomatoes, peeled, seeded and
   coarsely chopped

1. Preheat oven to 180°C/350°F/Gas Mark 4. Wrap aubergines in paper or foil and bake for 20 minutes to soften. Allow to cool, cut in half and scoop out the pulp leaving a 1.25cm/½ inch border to form a shell.

2. Melt butter or margarine and add the onion and garlic.

Step 1 Cut the cooked aubergines in half and scoop out the pulp with a spoon or melon baller.

Step 1 Leave a layer of pulp on the inside of the skin to form a shell.

Step 2 Chop the pulp roughly before adding to the onions.

Cook to soften slightly. Chop the aubergine pulp roughly and add to the pan. Cook for about 5 minutes and then add the remaining ingredients.

3. Fill the aubergine shells and place them in an ovenproof dish or on a baking sheet. Bake an additional 20 minutes in the oven. Garnish with chopped parsley or other herbs if desired.

Cook's Notes

Time
Preparation takes about 25 minutes, cooking takes about 40 minutes.

Preparation
Pre-cooking the aubergine makes it easier to remove the pulp.

Variation
The aubergines may be sprinkled with dry breadcrumbs and drizzled with olive oil before baking. Add cheese to the filling if desired.

Serving Ideas
Serve the aubergines hot or cold as a first course or a vegetable side dish.

SERVES 4

STUFFED PEPPERS

Stuffed vegetables are very popular in Mediterranean countries. The addition of lamb to the stuffing makes these a meal in themselves.

4 medium-sized red or green peppers
140ml/¼ pint olive oil
1 small onion, finely chopped
225g/8oz minced lamb or beef
15ml/1 tbsp chopped fresh dill
10ml/2 tsps chopped fresh coriander
10ml/2 tsps lemon juice
Grated rind of half a lemon
Salt and pepper
60g/2oz grated cheese
120g/4oz long-grain rice, cooked

1. Wash the peppers and place them in a pan of boiling water. Parboil for about 3 minutes and allow to drain and cool.

2. Cut about 2.5cm/1 inch off the tops and remove the core and seeds. Trim the bottoms of the peppers so that they will stand upright.

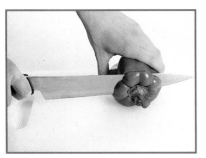

Step 2 Cut the tops off the peppers, but leave the stems attached.

Step 2 Remove the core and seeds with a teaspoon or small knife. If necessary, rinse to remove all the seeds.

Step 2 Slice a thin piece off the bottoms of the peppers so that they will stand level while cooking.

3. Heat 30ml/2 tbsps of the oil and cook the onions briefly. Add the lamb and cook until beginning to brown. Add the remaining filling ingredients and stuff the peppers. Put on the tops.

4. Stand the peppers upright close together in a baking dish. Pour over the remaining oil and add enough water to come halfway up the sides of the peppers. Cook 40-45 minutes or until the peppers are tender, basting often. Remove the peppers to a serving dish with a slotted spoon.

Cook's Notes

Preparation
Parboiling the peppers helps to speed up their cooking and makes it easier to remove the core and seeds.

Serving Ideas
Serve the peppers either hot or cold, as a first course or a vegetable side dish.

SERVES 4

OKRA CASSEROLE

This vegetable has always been popular in
Mediterranean cookery and is becoming easier
to find in supermarkets and greengrocers.

60ml/4 tbsps olive oil
1 small onion, sliced
225g/8oz okra
6 ripe tomatoes, peeled and quartered
Juice of half a lemon
Salt and pepper
Chopped parsley

1. Heat the olive oil in a sauté pan and cook the onion until soft but not coloured.

2. Remove just the stems from the okra, but leave on the tops and tails.

To slice onions, peel and cut in half lengthwise. Place cut side down on chopping board and use a sharp knife to cut across in thin slices.

Cook the onion in the olive oil until soft and transparent.

Step 2 Trim the stems from the tops of the okra, but do not top and tail.

3. Add the okra to the pan and cook for 10 minutes. Add remaining ingredients and cook to heat the tomatoes through. Spoon into a serving dish and serve hot or cold with lamb or chicken.

Cook's Notes

Variation
Substitute canned okra, but drain and rinse before use. Cut the cooking time in half. Green beans may be used instead of okra.

Preparation
If too much liquid is left at the end of cooking, remove the vegetables and boil to reduce the sauce.

Cook's Tip
Okra only needs brief cooking or it will become soggy.

SERVES 4

COURGETTE AND PEPPER SALAD

Salad dressing in Greece is most commonly made from olive oil and lemon juice instead of vinegar.

675g/1½ lbs very small courgettes
1 red pepper, cored, seeded and thinly sliced
90ml/6 tbsps olive oil
Juice and zest of 1 small lemon
Fresh basil
Salt and pepper
Pinch sugar
Whole basil leaves for garnish

1. Top and tail the courgettes. Use a cannelle knife to remove strips of peel from the courgettes. Cut the courgettes in half. If using baby courgettes, top and tail, but leave whole.

2. Place the courgettes and red pepper in boiling salted water and cook for 2 minutes. Allow to drain.

3. Strip the zest from the lemons with a zester. Alternatively, use a swivel peeler to take off strips and then cut the peel in very fine shreds. Blanch for 2 minutes.

4. Mix the oil, lemon juice, chopped basil, salt and pepper and sugar, if desired. Pour over the vegetables while they are still warm and sprinkle with the lemon zest. Garnish with whole basil leaves.

Step 3 Use a lemon zester to make thin strips of lemon peel.

Step 3 As an alternative method, use a swivel peeler to remove thin strips of peel and then cut into thin shreds.

Step 4 Mix the oil, lemon juice, basil, sugar, salt and pepper together well and pour over the warm vegetables.

Cook's Notes

 **Cook's Tip**
If serving the salad cold, rinse the vegetables under cold running water and leave to drain thoroughly

Time
Preparation takes about 25 minutes, cooking takes about 2 minutes.

 Serving Ideas
Serve as a side salad, first course, or part of an hors d'oeuvre selection.

SERVES 4

CAULIFLOWER AND OLIVES

Kalamata, where this dish is said to
have originated, is an area of Greece
well known for its black olives.

1 large cauliflower
60ml/4 tbsps olive oil
1 onion, cut in rings
140ml/¼ pint water
Juice of half a lemon
45ml/3 tbsps tomato purée
Salt and pepper
90g/3oz black olives
30ml/2 tbsps chopped parsley

1. Trim the leaves from the cauliflower and remove the core. Cut into medium sized pieces.

2. Heat the oil and sauté the cauliflower for 1-2 minutes. Remove to a plate and add the onion to the pan. Cook to soften and add the water and lemon juice. Bring to the boil and return the cauliflower to the pan. Cook until tender.

Step 1 Trim the leaves from the cauliflower and remove the core with a small, sharp knife. Cut the florets into even-sized pieces.

Step 2 When cutting an onion into rings, pierce with a fork and hold the handle to keep the onion steady while slicing.

Step 4 To pit olives, use a cherry pitter or roll them firmly on a flat surface to loosen the stones, then use a swivel peeler to remove them.

3. Remove the cauliflower to a serving dish and add the tomato purée to the liquid and boil to reduce.

4. Pit the olives, chop them roughly and add to the pan. Pour the sauce over the cauliflower and sprinkle with chopped parsley to serve.

Cook's Notes

Cook's Tip
A bay leaf may be added to the water while cooking the cauliflower. This reduces the cauliflower smell.

Variation
Add strips of tomato pulp with the olives if desired. Green olives may be substituted for black.

Time
Preparation takes about 25 minutes, cooking takes about 20 minutes.

SERVES 4-6

PEAS AND ARTICHOKES

Fresh peas are a springtime delicacy in
Greece. They are well worth the effort
of shelling for their taste and texture.

900g/2lbs fresh peas
Juice of 1 lemon
Pinch sugar
30ml/2 tbsps chopped fresh dill
30ml/2 tbsps olive oil
1 small bunch spring onions
1 can artichoke hearts, drained
Salt and pepper

1. Shell the peas and put them into boiling salted water
with the lemon juice, a pinch of sugar and the dill. Cover and
cook for about 20 minutes, or until the peas are tender.
Drain and keep warm.

2. Trim the root ends from the spring onions and trim down

Step 1 To shell
peas, break off
stem ends and
pull down strings.

Step 1 Press
open the pods
and push out the
peas with finger
or thumb.

Step 2 Trim the
root ends from
the spring onions
and about
2.5cm/1 inch of
the green tops. If
the onions are
very large, cut in
half lengthways.

the green tops leaving about 2.5cm/1 inch green attached.
Heat the olive oil in a saucepan or sauté pan and cook the
onions to soften. Cut the artichoke hearts into halves or
quarters and add to the onions.

3. Add the peas, salt and pepper and cook for 5 minutes.
Serve immediately.

Cook's Notes

 Variation
Add peeled and seeded
tomatoes, roughly chopped,
during the last 5 minutes of cooking.
Frozen peas may be substituted for
fresh ones, and the cooking time
reduced by half.

Cook's Tip
A pinch of sugar added to
peas while cooking brings out
their flavour.

 Serving Ideas
Serve as a vegetable side dish
with chicken or lamb.

SERVES 4-6

LEMON CHICKEN

Chicken, lemon and basil is an ideal flavour combination and one that is used often in Greek cookery.

1.5kg/3lb chicken, jointed
30ml/2 tbsps olive oil
30g/2 tbsps butter or margarine
1 small onion, cut in thin strips
2 sticks celery, shredded
2 carrots, cut in julienne strips
15ml/1 tbsp chopped fresh basil
1 bay leaf
Juice and grated rind of 2 small lemons
140ml/¼ pint water
Salt and pepper
Pinch sugar (optional)
Lemon slices for garnishing

1. Heat the oil in a large sauté pan. Add the butter or margarine and, when foaming, place in the chicken, skin side down, in one layer. Brown and turn over. Brown the other side. Cook the chicken in two batches if necessary. Remove the chicken to a plate and set aside.

2. Add the vegetables and cook 2-3 minutes over a moderate heat. Add the basil, bay leaf, lemon juice and rind, water, salt and pepper and replace the chicken. Bring the mixture to the boil.

3. Cover the pan and reduce the heat. Allow to simmer about 35-45 minutes or until the chicken is tender and the juices run clear when the thighs are pierced with a fork.

4. Remove the chicken and vegetables to a serving dish and discard the bay leaf. The sauce should be thick, so boil

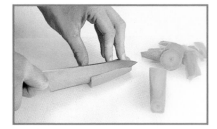

To cut the onion in thin strips, first cut in half through the root end. Using a sharp knife, follow the natural lines in the onion and cut through neatly to the flat base. Cut off the root end and the onion will fall apart in strips.

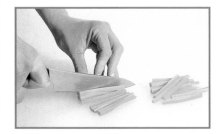

To make the carrots easier to cut into julienne strips, first cut them into rectangular blocks.

Cut the carrot blocks into thin slices and then stack them up to cut into strips quickly.

to reduce if necessary. If the sauce is too tart, add a pinch of sugar. Spoon the sauce over the chicken to serve and garnish with the lemon slices.

Cook's Notes

Watchpoint
Pat the chicken with paper towels to make sure it is really dry or it will spit when browning.

Variation
Use limes instead of lemons and oregano instead of basil.

Serving Ideas
There is a flat, square shaped pasta in Greece that is often served with chicken dishes. Rice is also a good accompaniment, along with a green salad.

Time
Preparation takes about 30 minutes, cooking takes about 45-55 minutes total, including browning of chicken.

SERVES 4-6

CHICKEN WITH OLIVES

This is a chicken sauté dish for olive lovers. Use more or less of them as your own taste dictates.

1.5kg/3lb chicken, jointed
30ml/2 tbsps olive oil
30g/2 tbsps butter or margarine
1 clove garlic, crushed
140ml/¼ pint white wine
140ml/¼ pint chicken stock
Salt and pepper
30ml/2 tbsps chopped parsley
20 pitted black and green olives
4 courgettes, cut in 1.25cm/½ inch pieces

1. Heat the oil in a large sauté pan and add the butter or margarine. When foaming, add the chicken skin side down in one layer. Brown one side of the chicken and turn over to brown the other side. Cook the chicken in two batches if necessary.

To peel a garlic clove easily, first crush it gently with the side of a large knife. The peel will split, making it easier to remove.

To cut the courgettes quickly into chunks, first top and tail them, then cut them in half if small, or quarters if large, lengthwise. Gather the strips together and cut crosswise into chunks of the desired size.

Step 1 Cook the chicken, skin side down first, until golden brown.

2. Turn the chicken skin side up and add the garlic, wine, stock, salt and pepper. Bring to the boil, cover the pan and allow to simmer over gentle heat for about 30-35 minutes.

3. Add the courgettes and cook 10 minutes. Once the chicken and courgettes are done, add the olives and cook to heat through. Add the parsley and remove to a dish to serve.

Cook's Notes

 Time
Preparation takes about 25 minutes, cooking takes about 50-55 minutes.

 Serving Ideas
Serve with rice or pasta and tomato salad.

 Variation
Artichoke hearts may be used in place of the courgettes.

SERVES 4

MARINATED CHICKEN WITH WALNUT SAUCE

Offer your guests a walnut sauce that tastes
delicious and is very easy to make.

2 900g/2lb chickens, cut in half
140ml/¼ pint olive oil
Juice and grated rind of 2 lemons
15ml/1 tbsp chopped fresh oregano
Pinch ground cumin
15ml/1 tbsp chopped fresh parsley
10ml/2 tsps chopped fresh thyme
Salt and pepper
Pinch sugar

Walnut Sauce

2 cloves garlic, peeled and roughly chopped
4 slices bread, crusts removed and soaked in water for 10
   minutes
30ml/2 tbsps white wine vinegar
Salt and pepper
60-75ml/4-5 tbsps olive oil
15-30ml/1-2 tbsps water (optional)
90g/3oz ground walnuts

Step 1 Remove the backbone from the chickens using a pair of sharp poultry shears or a cleaver.

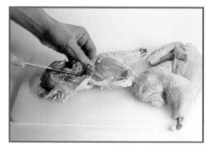

Step 1 Cut away some of the ribcage to make the chickens easier to flatten with a meat mallet or rolling pin.

1.   Remove the backbones from the chickens with poultry shears. Bend the legs backwards to break the ball and socket joint. Cut away some of the ribcage with a sharp knife. Flatten the chickens slightly with a meat mallet or rolling pin. Mix together the marinating ingredients in a large, shallow dish or a large plastic bag. Place in the chicken and turn to coat. If using a plastic bag, fasten securely and place in a dish to catch any drips. Refrigerate for at least 4 hours or overnight.

2.   Place the chicken on a grill and cook under low heat for about 30 minutes, basting frequently. Raise the heat and cook for a further 10 minutes, skin side up, to brown nicely.

3.   Meanwhile, place the garlic in a food processor and squeeze the bread to remove the water. Add the bread to the food processor along with the vinegar. With the machine running, pour the oil through the funnel in a thin, steady stream. Add water if necessary to bring the sauce to coating consistency. Add salt and pepper and stir in the walnuts by hand. When the chicken is cooked, remove it to a serving dish and pour over any remaining marinade. Serve with the walnut sauce.

Cook's Notes

Cook's Tip
If grill does not have an adjustable setting, pre-cook the chicken in the oven for about 30 minutes and then grill for the remaining time until done.

Serving Ideas
Garnish with lemon wedges and sprigs of parsley or other fresh herbs, if desired. Serve with rice and a green or tomato salad.

Time
Preparation takes about 30 minutes plus marinating time, cooking takes about 40 minutes.

SERVES 4-6

MOUSSAKA

There are many different recipes for this casserole dish. This one is light, with no potatoes and a soufflé-like topping.

2 large aubergines, thinly sliced
Oil for frying
30g/2 tbsps butter or margarine
2 onions, thinly sliced
1 clove garlic, crushed
450g/1lb minced lamb
400g/14oz canned tomatoes
30ml/2 tbsps tomato purée
Salt and pepper
10ml/2 tsps chopped oregano
1.25ml/¼ tsp ground cinnamon
1.25ml/¼ tsp ground cumin

White Sauce

60g/4 tbsps butter or margarine
60g/4 tbsps flour
570ml/1 pint milk
Salt and white pepper
30g/2 tbsps grated cheese
2 eggs, separated

Topping

60g/4 tbsps finely grated cheese
60g/4 tbsps dry breadcrumbs

Step 5 To assemble the Moussaka, layer up the meat and aubergines, ending with an even layer of aubergines on top.

1. Preheat the oven to 180°C/350°F/Gas Mark 4. Heat the oil in a large frying pan and fry the aubergine slices for about 3 minutes. Remove them and drain on paper towels.

2. Pour the oil from the pan and melt the butter or margarine. Fry the onion and garlic for about 4 minutes, or until golden brown. Add the lamb and cook for about 10 minutes, breaking up well with a fork. Add the tomatoes and their juice, tomato purée, oregano, spices, salt and pepper. Bring to the boil, cover the pan and allow to simmer over gentle heat for 20 minutes.

3. To prepare the white sauce, melt the butter in a deep saucepan and stir in the flour off the heat. Gradually pour in the milk and add a pinch of salt and pepper. Whisk or beat well and return the pan to the heat. Cook over moderate heat, stirring continuously until thickened. Add the cheese and allow the sauce to cool slightly. Beat the egg yolks with one spoonful of the hot sauce and then gradually add to the sauce.

4. Whip the egg whites until stiff peaks form and fold a spoonful into the hot sauce mixture. Make sure it is thoroughly incorporated and then gently fold in the remaining egg whites.

5. Layer the meat mixture and the aubergine slices in an ovenproof casserole, ending with a layer of aubergine. Spoon the white sauce on top and sprinkle on the topping of cheese and breadcrumbs. Cook for about 45 minutes to 1 hour or until the topping has risen slightly and formed a golden crust on top. Allow to stand for about 5 minutes before serving to make cutting easier.

Cook's Notes

Cook's Tip
If preparing and assembling the moussaka in advance, add whole eggs to the white sauce and omit the separate whisking of egg whites.

Economy
Use left-over roast lamb, minced in a food processor or cut into small dice by hand.

Time
Preparation takes about 30 minutes, cooking takes about 45 minutes to 1 hour.

SERVES 4

LAMB KEBABS

Meat kebabs are the typical Greek dish and these have all the characteristic flavours – oregano, garlic, lemon and olive oil.

675g/1½lbs lean lamb from the leg or neck fillet
Juice of 1 large lemon
90ml/6 tbsps olive oil
1 clove garlic, crushed
15ml/1 tbsp chopped fresh oregano
15ml/1 tbsp chopped fresh thyme
Salt and pepper
2 medium-sized onions
Fresh bay leaves

1. Trim the meat of excess fat and cut it into 5cm/2 inch cubes. Mix together the remaining ingredients except the bay leaves and the onions. Pour the mixture into a shallow dish or into a large plastic bag.

2. Place the meat in the dish or the bag with the marinade and turn to coat completely. If using a bag, tie securely and place in a dish to catch any drips. Leave to marinate for at least four hours, or overnight.

Step 1 Cut the meat into even-sized cubes.

Step 2 Marinade may be poured into a plastic bag. Add the meat, tie the bag securely and shake gently to coat the meat completely. Place the bag in a dish to catch any drips.

Step 3 Thread the meat and bay leaves onto skewers and slip the onion rings over the meat.

3. To assemble the kebabs, remove the meat from the marinade and thread onto skewers, alternating with the fresh bay leaves.

4. Slice the onions into rings and slip the rings over the meat on the skewers.

5. Place the kebabs on the grill pan and grill for about 3 minutes per side under a preheated grill. Baste the kebabs often. Alternatively, grill over hot coals. Pour over any remaining marinade to serve.

Cook's Notes

Time
Preparation takes about 20 minutes plus marinating time. Cooking takes about 3 minutes per side, but will vary according to desired doneness.

Variation
Rump or sirloin steak may be used in place of the lamb. The cooking time will have to be increased, but cook until desired doneness is reached.

Serving Ideas
A Greek country salad and rice make good accompaniments. Kebabs may also be served with stuffed vegetables.

SERVES 6-8

LAMB WITH PASTA AND TOMATOES

Lamb appears in many different guises in Greek cuisine;
this recipe offers a delicious blend of subtle tastes.

1 leg or shoulder of lamb
2 cloves garlic, peeled and cut into thin slivers
60ml/4 tbsps olive oil
50g/1lb fresh tomatoes or 400g/14oz canned tomatoes
15ml/1 tbsp chopped fresh oregano
Salt and pepper
570ml/1 pint lamb or beef stock or water
225g/8oz pasta shells, spirals or other shapes
Finely grated Parmesan cheese

1. Cut slits at about 5cm/2 inch intervals all over the lamb.
Insert small slivers of garlic into each slit. Place the lamb in
a large baking dish and rub the surface with the olive oil.

2. Cook in a preheated oven at 220°C/425°F/Gas Mark 7
for about 50 minutes, basting occasionally.

3. Meanwhile, parboil the pasta for about 5 minutes and
rinse in hot water to remove the starch.

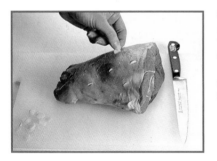

Step 1 Cut slits at
intervals all over
the lamb with a
small, sharp knife.
Insert slivers of
garlic into each
cut.

Step 4 Mix the
tomatoes with
oregano, salt and
pepper and pour
over the lamb.

Step 4 Once the
pasta is added to
the lamb, take the
dish out of the
oven occasionally
and stir so that
the pasta cooks
evenly.

4. Turn the meat over and add the stock or water, pasta and
additional seasoning. Mix the tomatoes with the oregano,
salt and pepper and pour over the lamb. Stir well. Cook an
additional 20-30 minutes, stirring the pasta occasionally to
ensure even cooking.

5. When the pasta is completely cooked, turn the lamb
over again and sprinkle with cheese to serve. Serve directly
from the dish or transfer to a large, deep serving plate.

Cook's Notes

Cook's Tip
If the meat reaches desired
doneness before the pasta is
cooked, remove it to a serving plate
and keep it warm. Continue cooking
the pasta, covering the dish to speed
things up.

Variation
The dish can be made without
tomatoes, if desired. Beef can
be substituted for the lamb and the
cooking time increased.

Time
Preparation takes about 20
minutes, cooking takes about
1 hour 35 minutes.

SERVES 4

FRIED FISH WITH GARLIC SAUCE

Fish in such an attractive shape makes an excellent first course.

900g/2lbs fresh anchovies or whitebait
120g/4oz plain flour
60-90ml/4-6 tbsps cold water
Pinch salt
Oil for frying

Garlic Sauce

4 slices bread, crusts trimmed, soaked in water for 10 minutes
4 cloves garlic, peeled and roughly chopped
30ml/2 tbsps lemon juice
60-75ml/4-5 tbsps olive oil
15-30ml/1-2 tbsps water (optional)
Salt and pepper
10ml/2 tsps chopped fresh parsley
Lemon wedges for garnishing (optional)

---

1. Sift the flour into a deep bowl with a pinch of salt. Gradually stir in the water in the amount needed to make a very thick batter.

2. Heat enough oil for frying in a large, deep pan. A deep-sided sauté pan is ideal.

3. Take 3 fish at a time and dip them into the batter together. Press their tails together firmly to make a fan shape.

4. Lower them carefully into the oil. Fry in several batches until crisp and golden. Continue in the same way with all the remaining fish.

Step 3 Dip three fish at a time into the batter and when coated press the tails together firmly to form a fan shape.

Step 4 Lower the fish carefully into the hot oil to preserve the shape.

5. Meanwhile, squeeze out the bread and place in a food processor with the garlic and lemon juice. With the processor running, add the oil in a thin, steady stream. Add water if the mixture is too thick and dry. Add salt and pepper and stir in the parsley by hand. When all the fish are cooked, sprinkle lightly with salt and arrange on serving plates with some of the garlic sauce and lemon wedges, if desired.

Cook's Notes

Time
Preparation takes about 30 minutes, cooking takes about 3 minutes per batch for the fish.

Preparation
Coat the fish in the batter just before ready for frying.

Cook's Tip
The fish should be eaten immediately after frying. If it is necessary to keep the fish warm, place them on a wire cooling rack covered with paper towels in a slow oven with the door open. Sprinkling fried food lightly with salt helps to absorb excess fat.

Variation
Fish may be dipped in the batter and fried singly if desired. Other fish, such as smelt or sardines, may also be used. Use thin strips of cod or halibut as well. Vary the amount of garlic in the sauce to your own taste.

SERVES 4

BAKED RED MULLET WITH GARLIC AND TOMATOES

This is a fish that appears often in Mediterranean cookery.

4 even-sized red mullet
45ml/3 tbsps olive oil
45ml/3 tbsps dry white wine
1 lemon
2 cloves garlic, crushed
Salt and pepper
340g/12oz fresh tomatoes, thinly sliced or 400g/14oz
  canned tomatoes, strained
Sprigs of fresh dill for garnish

1. Preheat the oven to 190°C/375°F/Gas Mark 5. First scale the fish by running the blunt edge of a large knife over the skin of the fish going from the tail to the head.

2. Using a filleting knife, cut along the belly of the fish from just under the head to the vent, the small opening near the tail. Clean out the cavity of the fish, leaving in the liver if desired. Rinse the fish well inside and out and pat dry.

Step 1 To scale the fish, hold it by the tail and run the blunt side of a knife down the length of the body from the tail to the head.

Step 2 To gut the fish, cut with a filleting knife from just under the head to the vent and remove the insides of the fish.

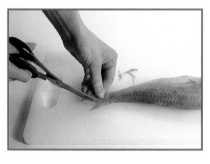

Step 3 Rinse the fish well under cold running water and, using kitchen scissors, trim the tail and fins.

3. Trim the fins and neaten the tail with kitchen scissors. Place the fish head to tail in an ovenproof dish. Mix the oil and the wine together and squeeze the juice from one of the lemons. Add the garlic, salt and pepper and pour over the fish. Place on the tomato slices or if using canned tomatoes, crush them slightly and spoon over. Bake for about 25 minutes, basting frequently until the fish is tender. Garnish with dill.

Cook's Notes

Variation
Add thinly sliced fennel to the fish before baking, in addition to the tomatoes. Substitute other fish such as sea bass, grey mullet, or fish steaks such as cod or halibut.

Time
Preparation takes about 20 minutes, cooking takes about 25 minutes.

Cook's Tip
Red mullet spoils quickly, so use on the day of purchase.

SERVES 4

GRILLED FISH

Grilling fish with herbs and lemon is one of the most delightful ways of preparing it, and is particularly common in the Greek Islands.

2 large bream or other whole fish
Fresh thyme and oregano
Olive oil
Lemon juice
Salt and pepper
Lemon wedges
Vine leaves

1. Preheat a grill. Gut the fish and rinse it well. Pat dry and sprinkle the cavity with salt, pepper and lemon juice. Place sprigs of herbs inside.

2. Make 3 diagonal cuts on the sides of the fish with a sharp knife. Place the fish on the grill rack and sprinkle with olive oil and lemon juice.

3. Cook on both sides until golden brown and crisp. This should take about 8-10 minutes per side, depending on the thickness of the fish.

To make perfect lemon wedges, first cut the ends off the lemons, then cut in 4 or 8 wedges and remove the membrane and seeds.

Step 1 Open the cavity of the fish and sprinkle with salt, pepper and lemon juice.

Step 2 Use a sharp knife to make diagonal cuts on both sides of each fish.

4. If using vine leaves preserved in brine, rinse them well. If using fresh vine leaves, pour over boiling water and leave to stand for about 10 minutes to soften slightly. Drain and allow to cool. Line a large serving platter with the vine leaves and when the fish is cooked place it on top of the leaves. Serve surrounded with lemon wedges.

Cook's Notes

Time
Preparation takes about 20 minutes, cooking takes about 16-20 minutes, depending upon the size of the fish.

Cook's Tip
When grilling large whole fish, slit the skin on both sides to help the fish cook evenly.

Variation
The fish may be wrapped in vine leaves before grilling. This keeps the fish moist and adds extra flavour. Other fish suitable for cooking by this method are red mullet, trout, sea bass, grey mullet, sardines, herring or mackerel.

Preparation
If desired, the fish may be cooked on an outdoor barbecue grill. Wait until the coals have white ash on the top and be sure to oil the racks before placing on the fish, or use a special wire cage for cooking fish.

SERVES 4

FIGS AND CURRANTS WITH ORANGE

Fruit is the most popular sweet in Greece, and fresh figs are a favourite choice.

4 fresh figs
Small bunches of fresh redcurrants
6 oranges
5ml/1 tsp orange flower water

1. Cut the stalks off the tops of the figs but do not peel them.

2. Cut the figs in quarters but do not cut completely through the base. Open the figs out like flowers and stand them on their bases on serving dishes. Arrange small bunches of redcurrants on the figs. Squeeze the juice from 2 of the oranges. Peel and segment the other 4 and arrange segments around each fig.

Step 2 Peel the oranges and cut into segments.

Step 2 With a small, sharp knife, cut the figs into quarters, but not all the way through the base.

Step 2 Open the figs out like flowers.

3. Pour over the orange juice mixed with the orange flower water and chill before serving.

Cook's Notes

Variation
Orange flower water may be omitted if desired.
Blackcurrants may be substituted for the redcurrants.

Serving Ideas
Yogurt and honey may be served as an accompaniment.

Time
Preparation takes about 15 minutes.

SERVES 6-8

BAKLAVA

Fyllo pastry is used for sweet dishes as well as savoury ones. Serve baklava in small portions; it is buttery and rich.

Syrup

340g/12oz granulated sugar
90ml/6 tbsps liquid honey
340ml/¾ pint water
15ml/1 tbsp lemon juice
15ml/1 tbsp orange flower water

Pastry

450g/1lb package fyllo pastry
120g/4oz unsalted butter, melted
120g/4oz chopped walnuts, almonds or pistachio nuts
2.5ml/½ tsp ground cinnamon
25g/1½ tbsps sugar

1. First make the syrup by combining all the ingredients in a heavy-based saucepan. Place over low heat until the sugar dissolves. Stir occasionally. Once the sugar is dissolved, raise the heat and allow the syrup to boil until it is thick enough to coat a spoon. This should take about 2 minutes. Allow the syrup to cool and then chill thoroughly.

2. Preheat the oven to 180°C/350°F/Gas Mark 4. Brush a rectangular baking dish, about 30x20cm/12x18 inches, with some of the melted butter. Place about 8 of the pastry sheets in the dish, brushing the top of each with melted butter.

3. Mix the nuts, sugar and cinnamon together and spread half of the mixture over the top of the pastry. Place two more layers of the buttered pastry on top and then cover with the remaining nuts. Layer up the remaining pastry, brushing each layer with butter.

Step 1 Cook the syrup slowly until the sugar dissolves and the liquid looks clear.

Step 1 Bring the syrup to a rapid boil and allow to boil for about 2 minutes, until thick enough to coat a spoon.

4. With a sharp knife, score a diamond pattern in the top. Sprinkle the pastry with water to keep it moist and prevent curling. Bake for 30 minutes and then raise the oven temperature to 220°C/425°F/Gas Mark 7. Continue baking for 10-15 minutes longer, or until the pastry is cooked and the top is golden brown and crisp.

5. Remove the pastry from the oven and immediately pour over the syrup. Leave the pastry to cool and when thoroughly cold, cut into diamond shapes to serve.

Cook's Notes

Time
Preparation takes about 30 minutes, cooking takes about 40-45 minutes. Preparation time does not include chilling the syrup or the pastry.

Cook's Tip
Baklava may be made several days in advance and kept in the refrigerator. Leave at room temperature for about 20 minutes before serving.

Watchpoint
When boiling the syrup, watch it constantly. Sugar syrups can turn to caramel very quickly. If this happens, discard the syrup and begin again.

HONEY SHORTBREAD

Sweets in a honey syrup are quite common
in Greece. Use hymettus honey, which is
dark and fragrant, for authenticity.

340g/12oz plain flour, sifted
5ml/1 tsp baking powder
5ml/1 tsp bicarbonate of soda
280ml/½ pint olive oil
60g/2oz sugar
140ml/¼ pint brandy
60ml/4 tbsps orange juice
1 tbsp grated orange rind
60g/2oz chopped walnuts
5ml/1 tsp cinnamon

Syrup

280ml/½ pint honey
120g/4oz sugar
280ml/½ pint water

1. Preheat the oven to 180°C/350°F/Gas Mark 4. Sift flour, baking powder and soda together.

2. Combine oil, sugar, brandy, orange juice and rind in a large bowl or food processor. Gradually add the dry ingredients, running the machine in short bursts. Work just until the mixture comes together.

Step 2 Add the dry ingredients to the liquid ingredients gradually, combining well after each addition.

Step 3 Flour hands well and shape mixture into ovals. Place well apart on baking sheets.

Step 5 Dip the shortbread into the syrup and sprinkle on nuts and cinnamon while still wet.

3. Grease and flour several baking sheets. Shape the shortbread mixture into ovals about 7.5cm/3 inches long. Place well apart on prepared baking sheets and cook about 20 minutes. Cool on the baking sheet.

4. Mix the syrup ingredients together and bring to the boil. Boil rapidly for 5 minutes to thicken. Allow to cool.

5. Dip the cooled shortbread into the syrup and sprinkle with nuts and cinnamon. Allow to set slightly before serving.

Cook's Notes

Freezing
Do not dip the biscuits in syrup. Wrap them well, label and store for up to 2 months. Defrost thoroughly before coating with syrup, nuts and cinnamon.

Watchpoint
If the mixture is overworked it becomes too soft to shape and will spread when baked. Chill in the refrigerator to firm up.

Time
Preparation takes about 20 minutes, cooking takes 10 minutes for the syrup to boil and about 20 minutes for the biscuits to bake.

SPANISH COOKING

INTRODUCTION

Spanish cuisine has been a very well kept secret for a long time. There were few Spanish restaurants in Northern Europe, Great Britain or the United States, and there were many misconceptions about the taste of Spanish food.

However, when a country becomes a popular holiday destination, its cuisine quite naturally comes under scrutiny. People discovered there was a lot to like about Spanish food, and that the old myths about the food being fiery-hot and very oily were untrue. While the food is flavourful, this comes mostly from a subtle blend of herbs and spices rather then a heavy-handed use of chilli peppers. Olive oil is the usual choice for frying, sautéeing and salad dressing, but there is no oil more fragrant.

Spanish cuisine is made up of foods that most of us know and like, and ones that are easy to find. It is the different combinations of those familiar ingredients that truly reflect Spanish flavour.

Although the style of eating in Spain is evolving just as it is everywhere else, and food is getting lighter, it still maintains a connection with culinary tradition. The recipes we have included reflect both the traditions and the new trends that make up the best of Spanish cuisine.

SERVES 6-8

GAZPACHO

A typically Spanish soup, this is the
perfect summer first course. The recipe
comes from Andalusia, in Southern Spain.

1 medium green pepper, seeded and roughly chopped
8 medium tomatoes, peeled, seeded and roughly
   chopped
1 large cucumber, peeled and roughly chopped
1 large onion, roughly chopped
90-150g/3-5oz French bread, crusts removed
45ml/3 tbsps red wine vinegar
850ml/1½ pints water
Pinch salt and pepper
1-2 cloves garlic, crushed
45ml/3 tbsps olive oil
10ml/2 tsps tomato purée (optional)

Garnish

1 small onion, diced
½ small cucumber diced, but not peeled
3 tomatoes, peeled, seeded and diced
½ green pepper, seeded and diced

1. Combine all the prepared vegetables in a deep bowl
and add the bread, breaking it into small pieces by hand.
Mix together thoroughly.

2. Add the vinegar, water, salt, pepper and garlic.

3. Pour the mixture, a third at a time, into a blender or food
processor and purée for about 1 minute, or until the soup is
smooth.

4. Pour the purée into a clean bowl and gradually beat in
the olive oil using a whisk. Add enough tomato purée for a
good red colour.

5. Cover the bowl tightly and refrigerate for at least 2 hours,
or until thoroughly chilled. Before serving, whisk the soup
to make sure all the ingredients are blended and then pour
into a large chilled soup tureen or into chilled individual
soup bowls. Serve all the garnishes in separate bowls to be
added to the soup if desired.

Step 2
Add the liquid,
seasoning and
garlic and stir the
mixture well.

Step 4
After puréeing the
soup, pour back
into a bowl and
whisk in the olive
oil by hand.

Cook's Notes

 Time
Preparation takes about 20
minutes and the soup must
chill for at least 2 hours.

 Preparation
Gazpacho may be prepared a
day in advance and kept
overnight in the refrigerator. To quickly
chill the soup, omit 280ml/½ pint water
from the recipe and use crushed ice
instead. Leave refrigerated for 30
minutes, stirring frequently to melt the
ice.

 Variation
Use only enough garlic to suit
your own taste, or omit if
desired. Vary the garnishing
ingredients by using croûtons,
chopped spring onions, or red onions,
red or yellow peppers.

SERVES 6

ANCHOVY STUFFED EGGS

A perfect 'tapa' or hors d'oeuvre with cocktails or
wine, these also make good picnic food.

6 eggs
6 anchovy fillets
½ fresh red chilli, finely chopped
10ml/2 tsps finely chopped parsley or coriander
15ml/1 tbsp lemon juice
45-60ml/3-4 tbsps double cream
Salt
6 black olives, pitted

Step 3
Use the bowl of a
large spoon to roll
the eggs in the
hot water to set
the yolks in the
middle of the
whites.

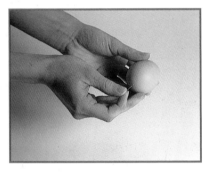

Step 1
Use an egg
pricker or needle
to make a small
hole in the round-
ed end of each
egg to prevent
cracking.

Step 5
To fill the eggs,
use a small
teaspoon or a
piping bag.

1. Prick the rounded end of each egg with a sharp needle
or an egg pricker. Lower the eggs carefully into boiling
water and bring back to the boil.

2. Using a large metal spoon, roll the eggs around in the
pan, gently, while the water comes up to the boil to set the
yolk in the middle of the white. Once the water is boiling,
allow the eggs to cook for about 9-10 minutes.

3. When the eggs are cooked, pour off the hot water and
rinse them under cold running water. Leave in the cold

water until ready for use.

4. Chop the anchovies finely and set them aside in a bowl.
When the eggs have cooled, peel them and cut them in half
lengthways. Scoop out the yolks and add these to the
anchovies. Add all the remaining ingredients, except the
olives, and mix thoroughly. Do not over mix. The filling
should not be a uniform colour.

5. Spoon or pipe the filling back into the hollow of each
egg white and top with half a black olive. Serve chilled.

Cook's Notes

Time
Preparation takes about 20
minutes and cooking takes
9-10 minutes.

Variation
Decorate the tops of the eggs
in various different ways. Use
stuffed green olives, small pieces of red
or green pepper or capers, for
example.

Serving Ideas
Serve as a tapa. The eggs are
also perfect for picnics.

SERVES 6

WHITE GAZPACHO

Often called Ajo Blanco, this soup is
prepared in much the same way as the
Gazpacho based on tomatoes.

180g/6oz blanched almonds
450g/1lb loaf white bread
1-2 cloves garlic, crushed
2 eggs
280ml/½ pint olive oil
140ml/¼ pint white wine vinegar
Pinch of salt and white pepper
1 small bunch of seedless white grapes

Step 6
Beat the reserved
water into the
soup gradually.

Step 3
Purée the
almonds and the
garlic to form a
smooth paste.

Step 5
Squeeze the
bread to remove
all the water.

1. Place the almonds in a bowl and cover with boiling
water. Leave to soak for about 30-45 minutes.

2. Cut the crusts from the bread and cut the bread into
slices or cubes. Place in a bowl and cover with 1 litre/2 pints
cold water.

3. Drain the almonds and place them in a food processor
or blender with the garlic. Process to a smooth paste.

4. Add the eggs and blend well. With the machine running, add the oil in a thin, steady stream.

5. Drain the bread, wringing it out with your hands and reserve the water. Add the bread to the other ingredients in
the food processor or blender and purée. Add vinegar, salt
and white pepper and transfer the mixture to a bowl.

6. Gradually add the water, stirring constantly to the
desired consistency. The soup should be as thick as single
cream. Cover the soup and chill for at least 4 hours or
overnight in the refrigerator. Garnish the soup with halved
grapes to serve.

Cook's Notes

Time
Preparation takes about 25
minutes, with 4 hours
minimum chilling time.

Variation
Use other light coloured fruit
such as melon, apples, pears
or pineapple for garnish. Peeled
cucumber, cut into small dice, may also
be used. Vary the amount of garlic to
suit your taste.

Cook's Tip
Be sure to add the oil in a thin,
steady stream. If added too
quickly, the soup may curdle. Adding
extra bread will sometimes bring the
mixture back together.

SERVES 4-6

TORTILLA
(SPANISH POTATO OMELETTE)

Unlike the usual French omelette, this one
isn't folded, so it's easier to prepare.

90ml/6tbsps olive oil
225g/½lb potatoes, peeled and thinly sliced
1 large onion, peeled and thinly sliced
Salt and pepper
4 eggs
2 tomatoes, peeled, seeded and roughly chopped or
    sliced
2 spring onions, chopped

Step 4
Push the eggs
and potatoes
back from the
sides of the pan
using a fork.

Step 3
Pour the potato,
onion and egg
mixture into a
large frying pan.

Step 5
Slide pan under a
preheated grill to
brown the top of
the omelette.

1. Heat the oil in a large frying pan and add the potatoes. Sprinkle lightly with salt and pepper and cook over medium heat until golden brown and crisp.

2. Add the onion once the potatoes begin to brown slightly. Turn the potatoes and onions over occasionally so that they brown evenly. They should take about 20 minutes to soften and brown.

3. Beat the eggs with a pinch of salt and pepper and stir the potatoes and onions into the eggs and pour the mixture

back into the pan.

4. Cook over gentle heat until the bottom browns lightly.

5. Invert a large plate over the top of the pan and carefully turn the omelette out onto it.

6. Slide the omelette back into the pan so the uncooked side has a chance to brown. Cook until the eggs are set. Garnish with the tomatoes and spring onions and serve warm.

Cook's Notes

Time
Preparation takes about 30 minutes, cooking takes about 30-40 minutes.

Preparation
As the potatoes cook, turn them frequently to prevent them sticking together. They will, however, stick slightly, which is not a problem.

Serving Ideas
The omelette may be cut into small squares and served as a tapa. It can also be served with a salad and bread for a light lunch or supper. Serve hot or cold.

SERVES 4

AVOCADO, ORANGE AND BLACK OLIVE SALAD

A light and colourful salad combining three of
Spain's abundant ingredients.

2 oranges, peeled and segmented
2 avocados
20 black olives, pitted
Basil leaves
½ small red onion, thinly sliced

Dressing

15ml/1 tbsp white wine or sherry vinegar
60ml/4 tbsps olive oil
2.5ml/½ tsp mustard
Pinch of salt and pepper

Step 1
Hit the stone with
the sharp edge of
a large knife and
twist to remove it.

Step 1
Cut the avocados
in half and twist to
separate.

Step 1
To peel the av-
ocado, lightly
score the skin in
two or three
places, place the
half cut side down
on a chopping
board and gently
pull back the
peel.

1. Make sure all the white pith is removed from each segment of orange. Cut the avocados in half and remove the
stone. Peel them and cut into slices.

2. Cut the olives in half and slice them thinly or chop them.

Use kitchen scissors to shred the basil leaves finely.

3. Arrange the orange segments, avocado slices, sliced
onion and olives on serving plates and sprinkle over the
shredded basil leaves. Mix the dressing ingredients
together well and pour over the salad to serve.

Cook's Notes

Time
Preparation takes about 30
minutes.

Cook's Tip
Do not peel the avocados
more than 30 minutes before
serving time unless you prepare the
dressing beforehand and coat the
avocados with it to prevent
discolouration

Variation
Spring onions may be used
instead of the red onions. Use
different varieties of herbs. Substitute
grapefruit for the orange.

SERVES 6

CARROT AND COURGETTE SALAD

This salad couldn't be easier. It is colourful, inexpensive
and can be made almost all year round.

340g/12oz carrots, peeled
340g/12oz courgettes, topped and tailed
Grated rind and juice of 2 oranges
45ml/3 tbsps olive oil
Salt and pepper
60g/4 tbsps unblanched almonds, chopped

Step 2
Grate the
courgettes
coarsely and add
to the carrots.

Step 1
Grate the carrots
on the coarse
side of a grater.

Step 3
When grating
oranges or other
citrus fruit, use a
pastry brush to
remove all the
zest from holes in
grater.

1. Shred the carrots on the coarse side of a grater or use
the coarse grating blade of a food processor. Place in a
large bowl.

2. Grate the courgettes in the same way and add to the
carrots.

3. Grate the orange on the fine side of the grater and then
cut in half to squeeze the juice. Mix the juice and rind with

the olive oil and salt and pepper. Pour over the carrots and
the courgettes and stir well. Leave to marinate for about 15
minutes.

4. Sprinkle over the almonds and toss just before serving.

Cook's Notes

Time
Preparation takes about 15-25
minutes. Vegetables should
marinate for about 15 minutes.

Preparation
The salad may be prepared in
advance and left to stand
longer than 15 minutes. Cover well and
refrigerate.

Serving Ideas
Serve in individual bowls with
a selection of other tapas.
Spoon on to lettuce leaves for a first
course or serve as a side salad.

SERVES 6

ROAST PEPPER SALAD

Charring the peppers makes the skins
easier to remove and gives a slightly
smoky taste that is very pleasant.

6 red peppers
90ml/6 tbsps olive oil
1 clove garlic, roughly chopped
30ml/2 tbsps red or white wine vinegar
Salt and pepper
1 spring onion, diagonally sliced

Step 3
Grill the lightly-
oiled peppers
until the skins are
very charred.

Step 2
Flatten the
peppers by
pushing down
with the palm of
the hand.

Step 4
Use a small,
sharp knife to
peel away the
skin.

1. Preheat a grill and cut the peppers in half, removing the seeds, stems and cores.

2. Flatten the peppers with the palm of your hand and brush the skin side of each pepper lightly with oil. Place the peppers on the grill rack under the grill.

3. Grill the peppers until the skins are well charred on top. Do not turn the peppers over.

4. Wrap the peppers in a clean towel and leave to stand for about 15-20 minutes.

5. Unwrap the peppers and peel off the skin using a small, sharp knife. Cut the peppers into strips or into 2.5cm/1 inch pieces. Mix the remaining oil with the vinegar, salt and pepper. Place the peppers in a serving dish and pour over the dressing. Sprinkle over the garlic and spring onion and leave the peppers to stand for about 30 minutes before serving.

Cook's Notes

Time
Preparation takes about 20 minutes. Grilling time for the peppers is approximately 10-12 minutes.

Preparation
The peppers must be well charred for the skin to loosen easily. Wrapping peppers in a tea towel creates steam, which helps to loosen the skin more easily.

Serving Ideas
Serve as a tapa or mix with cooked cold rice for a more substantial salad.

SERVES 4

SALMON AND VEGETABLE SALAD

The fish in this salad 'cooks' in the refrigerator in its vinegar marinade. Insist on very fresh fish for this recipe.

340g/12oz salmon or salmon trout fillets
2 carrots, peeled and diced
1 large courgette, peeled and diced
1 large turnip, peeled and diced
Chopped fresh coriander
45ml/3 tbsps tarragon or sherry vinegar
Salt and pepper
Pinch cayenne pepper
45ml/3 tbsps olive oil
Whole coriander leaves to garnish

Step 2
Cut all the vegetables into 2.5cm/1 inch dice.

Step 1
Place the salmon in a bowl with the vinegar and stir to coat well.

Step 3
When the salmon has marinated, it will become opaque and look cooked. Mix with the other ingredients.

1. Skin the salmon fillet and cut the fish into 2.5cm/1 inch pieces. Place in a bowl and add the vinegar, stirring well. Leave to stand for at least 2 hours.

2. Cut the vegetables into 1.25cm/½ inch dice and place the carrots in boiling water for about 5 minutes. Add the courgette and turnip during the last minute of cooking time.

3. Add the coriander, oil, salt and pepper and pinch cayenne pepper to the fish. Combine with the vegetables, mixing carefully so the fish does not break up. Chill briefly before serving and garnish with coriander.

Cook's Notes

Time
Preparation takes about 30 minutes, with 2 hours for the salmon to marinate.

Cook's Tip
Fish allowed to marinate in vinegar, lemon or lime juice will appear opaque and 'cooked' after standing for about 2 hours.

Serving Ideas
Serve as a tapa or as a first course.

SERVES 6

FISH ESCABECH

Originally, this method of marinating sautéed fish in vinegar was simply a way of preserving it. All kinds of fish and even poultry and game were prepared this way.

900g/3lb monkfish
90g/6 tbsps flour
Pinch salt and pepper
1 medium carrot, peeled and thinly sliced
1 medium onion, thinly sliced
1 bay leaf
2 sprigs parsley
¼-½ fresh red chilli, finely chopped
340ml/12 fl oz white wine vinegar
6 cloves garlic, peeled and thinly sliced
Olive oil

1. Peel the brownish membrane from the outside of the monkfish tails.

2. Cut along the bone with a sharp filleting knife to separate the flesh from it.

3. Cut the monkfish into slices about 2.5cm/1 inch thick. Mix the salt and pepper with the flour and dredge the slices of monkfish, shaking off the excess. Fry in olive oil until golden brown. Remove and drain on paper towels.

4. Add the carrot and onion and fry gently for about 5 minutes. Add the bay leaf, parsley, vinegar, chilli pepper and 280ml/½ pint water. Cover and simmer gently for about 20 minutes.

5. Place the fish in a shallow casserole dish and pour over the marinade. Sprinkle on the sliced garlic and cover well. Refrigerate for 24 hours, turning the fish over several times.

6. To serve, remove the fish from the marinade and arrange on a serving plate. Pour the marinade on top of the fish and garnish with parsley, if desired.

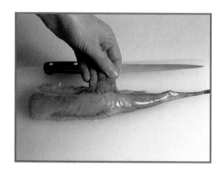

Step 1
Remove the brownish membrane from the outside of the monkfish tails.

Step 2
Using a sharp filleting knife, cut along the bone to separate one side of the tail. Repeat with the other side.

Step 3
Slice the tails into 2.5cm/1 inch thick pieces.

Cook's Notes

Time
Preparation takes about 25 minutes, with 24 hours refrigeration, cooking takes about 25 minutes.

Variation
Other fish, such as whole small trout or trout fillets or fish steaks such as cod or salmon, may be used.

Serving Ideas
Serve as a first course or for a light lunch with a salad and bread.

SERVES 6

PAELLA

This dish has as many variations as Spain has cooks! Fish, meat and poultry combine with vegetables and rice to make a complete meal.

12 mussels in their shells
6 clams (if not available use 6 more mussels)
180g/6oz cod, skinned and cut into 5cm/2 inch pieces
12 Mediterranean prawns
3 chorizos or other spicy sausage
900g/2lb chicken cut in 12 serving-size pieces
1 small onion, chopped
1 clove garlic, crushed
2 small peppers, red and green, seeded and shredded
450g/1lb long grain rice
Large pinch saffron
Salt and pepper
1150ml/2 pints boiling water
120g/5oz frozen peas
3 tomatoes, peeled, seeded and chopped or shredded

1. Scrub the clams and mussels well to remove beards and barnacles. Discard any with broken shells or those that do not close when tapped. Leave the mussels and clams to soak in water with a handful of flour for 30 minutes.

2. Remove the heads and legs from the prawns, if desired, but leave on the tail shells.

3. Place the sausage in a saucepan and cover with water. Bring to the boil and then simmer for 5 minutes. Drain and slice into 5mm/¼ inch rounds. Set aside.

4. Heat the oil and fry the chicken pieces, browning evenly on both sides. Remove and drain on paper towels.

5. Add the sausage, onions, garlic and peppers to the oil in the frying pan and fry briskly for about 3 minutes.

6. Combine the sausage mixture with uncooked rice and saffron and place in a special Paella dish or a large oven-and flame-proof casserole. Pour on the water, season with salt and pepper and bring to the boil. Stir occasionally and allow to boil for about 2 minutes.

7. Add the chicken pieces and place in a preheated 200°C/400°F/Gas Mark 6 oven for about 15 minutes.

8. Add the clams, mussels, prawns, cod and peas and cook a further 10-15 minutes or until the rice is tender, chicken is cooked and mussels and clams open. Discard any that do not open. Add the tomatoes 5 minutes before the end of cooking time and serve immediately.

Step 5
Cook the sausages, onions, garlic and peppers briefly in oil.

Step 6
Combine the sausage mixture, rice and water in a special Paella dish or flame-proof casserole.

Cook's Notes

 Time
Preparation takes about 30-40 minutes, cooking takes about 35-40 minutes.

 Variation
Vary the ingredients to suit your own taste. Use other kinds of fish and shellfish. Omit chicken or substitute pork for part of the quantity. Use red or spring onions if desired and add more sausage.

 Watchpoint
Do not stir the Paella once it goes into the oven.

SERVES 4

MUSSELS IN RED WINE

Red wine makes an unusual, but very pleasant, combination with seafood. This recipe is equally good with clams or cockles.

1.5kg/3lb mussels, well scrubbed
280ml/½ pint dry red wine
90ml/6 tbsps olive oil
4 cloves garlic, finely chopped
2 bay leaves
30ml/2 tbsps fresh thyme, chopped
90ml/6 tbsps red wine vinegar
5ml/1 tsp paprika
Grated rind and juice of 1 lemon
Salt and pepper
Pinch cayenne pepper
Pinch sugar (optional)
Chopped parsley

1. Prepare the mussels as in the recipe for Paella. Place the wine in a large saucepan and bring to the boil. Add the mussels, cover the pan and cook briskly for about 4-5 minutes, stirring frequently, until the shells open. Discard any that do not open.

2. Transfer the mussels to a bowl and pour the cooking liquid through a fine strainer and reserve it.

3. In a clean saucepan, heat the oil and fry the garlic over gentle heat until golden brown. Add the bay leaves, thyme, vinegar, paprika, lemon juice and rind, salt, pepper and cayenne pepper. Pour on the wine, add sugar, if using, and bring to the boil. Cook to reduce to about 180ml/6 fl oz. Allow to cool completely.

4. Remove the mussels from their shells and add them to the liquid, stirring to coat all the mussels. Cover and place in the refrigerator for at least 2 hours. Allow to stand at room temperature for about 30 minutes before serving. Sprinkle with parsley.

Step 1
Cook the mussels over high heat, stirring frequently, until the shells begin to open.

Step 2
Transfer the mussels to a plate and pour the liquid through a fine strainer or through muslin.

Step 4
Remove the mussels from their shells with your fingers or by using a small teaspoon.

Cook's Notes

Time
Preparation takes about 30 minutes and cooking takes about 9-10 minutes.

Serving Ideas
Serve in small dishes as tapas. To serve as a more formal first course, place lettuce leaves on individual plates and spoon on the mussels. Sprinkle with chopped parsley, if desired.

Variation
Shelled mussels, purchased from a fishmonger, or frozen mussels may be used instead. If using frozen mussels, allow a further 2-3 minutes cooking time.

SERVES 4

GRILLED FISH WITH ROMESCU

Romescu is a sauce that evolved from a fish stew recipe
and is still often considered a dish on its own. It is
simple to make and has a strong, pungent taste.

900g/2lbs whole fish such as trout, red mullet, herring,
  sardines or mackerel, allowing 1-4 fish per person,
  depending on size.
Bay leaves
Salt and pepper
Olive oil
Lemon juice

Romescu (Almond and Hot Pepper Sauce)

1 tomato, peeled, seeded and chopped
45g/3 tbsps ground almonds
½ clove garlic, crushed
2.5ml/½ tsp cayenne pepper
Pinch salt
45ml/3 tbsps red wine vinegar
180ml/6 fl oz olive oil

with a wire whisk or a wooden spoon. Make sure each
addition of oil is absorbed before adding more. Once about
half the oil is added, the remainder may be poured in in a
thin, steady stream. Adjust the seasoning and set the sauce
aside.

3. Wash the fish well, sprinkle the cavities with salt and
pepper and place in a bay leaf. Brush the skin with olive oil
and sprinkle with lemon juice. Place under a preheated grill
and cook for about 2-5 minutes per side, depending on the
thickness of the fish. Brush with lemon juice and olive oil
while the fish is grilling. Serve with the sauce and lemon or
lime wedges if desired.

Step 2
Transfer the paste
to a bowl and
whisk in the wine
vinegar.

Step 1
Mix all the
ingredients
together into a
smooth paste
using a mortar
and pestle.

Step 2
Once half the oil
has been added,
add the remain-
der in a thin,
steady stream,
whisking by hand.

1. To prepare the sauce, combine all the ingredients,
except the olive oil and vinegar, in a mortar and pestle and
work to a smooth mixture.

2. Transfer to a bowl, whisk in red wine vinegar and add
the oil gradually, a few drops at a time, mixing vigorously

Cook's Notes

Time
Preparation takes about 20
minutes and cooking takes
about 10-20 minutes.

Preparation
The sauce may be made
several days in advance and
stored tightly sealed in the refrigerator.
Allow the sauce to come to room
temperature and whisk again before
serving.

Serving Ideas
Serve with boiled or fried
potatoes and a salad.

SERVES 6

SEAFOOD STEW

This makes the most of the delicious
and varied fish and shellfish found
off Spain's beautiful coastline.

24 clams or mussels in the shell
3 squid
900g/2lb firm whitefish, filleted into 5cm/2 inch pieces
3 medium-sized tomatoes, peeled, seeded and chopped
½ green pepper, seeded and chopped
1 small onion, chopped
1 clove garlic, finely chopped
280ml/½ pint dry white wine
Salt and pepper
140ml/¼ pint olive oil
6 slices French bread
45ml/3 tbsps chopped parsley

1. Scrub the clams or mussels well to remove the beards and barnacles. Discard any shellfish with broken shells or ones that do not close when tapped. Place the mussels or clams in a large saucepan or heatproof casserole, scatter over about half of the vegetables and garlic and spoon over 60ml/4 tbsps of the olive oil.

2. To clean the squid, hold the tail section in one hand and the head section in the other to pull the tail away from the head.

3. Cut the tentacles free from the head just above the eyes. Discard the head, entrails and ink sack.

4. Remove the quill from the body of the squid and peel away the reddish-purple outer skin.

5. Slice the tail into strips about 1.25cm/½ inch thick. Cut the tentacles into individual pieces.

6. Scatter the squid and the prepared whitefish over the vegetables in the pan and top with the remaining vegetables. Pour over the white wine and season with salt and

pepper. Bring to the boil over high heat and then reduce to simmering. Cover the pan and cook for about 20 minutes or until the clams open, the squid is tender and the fish flakes easily. Discard any clams or mussels that do not open.

7. Heat the remaining olive oil in a frying pan and when hot, add the slices of bread, browning them well on both sides. Drain on paper towels.

8. Place a slice of bread in the bottom of a soup bowl and ladle the fish mixture over the bread. Sprinkle with parsley and serve immediately.

Step 2
To clean the squid, separate the head from the tail by pulling them in opposite directions

Step 4
Remove the quill from the tail and peel the reddish-purple skin from the outside.

Cook's Notes

 Time
Preparation takes about 35 minutes and cooking takes about 20 minutes.

Preparation
Fry the bread while the fish stew is cooking. The stew must be served immediately and not reheated.

Variation
Different kinds of fish, such as haddock, cod, halibut or sea bass can be used.

SERVES 4

MARINATED TROUT WITH EGG SAUCE

This recipe came from Navarre, an area famous for its brook trout.
The simply-prepared sauce allows the flavour of the fish to shine through.

4 even-sized trout, gutted but heads and tails left on
90ml/6 tbsps red wine
45ml/3 tbsps olive oil
45ml/3 tbsps water
1 clove garlic, crushed
2 sprigs fresh mint, 1 sprig fresh rosemary, 1 sprig fresh
    thyme, 1 small bay leaf, crumbled
6 black peppercorns
Pinch salt
3 egg yolks, lightly beaten
15ml/1 tbsp fresh herbs
Lemon or lime slices to garnish

1. Place the fish in a roasting pan and pour over the wine, oil, water and add the garlic and herbs. Sprinkle over the peppercorns and the salt and turn the fish several times to coat them thoroughly with the marinade. Leave at room temperature for about 30 minutes.

2. Place the roasting pan with the fish on top of the stove and bring the marinade just to the simmering point. Cover the pan and place in a preheated 180°C/350°F/Gas Mark 4 oven and cook for about 20 minutes or until the fish is firm.

3. Transfer the fish to a serving dish and peel off the skin on one side. Cover and keep warm.

4. Strain the fish cooking liquid into a bowl or the top of a double boiler and discard the herbs and garlic. Mix about 45ml/3 tbsps of the liquid into the egg yolks and then return to the bowl or double boiler.

5. Heat slowly, whisking constantly until the sauce thickens. Do not allow the sauce to boil. Add the chopped herbs and adjust the seasoning.

6. Coat the sauce over the skinned side of each trout and garnish the plate with lemon or lime wedges. Serve the rest of the sauce separately.

Step 2
Bring the marinade and fish to the simmering point on top of the stove. Allow to boil.

Step 3
When the fish is cooked, transfer to a serving dish and peel off one side of the skin on each fish.

Step 5
Cook the strained marinade and egg yolks slowly in a double boiler, whisking constantly until the sauce thickens.

Cook's Notes

Time
Preparation takes about 30 minutes, cooking takes about 20 minutes for the fish and about 5 minutes to finish the sauce.

Variation
The sauce may be made with white wine instead of red wine if desired.

Serving Ideas
A classic accompaniment is boiled potatoes.

SERVES 4-6

CHORIZO SAUSAGES WITH PEAS AND MINT

Spicy sausages are a perfect foil for the mild flavour of peas
and the cooling tang of mint in this informal dish.

4 chorizos
120g/4oz green streaky bacon, finely diced
1 small onion, finely chopped
½ clove garlic, finely chopped
180ml/6 fl oz white wine
180ml/6 fl oz water
1 bay leaf
Pinch salt and pepper
10ml/2 tsps chopped fresh mint
450g/1lb shelled fresh peas or frozen peas

Step 3
Cook the onions
and garlic until
soft but not
coloured.

Step 2
Cook the bacon
in its own fat until
crisp and golden
brown.

Step 4
Add all the
ingredients and
cook, uncovered,
until tender.

1. Place the chorizo sausages in a saucepan or frying pan and add enough water to cover completely. Bring to the boil and then reduce the heat to simmering. Cook, uncovered, for about 5 minutes and drain on paper towels. Set the sausages aside.

2. Cook the bacon slowly in a frying pan or saucepan until the fat is rendered. Then turn up the heat and cook until crisp and golden brown. Place on paper towels to drain.

3. Add the onion and garlic to the bacon fat in the pan and cook until the onions are softened but not browned. Add the wine, water, bay leaf, bacon, mint, salt and pepper. Bring to the boil over high heat and then reduce to simmering. Add the sausages and cook, partially covered, for about 20 minutes.

4. If using fresh peas, add with the sausages. If using frozen peas, add during the last 5 minutes of cooking time. Remove sausages and slice. Add to the peas and re-heat if necessary. Using a draining spoon, place a serving on each plate.

Cook's Notes

Time
Preparation takes about 20 minutes, or slightly longer if shelling fresh peas. Cooking takes about 35 minutes.

Variation
Broad beans or French beans may be used instead of the peas.

Serving Ideas
Serve as a side dish to meat, poultry or fish. Add rice to serve as a main course.

SERVES 4

SWEETBREADS WITH PEPPERS AND SHERRY

Rich, velvety sweetbreads are perfectly complemented
by the sweet-sour taste of honey and vinegar.

1kg/2.2lbs lamb or calf sweetbreads
1 slice lemon
1 small red pepper, seeded and sliced
1 small green pepper, seeded and sliced
1 medium onion, peeled and thinly sliced
30ml/2 tbsps olive oil
15g/1 tbsp butter or margarine
60ml/4 tbsps dry sherry
30ml/2 tbsps tarragon vinegar
280ml/½ pint chicken or veal stock
15ml/1 tbsp lemon juice
30ml/2 tbsps clear honey
Salt and pepper

1. Soak the sweetbreads in enough water to cover with the lemon slice for at least 2 hours. Transfer the sweetbreads to a saucepan and pour over clean water to cover.

2. Bring to the boil and cook for 10 minutes. Drain the sweetbreads and rinse them under cold water. Place drained sweetbreads on a plate and cover with another plate to weight down slightly. Leave to stand for 15 minutes.

3. Using a small, sharp knife, peel away the outer membrane from the sweetbreads.

4. Heat the oil, add the butter and, when foaming, fry the sweetbreads until golden brown. Remove them to a plate.

5. Cook the peppers and onions until softened and set them aside with the sweetbreads. Pour off any remaining fat in the pan.

6. Add the sherry and vinegar to the pan and boil. Pour on the stock and boil rapidly to reduce by half. Add the lemon juice and honey and return the sweetbreads and vegetables to the pan. Heat through and serve immediately.

Step 1
Soak the sweetbreads with a slice of lemon in enough cold water to cover.

Step 2
Once the sweetbreads have boiled, place them between two plates to weight down slightly.

Step 3
Use a small, sharp knife to pull away the outer membrane from the sweetbreads to keep them from shrinking and toughening.

Cook's Notes

Time
Preparation takes about 45 minutes, with 2 hours soaking time for the sweetbreads. Cooking takes about 25 minutes.

Preparation
The method for preparing sweetbreads is designed to allow the outer membrane to be removed fairly easily. This prevents the sweetbreads from shrinking and toughening.

Buying Guide
Sweetbreads are the thymus or pancreas of lambs and calves. Lamb sweetbreads are more readily available and are less expensive. Sweetbreads have a mild flavour much like chicken.

SERVES 6

PORK WITH TOMATO AND BLACK OLIVE SAUCE

A recipe like this one is often served in a small amount
as one of a selection of tapas – hors d'oeuvres.

1.5kg/3lb pork fillet, cut into 1.25cm/½ inch slices
Salt and pepper
60g/4 tbsps flour
45ml/3 tbsps olive oil
1 medium-sized onion, thinly sliced
450g/1lb canned tomatoes, drained and juice reserved
90ml/6 tbsps white wine
180ml/6 fl oz light stock
3 slices cooked ham, shredded
1 hard-boiled egg
10-12 black olives, pitted and sliced
30ml/2 tbsps chopped parsley or coriander

Step 1
Place pieces of pork in a sieve with the flour and shake to coat evenly.

1. Mix the salt and pepper with the flour and coat the pieces of meat lightly, shaking off the excess. Heat the oil in a large frying pan and fry the meat, in several batches, until brown on both sides. Transfer the meat to a plate.

2. Add the onions to the pan and cook for about 5 minutes over low heat to soften but not brown. Add the tomatoes, wine and stock to the pan and bring to the boil.

3. Return the meat to the pan, cover and cook over low heat for about 30-40 minutes or until the meat is tender. Check the level of liquid and add some reserved tomato juice if necessary.

4. Cut the hard-boiled egg in half and remove the yolk. Cut the white into thin shreds. Five minutes before the end of cooking time, add the ham, egg white, olives and parsley to the sauce.

5. To serve, place pork fillets on individual plates or on a large serving dish and spoon over the sauce. Push the egg yolks through a metal sieve to garnish the top of the pork. Serve immediately.

Step 2
Cook the onions until soft, but not coloured.

Step 5
Push egg yolk through a sieve to garnish the pork.

Cook's Notes

Time
Preparation takes about 25 minutes and cooking takes about 30-40 minutes.

Serving Ideas
Serve with rice or potatoes and a green vegetable.

Buying Guide
Pitted black olives are available in delicatessens and large supermarkets.

SERVES 4

SHERRIED PORK WITH FIGS

Another popular Spanish fruit and meat combination.
Figs look especially attractive as a garnish and
really complement the sherry sauce.

900g/2lb pork fillet
45g/3 tbsps butter or margarine
1 bay leaf
1 sprig fresh thyme
140ml/¼ pint medium-dry sherry
280ml/½ pint brown stock
Juice and zest of 1 large orange
25ml/1½ tbsps cornflour
Pinch cinnamon
Salt and pepper
4 fresh figs

1. Slice the pork fillets into diagonal pieces about 1.25cm/½ inch thick. Melt the butter or margarine in a large sauté pan and, when foaming, place in the slices of pork fillet. Cook quickly on both sides to brown.

2. Pour away most of the fat and add the sherry. Bring to the boil and cook for about 1 minute. Pour on the stock and add the bay leaf and thyme. Bring to the boil and then lower the heat, cover and simmer for about 30 minutes or until the pork is tender.

3. When the pork is cooked, remove it from the pan and boil the liquid to reduce slightly. Add the orange zest to the liquid and mix the juice and cornflour together. Spoon in a bit of the hot liquid and then return the mixture to the pan. Bring to the boil, whisking constantly until thickened and cleared. Stir in a pinch of cinnamon, salt and pepper. Return the pork to the pan and cook to heat through.

4. If the figs are small, quarter them. If they are large, slice lengthways. Remove the pork to a serving dish and spoon over the sauce. Garnish with the sliced or quartered figs.

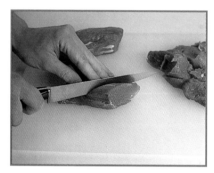

Step 1
Slice the pork fillet into diagonal pieces about 1.25cm/1/2 inch thick.

Step 1
Use a large sauté pan or frying pan to brown the slices of pork on both sides.

Step 3
Cook the pork over moderate heat until tender to the point of a knife. Do not allow the pork to boil rapidly.

Cook's Notes

Time
Preparation takes about 25 minutes and cooking takes about 45 minutes.

Preparation
Pork fillet can toughen if cooked too rapidly or over heat that is too high. Simmer gently in the liquid.

Serving Ideas
Serve with rice, either saffron or plain.

SERVES 4

PEPPERED FILLET OF LAMB WITH FRUIT

In Catalonia, on the border with France,
meat cooked with fruit is extremely popular.

1kg/2¼lbs lamb neck fillets
15g/1 tbsp coarsely crushed black peppercorns
225g/8oz dried fruit salad
60g/4 tbsps butter or margarine
30g/2 tbsps flour
280ml/½ pint light stock
140ml/¼ pint medium dry sherry
45ml/3 tbsps double cream
Pinch salt
Coriander leaves to garnish

brown slightly. Stir in the stock gradually to blend well and add the sherry. Bring to the boil.

5. Drain the fruit, add to the pan and return the lamb fillets. Cover and cook over gentle heat for about 15-20 minutes or until lamb and fruit are tender.

6. When the lamb is cooked, remove it from the pan and slice into diagonal pieces about 5mm/¼ inch thick. Arrange on a serving plate and add the cooked fruit.

7. Add the cream to the sauce and bring to the boil. Allow to boil 1 minute to thicken and cook the cream and spoon the sauce over the fruit and meat to serve.

Step 2
Press the peppercorns firmly into the surface of each lamb fillet using your hand, a meat mallet or rolling pin.

Step 3
Fry the lamb fillets in a sauté pan or frying pan to brown evenly on all sides.

1. Place the fruit salad in a saucepan, cover with water and bring to the boil. Once the water boils, remove from the heat and leave to soak for about 2 hours.

2. Sprinkle the black peppercorns on the lamb fillets and press them in firmly with the palm of your hand or bat them lightly with a meat mallet or rolling pin.

3. Melt the butter or margarine in a large sauté pan and when foaming, add the lamb fillets. Cook over moderately high heat to seal on both sides. When the lamb fillets are brown, remove them to a plate and set them aside.

4. Add the flour to the pan and cook over moderate heat to

Step 6
When lamb is cooked, slice it thinly on the diagonal.

Cook's Notes

Time
Preparation takes about 25 minutes, with 2 hours soaking time for the fruit. Cooking takes about 30-40 minutes.

Variation
Substitute pork fillets or fillet steaks for the lamb neck fillet. Lamb chops may also be used. Any combination of dried fruit may be used in this recipe.

Preparation
When coating the fillets with peppercorns, press firmly so that they stick well in the surface and do not fall off during cooking.

SERVES 4

CHICKEN WITH SAFFRON RICE AND PEAS

Saffron is frequently used in Spanish recipes. While it is expensive.
it gives rice and sauces a lovely golden colour and delicate taste.

30ml/2 tbsps oil
900g-1.5kg/2-3lb chicken, cut into 8 pieces and skinned if
    desired
Salt and pepper
1 small onion, finely chopped
10ml/2 tsps paprika
1 clove garlic, crushed
8 tomatoes, peeled, seeded and chopped
300g/10oz rice
700ml/1¼ pints boiling water
Large pinch saffron or 1.25ml/¼ tsp ground saffron
180g/6oz frozen peas
30ml/2 tbsps chopped parsley

1. Heat the oil in a large frying pan. Season the chicken
with salt and pepper and place it in the hot oil, skin side
down first. Cook over moderate heat, turning the chicken
frequently to brown it lightly. Set the chicken aside.

2. Add the onions to the oil and cook slowly until softened
but not coloured.

3. Add the paprika and cook about 2 minutes, stirring
frequently until the paprika loses some of its red colour. Add
the garlic and the tomatoes.

4. Cook the mixture over high heat for about 5 minutes to
evaporate the liquid from the tomatoes. The mixture should
be of dropping consistency when done. Add the rice, water
and saffron and stir together.

5. Return the chicken to the casserole and bring to the boil
over high heat. Reduce to simmering, cover tightly and
cook for about 20 minutes. Remove chicken and add the
peas and parsley. Cook a further 5-10 minutes, or until rice
is tender. Combine with the chicken to serve.

Step 3
Add the paprika
and cook until it
loses some of its
red colour.

Step 4
When the garlic
and tomatoes are
added, cook over
a high heat to
evaporate the
liquid until the
mixture is of a
dropping
consistency.

Step 5
Stir in the peas
and parsley and
cook for five
minutes.

Cook's Notes

Time
Preparation takes about 20-25
minutes and cooking takes
about 25-35 minutes.

Variation
If using fresh peas, allow
about 400g/14oz of peas in
their pods. Cook fresh peas with the
rice and chicken.

Serving Ideas
This is a very casual, peasant-
type dish which is traditionally
served in the casserole in which it was
cooked.

SERVES 4

SPRING CHICKENS WITH BITTER CHOCOLATE SAUCE

A small amount of unsweetened chocolate lends a rich depth of colour
and a delightfully mysterious flavour to a savoury sauce.

60ml/4 tbsps olive oil
4 poussins
Salt and pepper
45g/3 tbsps flour
1 clove garlic, crushed
280ml/½ pint chicken stock
60ml/4 tbsps dry white wine
10ml/2 tsps unsweetened cooking chocolate, grated
Lemon slices to garnish

Step 2
Cook the flour in the oil until it turns a pale straw colour.

Step 1
Brown the poussins in the hot oil, turning carefully to avoid tearing the skin.

Step 5
Stir the grated chocolate into the sauce and cook over low heat to melt it.

1. Heat the oil in a heavy-based pan or casserole. Season the poussins and place them, breast side down first, in the hot oil. Cook until golden brown on all sides, turning frequently.

2. Transfer the poussins to a plate and add flour to the casserole. Cook until a pale straw colour.

3. Add the garlic and cook to soften. Pour on the stock gradually, mixing well. Add the wine and bring to the boil.

4. Reduce to simmering, replace the poussins and cover the casserole. Cook 20-30 minutes, or until the poussins are tender.

5. Transfer the cooked poussins to a serving dish and skim any fat from the surface of the sauce. Add the grated chocolate and cook, stirring quickly, over low heat for 2-3 minutes. Pour some of the sauce over the poussins and garnish with lemon slices. Serve the rest of the sauce separately.

Cook's Notes

Time
Preparation takes about 20 minutes, cooking takes about 25-35 minutes.

Buying Guide
Unsweetened baking chocolate is not the same as plain chocolate, which must not be used as a substitute. Unsweetened chocolate is available in large supermarkets and speciality shops.

Serving Ideas
Serve with rice and a vegetable such as peas or asparagus, or with a green salad.

SERVES 4

VEAL WITH PEACHES AND PINENUTS

This dish is quite expensive, but very easy
and quick to prepare and cook.

4 ripe peaches
90ml/6 tbsps brandy or sherry
8 veal escalopes
Salt and pepper
140ml/¼ pint dry white wine
Pinch cinnamon
1 small bay leaf
30g/2 tbsps butter or margarine
60g/4 tbsps pinenuts
15ml/1 tbsps cornflour mixed with 30ml/2 tbsps water
Pinch sugar

1. Peel the peaches by dropping them into boiling water for about 30 seconds. Remove immediately to a bowl of cold water and leave to cool completely. Use a small, sharp knife to remove the peels.

2. Cut the peaches in half and twist the halves to separate. Remove the stones and place the peaches in a deep bowl with the brandy or sherry. Stir the peach halves to coat them completely.

3. Place the veal escalopes between 2 sheets of grease-proof paper and use a rolling pin or meat mallet to bat out to flatten slightly. This may not be necessary. Heat the oil and fry the escalopes on both sides until golden brown. Pour on the wine and add the cinnamon, bay leaf, salt, pepper and cover the pan. Cook over low heat for about 15 minutes or until the veal is tender and cooked through.

4. While the veal is cooking, melt the butter in a small frying pan and add the pinenuts. Cook over moderate heat, stir-ring continuously until they are golden brown. Remove from the butter and set them aside to drain.

5. When the veal is cooked, remove it to a serving dish and keep it warm. Add cornflour and water mixture to the pan and bring to the boil. Cook until thickened and cleared.

6. Remove the peaches from the brandy and slice them. Add the peaches and the brandy to the thickened sauce mixture and bring to the boil. Allow to cook rapidly for about 1 minute. Add the sugar, if using. Spoon the peaches and sauce over the veal escalopes and sprinkle on the browned pinenuts. Serve immediately.

Step 1
Place peaches in boiling water for 30 seconds.

Step 1
Transfer to cold water to cool completely – the peel will be easy to remove with a small knife.

Cook's Notes

Time
Preparation takes about 25-30 minutes, cooking takes about 25-30 minutes in total.

Variation
The recipe may be prepared with pork fillet, chicken breasts or duck breasts. Use nectarines or apricots instead of peaches and do not peel them.

CHOCOLATE ALMOND STUFFED FIGS

A positively luxurious pudding that is deceptively easy to prepare. Try it when an elegant sweet is needed.

4 ripe figs
30ml/2 tbsps liquid honey
30g/1oz unsweetened cooking chocolate
90g/3oz ground almonds

Cinnamon Sauce

280ml/½ pint single cream
1 stick cinnamon
2 egg yolks
60g/4 tbsps sugar
Ground cinnamon and blanched almond halves to
    garnish

1. Make a cross cut in each fig without cutting right down through the base. Carefully press the 4 sections of the fig out so that it looks like a flower.

2. Melt the honey and chocolate together over a very gentle heat in a small, heavy-based saucepan.

3. Set aside to cool slightly and then mix in the ground almonds.

4. When the mixture has cooled completely, spoon an equal amount into the centre of each fig.

5. Meanwhile, prepare the sauce. Pour the cream into a deep saucepan and add the cinnamon stick. Bring just to the boil, draw off the heat and leave to infuse.

6. Beat the egg yolks and the sugar together until light and gradually strain on the infused cream.

Step 6
Whisk egg yolks and sugar together until light.

Step 7
Combine cream and eggs and cook over gentle heat until mixture coats the back of a spoon.

7. Return the mixture to the saucepan and stir over gentle heat until it just coats the back of a spoon. Leave to cool until just warm.

8. To serve, pour some of the custard onto a serving plate and tilt the plate slowly to coat the base. Place a filled fig on top of the custard and sprinkle around some of the ground cinnamon, topping each fig with a blanched almond.

Cook's Notes

Time
Preparation takes about 20 minutes and cooking takes about 25 minutes.

Cook's Tip
While the custard is cooling, place a sheet of damp grease-proof paper, wax paper or clingfilm directly onto the surface of the custard. This will prevent a skin from forming. Alternatively, leave out half of the sugar quantity and sprinkle the remainder over the top of the custard skin.

Preparation
Cook the custard over very gentle heat or in a double boiler to prevent curdling. If the custard should curdle, whisk vigorously or process in a food processor or blender and then strain.

MAKES 1150ML/2 PINTS
FROZEN MERINGUE CREAM

This is a richer version of a typical
iced milk sweet found all over Spain.

1150ml/2 pints single cream
90g/3oz sugar
1 whole vanilla pod
60ml/4 tbsps brandy
2 egg whites

Step 6
Freeze the cream mixture in shallow containers or ice cube trays until slushy.

Step 5
Whisk the egg whites until stiff but not dry and fold into the cooled cream mixture.

Step 7
Mix with an electric mixer or in a food processor until the mixture is smooth, and then refreeze.

1. Combine the cream, sugar and vanilla pod in a deep, heavy-based saucepan.

2. Cook over very gentle heat for about 10 minutes, stirring frequently to dissolve the sugar. Do not allow the cream to boil.

3. Cover the pan and leave to infuse for about 15 minutes. Strain into a bowl to remove the vanilla pod and set aside to cool completely.

4. Beat the egg whites until stiff but not dry.

5. Fold them into the cooled cream mixture. Add brandy and chill completely.

6. Pour into a shallow pan or ice cube tray and freeze until slushy.

7. Spoon the mixture into a food processor and work until smooth. Alternatively, use an electric mixer. Return the mixture to the freezer and freeze until nearly solid. Repeat the mixing procedure and then freeze in a rigid plastic container until firm. Allow the container to stand at room temperature for about 10 minutes before serving.

Cook's Notes

Time
Preparation takes about 20 minutes. Allow at least 2 hours for the freezing and mixing procedure.

Preparation
The freezing and mixing procedure eliminates large ice crystals from the sorbet. If desired, the sorbet may be processed again just before serving, but this will result in a very soft mixture.

Serving Ideas
Serve with chocolate sauce, fruit sauce or fresh fruit, biscuits, or simply sprinkled with ground cinnamon or nutmeg.

SERVES 4-6

BANANA FRITTERS

Fritters, plain or made with fruit, are
a favourite sweet in Spain. Bananas are
especially nice prepared this way.

120g/4oz plain flour, sifted
Pinch salt
1.25ml/¼ tsp ground cinnamon
1 egg, beaten
15ml/1 tbsp oil
90ml/6 tbsps milk
1 egg white, stiffly beaten
90ml/6 tbsps brandy or rum
30g/2 tbsps sugar
15ml/1 tbsp lemon juice
6 ripe bananas, peeled and cut into sharp diagonal slices
    about 1.25cm/½ inch thick
Oil for frying
Icing sugar

3. While the batter is resting, place the brandy or rum and sugar in a large bowl and stir well to help the sugar dissolve. Add the lemon juice and then slice the bananas. Place the bananas in the bowl, stirring to coat them completely. Set the bananas aside for about 20 minutes, turning them occasionally.

4. Heat the oil in a deep fat fryer or a large, heavy-based frying pan to a temperature of 190°C/375°F.

5. Dip the bananas in the batter using tongs or two forks. Drain off excess and fry a few pieces at a time in the hot fat. Drain on paper towels and sprinkle with icing sugar before serving.

Step 2
When ready to use, fold in stiffly beaten egg white using a large metal spoon or rubber spatula.

Step 1
Mix the liquid ingredients in a well in the centre of the flour, gradually drawing in the dry ingredients from the outside.

Step 5
Dip the prepared banana slices into the batter using tongs or a fork. Allow the excess to drain away before frying.

1. Sift half the flour with the salt and cinnamon into a large bowl and make a well in the centre. Pour the beaten egg, oil and milk into the well and stir with a wooden spoon to gradually incorporate the flour from the outside. Stir just until the batter is smooth, but do not overbeat. Set the batter aside at room temperature for at least 30 minutes.

2. Whisk the egg white until stiff but not dry and fold into the batter just before ready to use.

Cook's Notes

Time
Preparation takes about 30 minutes and cooking takes about 2-3 minutes per batch of 5 or 6 fritters.

Preparation
When preparing batters for fritters or pancakes, it is best to let them stand for at least 30 minutes before using. This gives the batter a better consistency and makes it easier to use.

Variation
Pineapple, fresh or canned, or peeled apples may be used instead of the bananas.

MAKES 1 CAKE

Cinnamon Buttercream Cake

A cake that doesn't need baking is convenient any time, and perfect
for summer. It's very rich, though, so it will go a long way.

280g/10oz sugar
1 cinnamon stick
90ml/6 tbsps water
8 egg yolks
450g/1lb unsalted butter, softened
24 sponge fingers
90ml/6 tbsps brandy
90g/3oz toasted almonds, roughly chopped
90g/3oz plain chocolate, coarsely grated

1. Combine the sugar, water and cinnamon stick in a small, heavy-based saucepan and bring to the boil, stirring until the sugar dissolves.

2. Allow to boil briskly without stirring until the syrup reaches a temperature of 113°C/236°F on a sugar thermometer, or until a small amount dropped into cold water forms a soft ball.

3. While the sugar syrup is boiling, beat the egg yolks in a large bowl with an electric mixer until they are thick and lemon coloured. Soften the butter until light and fluffy.

4. When the syrup is ready, quickly pour it in a thin, steady stream into the egg yolks, beating constantly with an electric mixer.

5. Continue beating until the mixture is thick, smooth and creamy. This will take about 10-15 minutes. Allow to cool to room temperature.

6. Beat in the softened butter, a spoonful at a time. Chill the mixture until it is of spreading consistency.

7. Cut the sponge fingers to fit closely together in a 20cm/8 inch square pan. Line the pan with lightly greased foil or paper.

8. Spread some of the buttercream lightly on one side of the biscuits and place them, icing side down, in the pan. Cut small pieces of biscuit to fill in any corners, if necessary.

9. Sprinkle over half of the brandy, soaking each biscuit well. Spread over another layer of buttercream and place on the remaining biscuits, pushing them down to stick them into the cream. Sprinkle over the remaining brandy and cover the top with buttercream, reserving some for the sides. Place the cake in the refrigerator and chill until firm.

10. When the icing is firm, remove the cake from the refrigerator and lift it out of the pan using the foil or paper. Slide the cake off the paper onto a flat surface and spread the sides with the remaining buttercream. Press the chopped almonds into the sides and decorate the top with grated chocolate. Transfer to a serving dish and serve immediately.

Step 4
Pour the prepared syrup in a thin, steady stream onto the egg yolks while beating with an electric whisk.

Step 6
Beat in the softened butter, a spoonful at a time.

Cook's Notes

Time
Preparation takes about 45 minutes, with about 3 hours in the refrigerator to set the butter cream.

Variation
The icing may be flavoured with 10ml/2 tsps instant coffee powder. Add when making the syrup. 60g/2oz plain chocolate may be grated into the syrup once it is made and stirred to dissolve.

Preparation
The syrup must be at exactly the right temperature when it is beaten into the egg yolks or the icing will be soft and runny.

SERVES 8

CARAMEL CUSTARD WITH ORANGE AND CORIANDER

This is one of the best loved puddings in Spain. Fragrant coriander gives it
new appeal and its flavour is marvellous with orange.

180g/6oz sugar
90ml/6 tbsps water
3 small oranges
850ml/1½ pints milk
15ml/1 tbsp coriander seeds, crushed
6 eggs
2 egg yolks
180g/6oz sugar

Step 1
Dissolve the sugar
in water over
gentle heat until it
forms a clear
syrup.

Step 2
Bring the syrup to
the boil over high
heat and watch
carefully as it
begins to turn
brown.

1. To prepare the caramel, put the sugar and water in a heavy-based saucepan and bring to the boil over gentle heat to dissolve the sugar.

2. Once the sugar is dissolved, bring to the boil over high heat and cook to a golden brown, watching the colour carefully.

3. While the caramel is cooking, heat 8 ramekin dishes to warm them. When the caramel is brown, pour an equal amount into each dish and swirl the dish quickly to coat the base and sides with caramel. Leave the caramel to cool and harden in the dishes.

4. Grate the oranges and combine the rind, milk and crushed coriander seeds in a deep saucepan. Set the oranges aside for later use. Bring the milk almost to the boiling point and set it aside for the flavours to infuse.

5. Beat the eggs, yolks and sugar together until light and fluffy. Gradually strain on the milk, stirring well in between each addition. Pour the milk over the caramel in each dish. Place the dishes in a bain-marie and place in a preheated 170°C/325°F/Gas Mark 3 oven for about 40 minutes, or until a knife inserted into the centre of the custards comes out clean. Lower the oven temperature slightly if the water begins to boil around the dishes.

6. When the custards are cooked, remove the dishes from the bain-marie and refrigerate for at least 3 hours or overnight until the custard is completely cold and set.

7. To serve, loosen the custards from the sides of the dish with a small knife and turn them out onto individual plates. Peel the white pith from around the oranges and segment them. Place some of the orange segments around the custards and serve immediately.

Cook's Notes

Time
Preparation takes about 30-40 minutes, cooking time for the custards is about 40 minutes.

Watchpoint
The sugar and water can burn easily once it comes to the boil, so watch it carefully.

Preparation
A bain-marie literally means a water bath. To make one, pour warm water into a roasting pan, the level to come half way up the sides of the dish or dishes being used. This protects delicate egg custard mixtures from the direct heat of the oven. Check from time to time to see that the water is not boiling.

Cook's Tip
It is usual for some of the caramel to stick in the bottom of the dish when the custards are turned out. To make cleaning easier, pour boiling water into the bottom of each dish and leave until it dissolves the residue of caramel.

SERVES 6-8

FRIED MILK SQUARES

An unusual way with custard, this recipe requires
good organisation for delicious results.

30g/2 tbsps cornflour
700ml/1¼ pints milk
120g/4oz sugar
Vanilla essence
2 eggs, beaten
Dry breadcrumbs
Cinnamon sugar
Oil for deep frying

---

1. Place the cornflour in a heavy-based saucepan and gradually whisk in the milk until completely blended. Add the sugar, stir well and bring the mixture slowly to the boil, stirring constantly until thickened. Stir in the vanilla essence.

2. Pour the mixture into a 20cm/8 inch square dish lined with lightly buttered foil.

3. Chill the mixture for at least 4 hours in a refrigerator, or until completely firm.

4. When set, lift out the paper and cut the mixture into squares with a knife dipped in hot water.

5. Coat the squares carefully with egg, using a fish slice.

6. Coat carefully with crumbs, patting them in place with your hands. Place the coated squares on a plate and set them aside.

7. Heat the oil in a deep fat fryer or deep saucepan and place in the squares, one at a time. Brown for about 2 minutes per side, turning over carefully. Drain on paper towels and transfer to a serving dish. Repeat with remaining squares. Sprinkle with sugar and cinnamon and serve immediately.

Step 4
When set, cut through the mixture with a knife dipped in hot water.

Step 5
Coat the squares carefully with beaten egg.

Step 6
Place crumbs on a sheet of paper. Use paper to toss the crumbs over the egg-coated squares.

Cook's Notes

Time
Preparation takes about 25 minutes, with 4 hours chilling time. Cooking takes about 4 minutes or longer if the squares are cooked in several batches.

Preparation
The milk mixture must be chilled until very firm before slicing. The squares must be completely cold before frying or they will begin to melt and fall apart. Using a knife dipped in hot water makes it easier to slice cleanly through the mixture.

Serving Ideas
The fried milk squares may be served with cream, either pouring or whipped. Fresh fruit such as strawberries, raspberries or sliced peaches make a nice accompaniment.

SERVES 4-6

SANGRIA

This is the ideal drink with hors d'oeuvres
on warm summer evenings and the perfect complement
to the flavour of Spanish food anytime.

60-90g/4-6 tbsps sugar
1 lime
1 orange
1 lemon
60ml/4 tbsps brandy
1 bottle dry red wine
Soda water or sparkling mineral water
Ice cubes

4. Refrigerate the mixture for about 1 hour or until thoroughly chilled. Chill the soda or mineral water separately. Just before serving, pour in the soda or mineral water, adding about 700ml/1¼ pints. Pour over ice into large wine glasses, adding some of the sliced fruit to each glass, and serve immediately.

Step 1
Slice the fruit thinly and place in a bowl or jug with the sugar.

Step 3
Add the wine and brandy and mix all the ingredients to help dissolve the sugar.

1. Slice the lime and lemon into rounds about 5mm/¼ inch thick. Remove any pips.

2. Slice the oranges in half and then cut each half into 5mm/¼ inch thick slices, removing any pips. Place all the fruit in a large bowl or jug.

3. Add the sugar, brandy and wine and stir until well mixed. If desired, add a bit more sugar to taste.

Step 4
Just before serving, pour in soda water or carbonated mineral water.

Cook's Notes

Time
Preparation takes about 20 minutes, with 1 hour chilling time.

Cook's Tip
If Sangria is made more than an hour or two in advance, the fruit may discolour slightly because of the wine. This will not affect the taste, but fresh fruit may be substituted for serving.

Variation
May also be made with dry white wine.

SERVES 8

SPANISH LEMONADE

Spanish lemonade has a definite
kick, with the unusual combination
of both red and white wines.

180g/6oz sugar
6 lemons
1 litre dry red wine
1 litre dry white wine
Fresh mint

Step 1
Remove the peel
from the lemons
in thin strips,
using a serrated
knife or a
vegetable peeler.
Do not remove
the white pith.

Step 2
Slowly heat the
peel, sugar and
lemon juice, stirr-
ing occasionally
to dissolve the
sugar.

Step 3
Add the lemon
slices and the
other ingredients
and pour into a
glass serving jug.

1. Place the sugar in a heavy-based saucepan. Peel the
rind carefully from three of the lemons using a sharp
serrated knife or a vegetable peeler. Do not take any of the
white pith off with the peel. Squeeze the lemons for juice
and strain them into the saucepan.

2. Place the saucepan over gentle heat to dissolve the
sugar, stirring occasionally. Set aside to cool completely.

3. Slice the remaining lemons about 5mm/¼ inch thick.

Mix all the ingredients together and pour into a large glass
jug. Refrigerate for at least 4 hours or overnight, stirring
occasionally.

4. Add just the leaves or small sprigs of mint to the lemonade, stirring them in well. To serve, pour into tall glasses over
ice.

Cook's Notes

Time
Preparation takes about 20
minutes with overnight chilling
time.

Variation
Use 7 or 8 limes or 3 oranges
in place of the lemons.

Preparation
Taste and add more sugar, if
necessary, before chilling the
lemonade.

CHINESE COOKING

INTRODUCTION

To say China is vast seems a gross oversimplification. But it is this vastness that is the key to unlocking the mysteries of the country's cuisine. Because of the great land area, China has a great range of climates which influence the crops that grow and hence the dishes of the regions. It is usual, for culinary purposes, to divide the country into four regions: North or Peking, South or Cantonese, East or Shanghai, West or Szechuan.

In the North, noodles are eaten more often than rice, because that is the wheat growing region. Rich sauces and meat dishes are featured, as are pancakes and dumplings. From this region comes the legendary Peking duck.

In the South, the weather is warmer and the meals lighter. Stir-fried dishes with crisp vegetables are popular. The salty tang of fermented black beans or oyster sauce lends interest to meat and poultry stir-fries. Rice is the staple rather than wheat noodles.

In the East, rice and noodles compete for popularity. Noodles, combined with vegetables, poultry or sea-

food, make a favourite snack in tea houses. Fish, both freshwater and saltwater, are plentiful.

In the West, hearty dishes with a fiery taste are a speciality. The Szechuan peppercorn grows here, with a taste very different from the pepper we in the Western world are used to. The edible tree fungus — cloud ear — is a highly-prized ingredient.

Cooking Chinese food takes only minutes for most recipes, but preparation often involves much slicing and chopping, so it is best to have everything ready to go. Ingredients are generally cut to approximately the same size so that they cook in almost the same length of time. To slice meat to the necessary thinness, use it partially frozen.

Stir-frying is probably the most important Chinese cooking method used in this book. This involves cooking over high heat in a small amount of oil. A wok is best for this, but, if necessary, a large heavy-based frying pan can be used. Woks usually sit on a stand which keeps the base slightly elevated to give greater control over cooking.

Chinese food is becoming more and more popular, but some ingredients may still prove mystifying and in need of definition:

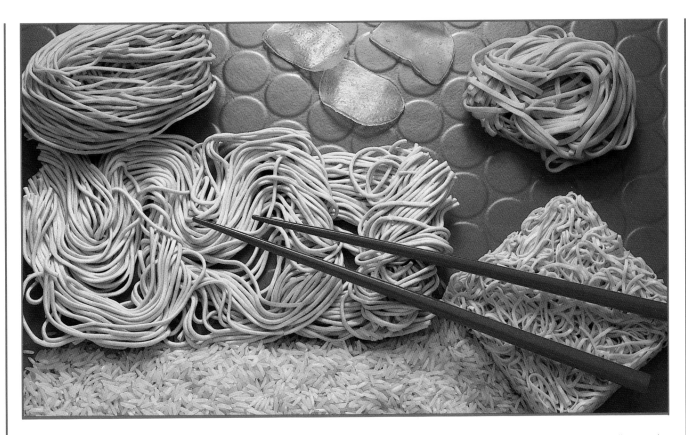

Bamboo shoots – first growth of the bamboo plant, cut just as it emerges from the ground. Crisp, ivory coloured and slightly sweet, usually sold canned, sliced or in whole pieces which can be cut to various shapes.

Baby corn – miniature variety of corn. Sold in cans and often available fresh. Needs very brief cooking.

Black beans – used often in Cantonese cooking. Available in pre-prepared sauce or salted to preserve them. Salted beans should be soaked.

Chilli peppers – available dried or fresh. Usually red, they are used in Szechuan cooking. Seeds are the hottest part, so remove for less heat.

Chilli sauce – available hot or sweet and made from fresh, red chilli peppers.

Chinese leaves – usually refers to Chinese celery cabbage. Some varieties have thicker, whiter spines. Readily available in greengrocers or supermarkets. Smaller, stronger-tasting bok choy is rarely seen outside Chinese markets.

Chinese parsley – also coriander leaves or cilantro. A pungent green herb with a leaf similar to flat parsley.

Five-spice powder – a combination of star anise, anise pepper, fennel, cloves and cinnamon. Use sparingly.

Ginger – knobbly root that must be peeled before use. Use in small amounts, grated or thinly sliced. Also available in powder form or preserved in sugar syrup.

Hoisin sauce – a thick, vegetable-based sauce used often in Chinese barbecue cooking. Useful for stir-fried dishes and as a dipping sauce.

Mushrooms, dried Chinese – brown-black in colour, must be soaked for 15-30 minutes before use. Stronger in taste than fresh mushrooms, they also have a chewier texture.

Red bean paste – made from boiled red beans or bean flour mixed with water and flour. Usually sweetened and used in desserts.

Rice wine – available from Chinese groceries, it has a flavour ranging from dry sherry to sweet white wine depending on the variety bought. Substitute either sherry or white wine.

Rice vinegar – made from rice and quite pale in colour. Substitute white wine vinegar.

Sesame oil – pressed from sesame seeds it is golden in colour with a nutty flavour. Expensive, so use as flavouring at the end of cooking.

Soy sauce – made from fermented soy beans. There are various strength, which will affect the colour and flavour of the finished dish.

Star anise – star-shaped seed pod with a liquorice taste. Used in meat, poultry and sweet dishes.

Szechuan peppercorns – also called wild pepper. Not readily available, so substitute black peppercorns.

Water chestnuts – fresh variety is very difficult to obtain. Usually found canned, peeled, sliced or whole. Creamy white in colour and crisp in texture.

White radish or mooli – very large, with a delicious, crisp texture and white, translucent appearance. Barely needs cooking.

Wonton skins or wrappers – thin sheets of egg noodle dough in large or small squares. The traditional wrapping for spring rolls and dumplings with various stuffings. Can be steamed or cooked in liquid.

Wood or tree ears – greyish-black tree fungus. Sold dried and must be soaked before use.

Yellow beans – whole in brine or in paste or sauce form. Golden brown in colour and very salty.

MAKES 12

SPRING ROLLS

One of the most popular Chinese hors
d'oeuvres, these are delicious dipped
in sweet-sour sauce or plum sauce.

Wrappers

120g/4oz strong plain flour
1 egg, beaten
Cold water

Filling

225g/8oz pork, trimmed and finely shredded
120g/4oz prawns, shelled and chopped
4 spring onions, finely chopped
10ml/2 tsps chopped fresh ginger
120g/4oz Chinese leaves, shredded
100g/3½oz bean sprouts
15ml/1 tbsp light soy sauce
Dash sesame seed oil
1 egg, beaten

1. To prepare the wrappers, sift the flour into a bowl and make a well in the centre. Add the beaten egg and about 15ml/1 tbsp cold water. Begin beating with a wooden spoon, gradually drawing in the flour from the outside to make a smooth dough. Add more water if necessary.

2. Knead the dough until it is elastic and pliable. Place in a covered bowl and chill for about 4 hours or overnight.

3. When ready to roll out, allow the dough to come back to room temperature. Flour a large work surface well and roll the dough out to about 5mm/¼ inch thick.

4. Cut the dough into 12 equal squares and then roll each piece into a larger square about 15x15cm/6x6 inches. The dough should be very thin. Cover while preparing the filling.

5. Cook the pork in a little of the frying oil for about 2-3 minutes. Add the remaining filling ingredients, except the beaten egg, cook for a further 2-3 minutes and allow to cool.

6. Lay out the wrappers on a clean work surface with the point of each wrapper facing you. Brush the edges lightly with the beaten egg.

7. Divide the filling among all 12 wrappers, placing it just above the front point. Fold over the sides like an envelope.

8. Then fold over the point until the filling is completely covered, Roll up as for a Swiss roll. Press all the edges to seal well.

9. Heat the oil in a deep fat fryer or in a deep pan to 190°C/375°F. Depending upon the size of the fryer, place in 2-4 spring rolls and fry until golden brown on both sides. The rolls will float to the surface when one side has browned and should be turned over. Drain thoroughly on paper towels and serve hot.

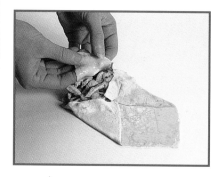

Step 7 Fill the dough and fold up sides like an envelope before rolling up.

Cook's Notes

Time
Preparation takes about 50 minutes for the wrapper dough, the filling and for rolling up. Dough must be allowed to rest for at least 4 hours before use. Cooking takes about 20 minutes.

Serving Ideas
Serve with a sauce dip. Sweet and sour sauce or hot mustard sauce are available bottled from speciality shops and Chinese supermarkets.

Freezing
Rolls may be frozen uncooked. Line a baking sheet with clingfilm, place on the rolls and freeze until nearly solid. Wrap each roll individually, place in a large plastic bag, seal, label and freeze for up to 2 months. Defrost completely before frying.

SERVES 4-6

HOT & SOUR SOUP

A very warming soup, this is a favourite in winter in Peking. Add chilli sauce and vinegar to suit your taste.

60g/2oz pork
3 dried Chinese mushrooms, soaked in boiling water for 5 minutes and chopped
60g/2oz peeled, uncooked prawns
1.5 litres/2½ pints chicken stock
30g/1oz bamboo shoots, sliced
3 spring onions, shredded
Salt and pepper
15ml/1 tbsp sugar
5ml/1 tsp dark soy sauce
2.5ml/½ tsp light soy sauce
5-10ml/1-2 tsps chilli sauce
25ml/1½ tbsps vinegar
Dash sesame seed oil and rice wine or sherry
1 egg, well beaten
30ml/2 tbsps water mixed with 15ml/1 tbsp cornflour

1. Trim any fat from the pork and slice it into shreds about 5cm/2 inches long and less than 5mm/¼ inch thick.

2. Soak the mushrooms in boiling water until softened. Place the pork in a large pot with the prawns and stock. Bring to the boil and then reduce the heat to allow to simmer gently for 4-5 minutes. Add all the remaining ingredients except for the egg and cornflour and water mixture. Cook a further 1-2 minutes over low heat.

3. Remove the pan from the heat and add the egg gradually, stirring gently until it forms threads in the soup.

4. Mix a spoonful of the hot soup with the cornflour and water mixture and add to the soup, stirring constantly.

5. Bring the soup back to simmering point for 1 minute to thicken the cornflour. Serve immediately.

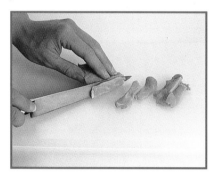

Step 1 Cut the pork into thin shreds, long enough to fit comfortably into a soup spoon.

Step 2 Soak the dry mushrooms in boiling water for 5 minutes until they soften and swell. Remove the stalks before chopping.

Step 3 Pour the egg into the hot soup and stir gently to form threads.

Cook's Notes

Time
Preparation takes about 25 minutes, cooking takes 7-8 minutes.

Preparation
Vary the amount of chilli sauce to suit your own taste.

Variation
Hot and Sour Soup is very versatile. Substitute other ingredients such as chicken, crabmeat, bean sprouts, spinach or green cabbage.

Watchpoint
The soup must be hot enough to cook the egg when it is added, but not so hot that the egg sets immediately.

MAKES 12

POT STICKER DUMPLINGS

So called because they are fried in very little
oil, they will stick unless they are brown and
crisp on the bottom before they are steamed.

Dumpling Pastry

180g/6oz plain flour
2.5ml/½ tsp salt
45ml/3 tbsps oil
Boiling water

Filling

120g/4oz finely minced pork or chicken
4 water chestnuts, finely chopped
3 spring onions, finely chopped
2.5ml/½ tsp five spice powder
15ml/1 tbsp light soy sauce
5ml/1 tsp sugar
5ml/1 tsp sesame oil

Step 3 Place a mound of filling on half of each dough circle.

1. Sift the flour and salt into a large bowl and make a well in the center. Pour in the oil and add enough boiling water to make a pliable dough. Add about 60ml/4 tbsps water at first and begin stirring with a wooden spoon to gradually incorporate the flour. Add more water as necessary. Knead the dough for about 5 minutes and allow to rest for 30 minutes.

2. Divide the dough into 12 pieces and roll each piece out

to a circle about 15cm/6 inches in diameter.

3. Mix all the filling ingredients together and place a mound of filling on half of each circle. Fold over the top and press the edges together firmly. Roll over the joined edges using a twisting motion and press down to seal.

4. Pour about 2.5mm/⅛ inch of oil in a large frying pan, preferably cast iron. When the oil is hot, add the dumplings flat side down and cook until nicely browned.

5. When the underside is brown, add about 90ml/3 fl oz water to the pan and cover it tightly. Continue cooking gently for about 5 minutes, or until the top surface of dumplings is steamed and appears cooked. Serve immediately.

Step 3 Fold over the dough and press edges to seal in filling.

Step 3 Twist the edges together to seal firmly.

Cook's Notes

Time
Preparation takes about 50 minutes including the standing time for the dough. Cooking takes about 10-20 minutes.

Preparation
The pan used for cooking must have a flat base. Do not use a wok.

Watchpoint
Make sure the dumplings are brown and crisp on the bottom before adding the water otherwise they really will be pot stickers!

SERVES 4-6

CRAB & SWEETCORN SOUP

Creamy sweetcorn and succulent crabmeat
combine to make a velvety rich soup. Whisked
egg whites add an interesting texture.

1 litre/1¾ pints chicken or fish stock
340g/12oz creamed sweetcorn
120g/4oz crabmeat
Salt and pepper
5ml/1 tsp light soy sauce
30ml/2 tbsps cornflour
45ml/3 tbsps water or stock
4 spring onions for garnish
2 egg whites, whisked
4 spring onions for garnish

Step 3 Whisk the egg whites until soft peaks form and stir into the hot soup.

Step 2 Mix the cornflour and water together with some of the hot soup and return the mixture to the pan.

1. Bring the stock to the boil in a large pan. Add the sweetcorn, crabmeat, seasoning and soy sauce. Allow to simmer for 4-5 minutes.

2. Mix the cornflour and water or stock and add a spoonful of the hot soup. Return the mixture to the soup and bring back to the boil. Cook until the soup thickens.

3. Whisk the egg whites until soft peaks form. Stir into the hot soup just before serving.

4. Slice the onions thinly on the diagonal and scatter over the top to serve.

Cook's Notes

Time
Preparation takes about 10 minutes, cooking takes about 8-10 minutes.

Preparation
Adding the egg whites is optional.

Watchpoint
Do not allow the sweetcorn and the crab to boil rapidly; they will both toughen.

Economy
Use crab sticks instead of crabmeat.

Variation
Chicken may be used instead of the crabmeat and the cooking time increased to 10-12 minutes.

SERVES 6-8

WONTON SOUP

Probably the best-known Chinese soup,
this recipe uses pre-made wonton
wrappers for ease of preparation.

20-24 wonton wrappers
30ml/2 tbsps chopped Chinese parsley
90g/3oz finely minced chicken or pork
3 spring onions, finely chopped
2.5cm/1 inch piece fresh ginger, peeled and grated
1 egg, lightly beaten
1.5 litres/2½ pints chicken stock
15ml/1 tbsps dark soy sauce
Dash sesame oil
Salt and pepper
Chinese parsley or watercress for garnish

Step 2 Place a spoonful of filling on half of each wrapper

Step 1 Place the wonton wrappers out on a clean surface. Brush edges with beaten egg.

Step 3 Fold over the tops and press firmly with the fingers to seal.

1. Place all the wonton wrappers on a large, flat surface. Mix together the chicken or pork, chopped parsley, spring onions and ginger. Brush the edges of the wrappers lightly with beaten egg.

2. Place a small mound of mixture on one half of the wrappers and fold the other half over the top to form a triangle.

3. Press with the fingers to seal the edges well.

4. Bring the stock to the boil in a large saucepan. Add the filled wontons and simmer 5-10 minutes or until they float to the surface. Add remaining ingredients to the soup, using only the leaves of the parsley or watercress for garnish.

Cook's Notes

 Time
Preparation takes 25-30 minutes and cooking takes about 5-10 minutes.

 Variation
Use equal quantities of crabmeat or prawns to fill the wontons instead of chicken or pork.

 Buying Guide
Wonton wrappers are sometimes called wonton skins. They are available in speciality shops, delicatessens and Chinese supermarkets. Chinese parsley is also known as coriander or cilantro and is available from greengrocers and supermarkets.

SERVES 4-6

BARBECUED SPARE RIBS

Although Chinese barbecue sauce is nothing like
the tomato-based American-style sauce, these
ribs are still tasty cooked on an outdoor grill.

1.8kg/4lbs fresh spare-ribs
45ml/3 tbsps dark soy sauce
90ml/6 tbsps hoisin sauce (Chinese barbecue sauce)
30ml/2 tbsps dry sherry
1.25ml/¼ tsp five spice powder
15g/1 tbsp brown sugar
4-6 spring onions for garnish

Step 2 Cut both
ends of the
onions into thin
strips, leaving the
middle whole.

Step 1 Trim the
root ends and the
green tops from
the onions.

Step 3 Place in
ice water and
leave to stand 4
hour or overnight
until the ends
curl.

1. First prepare the garnish. Trim the root ends and the
dark green tops from the onions.

2. Cut both ends into thin strips, leaving about 1.25cm/½
inch in the middle uncut.

3. Place the onions in ice water for several hours or
overnight for the ends to curl up.

4. Cut the spare-ribs into one-rib pieces. Mix all the
remaining ingredients together, pour over the ribs and stir

to coat evenly. Allow to stand for 1 hour.

5. Put the sparerib pieces on a rack in a roasting pan
containing 570ml/1 pint water and cook in a preheated
180°C/350°F/Gas Mark 4 oven for 30 minutes. Add more
hot water to the pan while cooking, if necessary.

6. Turn the ribs over and brush with the remaining sauce.
Cook 30 minutes longer, or until tender. Serve garnished
with the onion brushes.

Cook's Notes

Time
Preparation takes about 45
minutes. The onion brushes
must soak for at least 4 hours and the
ribs must marinate for 1 hour. Cooking
takes about 1 hour.

Preparation
If the ribs are small and not
very meaty, cut into two-rib
pieces before cooking, then into one-
rib pieces just before serving.

Cook's Tip
The ribs may be prepared in
advance and reheated at the
same temperature for about 10
minutes.

SERVES 8

SESAME CHICKEN WINGS

This is an economical starter that is
also good as a cocktail snack or as a
light meal with stir-fried vegetables.

12 chicken wings
15ml/1 tbsp salted black beans
15ml/1 tbsp water
15ml/1 tbsp oil
2 cloves garlic, crushed
2 slices fresh ginger, cut into fine shreds
45ml/3 tbsps soy sauce
25ml/1½ tbsps dry sherry or rice wine
Large pinch black pepper
15ml/1 tbsp sesame seeds

1. Cut off and discard the wing tips. Cut between the joint to separate into two pieces.

2. Crush the beans and add the water. Leave to stand.

3. Heat the oil in a wok and add the garlic and ginger. Stir briefly and add the chicken wings. Cook, stirring, until lightly browned, about 3 minutes. Add the soy sauce and wine and cook, stirring, about 30 seconds longer. Add the soaked black beans and pepper.

4. Cover the wok tightly and allow to simmer for about 8-10 minutes. Uncover and turn the heat to high. Continue cooking, stirring until the liquid is almost evaporated and the chicken wings are glazed with sauce. Remove from the

Step 1 Use a knife or scissors to cut through thick joint and separate the wing into two pieces.

Step 3 Fry garlic and ginger briefly, add the chicken wings and cook, stirring, until lightly browned.

heat and sprinkle on sesame seeds. Stir to coat completely and serve. Garnish with spring onions or Chinese parsley, if desired.

Cook's Notes

Time
Preparation takes about 25 minutes, cooking takes about 13-14 minutes.

Watchpoint
Sesame seeds pop slightly as they cook.

Cook's Tip
You can prepare the chicken wings ahead of time and reheat them. They are best reheated in the oven for about 5 minutes at 180°C/350°F/Gas Mark 4.

Serving Ideas
To garnish with scallion brushes, trim the roots and green tops of spring onions and cut both ends into thin strips, leaving the middle intact. Place in ice water for several hours or overnight for the cut ends to curl up. Drain and use to garnish.

SERVES 4-6

QUICK FRIED PRAWNS

Prepared with either raw or cooked
prawns, this is an incredibly delicious
starter that is extremely easy to cook.

900g/2lbs cooked prawns in their shells
2 cloves garlic, crushed
2.5cm/1 inch piece fresh ginger, finely chopped
15ml/1 tbsp chopped fresh Chinese parsley (coriander)
45ml/3 tbsps oil
15ml/1 tbsp rice wine or dry sherry
25ml/1½ tbsps light soy sauce
Chopped spring onions to garnish

Step 2 Peel the
shells from the
prawns, leaving
only the tail ends
on.

Step 1 Carefully
pull the head of
the prawn away
from the body.

1. Shell the prawns except for the very tail ends. Place the
prawns in a bowl with the remaining ingredients, except for
the garnish, and leave to marinate for 30 minutes.

2. Heat the wok and add the prawns and their marinade.
Stir-fry briefly to heat the prawns.

3. Chop the onions roughly or cut into neat rounds.
Sprinkle over the prawns to serve.

Cook's Notes

 Time
Preparation takes about 30
minutes for the prawns to
marinate. Cooking takes about 2
minutes.

 Watchpoint
Do not overcook the prawns
as they will toughen.

 **Variation**
If uncooked prawns are
available, stir-fry with their
marinade until they turn pink.

SERVES 4

AUBERGINES & PEPPERS SZECHUAN STYLE

Authentic Szechuan food is fiery hot.
Outside China, restaurants often tone down the taste for Western palates.

1 large aubergine
2 cloves garlic, crushed
2.5cm/1 inch piece fresh ginger, shredded
1 onion, cut into 2.5cm/1 inch pieces
1 small green pepper, seeded, cored and cut into 2.5cm/1 inch pieces
1 small red pepper, seeded, cored and cut into 2.5cm/1 inch pieces
1 red or green chilli, seeded, cored and cut into thin strips
120ml/4 fl oz chicken or vegetable stock
5ml/1 tsp sugar
5ml/1 tsp vinegar
Pinch salt and pepper
5ml/1 tsp cornflour
15ml/1 tbsp soy sauce
Dash sesame oil
Oil for cooking

Step 1 Cut aubergine in half and lightly score the surface.

Step 2 Sprinkle lightly with salt and leave on paper towels or in a colander to drain.

1. Cut the aubergines in half and score the surface.

2. Sprinkle lightly with salt and leave to drain in a colander or on paper towels for 30 minutes.

3. After 30 minutes, squeeze the aubergine gently to extract any bitter juices and rinse thoroughly under cold water. Pat dry and cut the aubergine into 2.5cm/1 inch cubes.

4. Heat about 45ml/3 tbsps oil in a wok. Add the aubergine and stir-fry for about 4-5 minutes. It may be necessary to add more oil as the aubergine cooks. Remove from the wok and set aside.

5. Reheat the wok and add 30ml/2 tbsps oil. Add the garlic and ginger and stir-fry for 1 minute. Add the onions and stir-fry for 2 minutes. Add the green pepper, red pepper and chilli pepper and stir-fry for 1 minute. Return the aubergine to the wok along with the remaining ingredients.

6. Bring to the boil, stirring constantly, and cook until the sauce thickens and clears. Serve immediately.

Cook's Notes

Time
Preparation takes about 30 minutes, cooking takes about 7-8 minutes.

Cook's Tip
Lightly salting the aubergine will help draw out any bitterness.

Serving Suggestions
Serve as a vegetarian stir-fry dish with plain or fried rice, or serve as a side dish.

SERVES 4

SPECIAL MIXED VEGETABLES

This dish illustrates the basic stir-frying
technique for vegetables. Use other varieties
for an equally colourful side dish.

15ml/1 tbsps oil
1 clove garlic, crushed
2.5cm/1 inch piece fresh ginger, sliced
4 Chinese leaves, shredded
60g/2oz flat mushrooms, thinly sliced
60g/2oz bamboo shoots, sliced
3 sticks celery, diagonally sliced
60g/2oz baby corn, cut in half if large
1 small red pepper, cored, seeded and thinly sliced
60g/2oz bean sprouts
30ml/2 tbsps light soy sauce
Dash sesame oil
Salt and pepper
3 tomatoes, peeled, seeded and quartered

1. Heat the oil in a wok and add the ingredients in the order
given, reserving the tomatoes until last.

2. To make it easier to peel the tomatoes, remove the stems
and place in boiling water for 5 seconds.

3. Remove from the boiling water with a draining spoon
and place in a bowl of cold water. This will make the peels
easier to remove. Cut out the core end using a small sharp
knife.

4. Cut the tomatoes in half and then in quarters. Use a
teaspoon or a serrated edged knife to remove the seeds
and the cores.

5. Cook the vegetables for about 2 minutes. Stir in the soy
sauce and sesame oil and add the tomatoes. Heat through
for 30 seconds and serve immediately.

Step 2 To peel
the tomatoes,
place them first in
a pan of boiling
water for 5
seconds.
Tomatoes that are
very ripe need
less time.

Step 3 Place in
cold water to stop
the cooking. The
skin will then peel
away easily.

Step 4 Cut into
quarters and
remove the seeds,
core and juice
with a teaspoon,
or use a serrated
edged knife.

Cook's Notes

 Time
Preparation takes about 25
minutes, cooking takes about
2½-3 minutes.

 Variation
Other vegetables such as
broccoli florets, cauliflower
florets, mangetout, courgettes or
French beans may be used.

 Serving Ideas
Serve as a side dish or as a
vegetarian main dish with
plain or fried rice.

SERVES 4-6

PORK & PRAWN CHOW MEIN

Chinese chow mein dishes are usually based on
noodles, using more expensive ingredients in small
amounts. This makes economical everyday fare.

225g/8oz medium dried Chinese noodles
225g/8oz pork fillet, thinly sliced
1 carrot, peeled and shredded
1 small red pepper, cored, seeded and thinly sliced
90g/3oz bean sprouts
60g/2oz mangetout (snow peas)
15ml/1 tbsp rice wine or dry sherry
30ml/2 tbsps soy sauce
120g/4oz peeled, cooked prawns

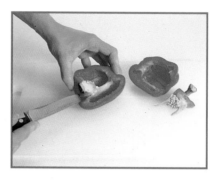

Step 3 Cut peppers in half and remove the cores and seeds. Make sure all the white pith is also removed before slicing thinly.

Step 1 Place whole sheets of noodles into rapidly boiling salted water. Stir as the noodles start to soften.

Step 4 Add the cooked noodles to the other ingredients in the wok and use chopsticks or a fish slice to toss over high heat.

1. Cook the noodles in plenty of boiling salted water for about 4-5 minutes. Rinse under hot water and drain thoroughly.

2. Heat the wok and add oil. Stir-fry the pork 4-5 minutes or until almost cooked. Add the carrots to the wok and cook for 1-2 minutes.

3. Core, seed and slice the red pepper and add the remaining vegetables, wine and soy sauce. Cook for about 2 minutes.

4. Add the cooked, drained noodles and prawns and toss over heat for 1-2 minutes. Serve immediately.

Cook's Notes

Time
Preparation takes about 20 minutes. The noodles take 4-5 minutes to cook and the stir-fried ingredients need to cook for about 5-6 minutes for the pork and about 3 minutes for the vegetables.

Variation
Use green pepper instead of red, or add other vegetables such as baby corn ears, mushrooms or peas.

Buying Guide
Dried Chinese noodles are available in three thicknesses. Thin noodles are usually reserved for soup, while medium and thick noodles are used for fried dishes.

SERVES 2-3

CANTONESE EGG FU YUNG

As the name suggests, this dish is from
Canton. However, fu yung dishes are popular
in many other regions of China, too.

5 eggs
60g/2oz shredded cooked meat, poultry or fish
1 stick celery, finely shredded
4 Chinese dried mushrooms, soaked in boiling water for
    5 minutes
60g/2oz bean sprouts
1 small onion, thinly sliced
Pinch salt and pepper
5ml/1 tsp dry sherry
Oil for frying

Sauce

15g/1 tbsp cornflour dissolved in 45ml/3 tbsps cold water
280ml/½ pint chicken stock
5ml/1 tsp tomato ketchup
15ml/1 tbsp soy sauce
Pinch salt and pepper
Dash sesame oil

1. Beat the eggs lightly and add the shredded meat and celery.

2. Squeeze all the liquid from the dried mushrooms. Remove the stems and cut the caps into thin slices. Add to the egg mixture along with the bean sprouts and onion. Add a pinch of salt and pepper and the sherry and stir well.

3. Heat a wok or frying pan and pour in about 60ml/4 tbsps oil. When hot, carefully spoon in about 90ml/3 fl oz of the egg mixture.

4. Brown on one side, turn gently over and brown the other side. Remove the cooked patties to a plate and continue until all the mixture is cooked.

5. Combine all the sauce ingredients in a small, heavy-based pan and bring slowly to the boil, stirring continuously until thickened and cleared. Pour the sauce over the Egg Fu Yung to serve.

Step 3 Heat the oil in a wok and spoon in the egg mixture to form patties.

Step 5 Bring sauce ingredients to the boil and cook until thick and clear.

Cook's Notes

Time
Preparation takes 25 minutes, cooking takes about 5 minutes for the patties and 8 minutes for the sauce.

Variation
Use cooked shellfish such as crab, shrimp or lobster, if desired. Fresh mushrooms may be used instead of the dried ones. Divide mixture in half or in thirds and cook one large patty per person.

Economy
Left-over cooked meat such as beef, pork or chicken can be used as an ingredient.

SERVES 6-8

FRIED RICE

A basic recipe for a traditional Chinese accompaniment
to stir-fried dishes, this can be more substantial
with the addition of meat, poultry or seafood.

450g/1lb cooked rice, well drained and dried
45ml/3 tbsps oil
1 egg, beaten
15ml/1 tbsp soy sauce
60g/2oz cooked peas
2 spring onions, thinly sliced
Dash sesame oil
Salt and pepper

1. Heat a wok and add the oil. Pour in the egg and soy sauce and cook until just beginning to set.

2. Add the rice and peas and stir to coat with the egg mixture. Allow to cook for about 3 minutes, stirring continuously. Add seasoning and sesame oil.

3. Spoon into a serving dish and sprinkle over the spring onions.

Step 2 Add rice and peas on top of egg mixture.

Step 2 Stir to coat the rice with egg, and toss mixture over heat to separate grains of rice.

Cook's Notes

Time
The rice will take about 10 minutes to cook. Allow at least 20 minutes for it to drain as dry as possible. The fried rice dish will take about 4 minutes to cook.

Variation
Cooked meat, poultry or seafood may be added to the rice along with the peas.

Cook's Tip

The 450g/1lb rice measurement is the cooked weight.

SERVES 4

SHANGHAI NOODLES

In general, noodles are more popular in northern and eastern China, where wheat is grown, than in other parts of the country. Noodles make a popular snack in Chinese tea houses.

45ml/3 tbsps oil
120g/4oz chicken breasts
120g/4oz Chinese leaves
4 spring onions, thinly sliced
30ml/2 tbsps soy sauce
Freshly ground black pepper
Dash sesame oil
450g/1lb thick Shanghai noodles, cooked

Step 3 Stack up the Chinese leaves and, using a large, sharp knife, cut across into thin strips.

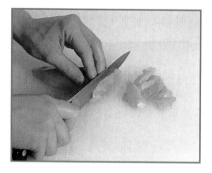

Step 1 Cut the chicken into thin strips across the grain.

Step 3 Toss in the cooked noodles, stir well and heat through.

1. Heat the oil in the wok and add the chicken cut into thin shreds. Stir-fry for 2-3 minutes.

2. Meanwhile, cook the noodles in boiling salted water until just tender, about 6-8 minutes. Drain in a colander and rinse under hot water. Toss in the colander to drain and leave to dry.

3. Add the shredded Chinese leaves and spring onions to the chicken in the wok along with the soy sauce, pepper and sesame oil. Cook about 1 minute and toss in the cooked noodles. Stir well and heat through. Serve immediately.

Cook's Notes

Time
Preparation takes about 10 minutes, cooking takes 6-8 minutes.

Variation
Pork may be used instead of the chicken. Add fresh spinach, shredded, if desired and cook with the Chinese leaves.

Buying Guide
Shanghai noodles are available in Chinese supermarkets and also some delicatessens. If unavailable, substitute tagliatelle or dried Chinese noodles.

SERVES 2

SWEET-SOUR FISH

In China this dish is almost always
prepared with freshwater fish, but
sea bass is also an excellent choice.

1 sea bass, grey mullet or carp, weighing about
    900g/2lbs, cleaned
15ml/1 tbsp dry sherry
Few slices fresh ginger
120g/4oz sugar
90ml/6 tbsps cider vinegar
15ml/1 tbsp soy sauce
30g/2 tbsps cornflour
1 clove garlic, crushed
2 spring onions, shredded
1 small carrot, peeled and finely shredded
30g/1oz bamboo shoots, shredded

1. Rinse the fish well inside and out. Make three diagonal
cuts on each side of the fish with a sharp knife.

2. Trim off the fins, leaving the dorsal fin on top.

3. Trim the tail to two neat points.

4. Bring enough water to cover the fish to the boil in a wok.
Gently lower the fish into the boiling water and add the
sherry and ginger. Cover the wok tightly and remove at
once from the heat. Allow to stand 15-20 minutes to let the
fish cook in the residual heat.

5. To test if the fish is cooked, pull the dorsal fin – if it comes
off easily the fish is done. If not, return the wok to the heat
and bring to the boil. Remove from the heat and leave the
fish to stand a further 5 minutes. Transfer the fish to a heated
serving dish and keep it warm. Take all but 60ml/4 tbsps of
the fish cooking liquid from the wok. Add the remaining
ingredients including the vegetables and cook, stirring
constantly, until the sauce thickens. Spoon some of the
sauce over the fish to serve and serve the rest separately.

Step 1 Rinse the
fish well and
make three
diagonal cuts on
each side.

Step 2 Using
kitchen scissors,
trim all of the fins
except the dorsal
fin at the top.

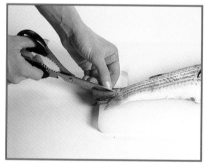

Step 3 Using
kitchen scissors
again, trim the
ends of the tail to
two sharp points.

Cook's Notes

Time
Preparation takes about 25
minutes, cooking takes about
15-25 minutes.

Cook's Tip
The diagonal cuts in the side
of the fish ensure even
cooking.

Variation
If desired, use smaller fish
such as trout or red mullet and
shorten the cooking time to 10-15
minutes.

Preparation
The fish may also be cooked
in the oven in a large roasting
pan or in greased foil sprinkled with
sherry. Cook at 190°C/375°F/Gas Mark
5 for 10 minutes per 1.25cm/½ inch
thickness, measured around the
middle of the fish.

SERVES 6

SINGAPORE FISH

The cuisine of Singapore was much influenced by
that of China. In turn, the Chinese brought
ingredients like curry powder into their own cuisine.

450g/1lb whitefish fillets
1 egg white
15g/1 tbsp cornflour
10ml/2 tsps white wine
Salt and pepper
Oil for frying
1 large onion, cut into 1.25cm/½ inch-thick wedges
15ml/1 tbsp mild curry powder
1 small can pineapple pieces, drained and juice
  reserved, or ½ fresh pineapple, peeled and cubed
1 small can mandarin orange segments, drained and
  juice reserved
1 small can sliced water chestnuts, drained
15g/1 tbsp cornflour mixed with juice of 1 lime
10ml/2 tsps sugar (optional)
Pinch salt and pepper

1. Starting at the tail end of the fillets, skin them using a
sharp knife.

2. Slide the knife back and forth along the length of each
fillet, pushing the fish flesh along as you go.

3. Cut the fish into even-sized pieces, about 5cm/2 inches.

4. Mix together the egg white, cornflour, wine, salt and
pepper. Place the fish in the mixture and leave to stand
while heating the oil.

5. When the oil is hot, fry a few pieces of fish at a time until
light golden brown and crisp. Remove the fish to paper
towels to drain, and continue until all the fish is cooked.

6. Remove all but 15ml/1 tbsp of the oil from the wok and
add the onion. Stir-fry the onion for 1-2 minutes and add the

curry powder. Cook the onion and curry powder for a
further 1-2 minutes. Add the juice from the pineapple and
mandarin oranges and bring to the boil.

7. Combine the cornflour and lime juice and add a
spoonful of the boiling fruit juice. Return the mixture to the
wok and cook until thickened, about 2 minutes. Taste and
add sugar if desired. Add the fruit, water chestnuts and
fried fish to the wok and stir to coat. Heat through 1 minute
and serve immediately.

Step 2 Hold
filleting knife at a
slight angle and
slide knife along
length of fillet in a
sawing motion.

Step 3 Cut fish
into even-sized
pieces, about
5cm/2 inches.

Cook's Notes

Time
Preparation takes about 25
minutes, cooking takes about
10 minutes.

Variation
Chicken may be used in place
of the fish and cooked in the
same way. Garnish with Chinese
parsley leaves if desired.

Serving Ideas
Serve with plain rice, fried rice
or cooked Chinese noodles.

SERVES 2-4

SNOW PEAS WITH PRAWNS

Snow peas, peapods and mangetout are
all names for the same vegetable – bright
green, crisp and edible, pods and all.

45ml/3 tbsps oil
60g/2oz split blanched almonds, halved
120g/4oz mangetout (snow peas)
60g/2oz bamboo shoots, sliced
10g/2 tsps cornflour
10ml/2 tsps light soy sauce
180ml/6 fl oz chicken stock
30ml/2 tbsps dry sherry
Salt and pepper
450g/1lb cooked, peeled prawns

with the almonds.

3. Drain all the oil from the wok and mix together the corn-flour and the remaining ingredients, except the prawns and bamboo shoots. Pour the mixture into the wok and stir constantly while bringing to the boil. Allow to simmer for 1-2 minutes until thickened and cleared. Stir in the prawns and all the other ingredients and heat through for about 1 minute. Serve immediately.

Step 2 If mangetout are very large, cut in half on the diagonal.

Step 2 Tear stems downward to remove strings from mangetout.

1. Heat the oil in a wok. Add the almonds and cook over moderate heat until golden brown. Remove from the oil and drain on paper towels.

2. To prepare the mangetout, tear off the stems and pull them downwards to remove any strings. If the mangetout are small, just remove the stalks. Add the mangetout to the hot oil and cook for about 1 minute. Remove and set aside

Step 3 Add all the ingredients to the wok and stir-fry, tossing with chopsticks or a fish slice.

Cook's Notes

Time
Preparation takes about 10 minutes, cooking takes 6-8 minutes.

Variation
If using spring onions, celery or water chestnuts, cook with the mangetout.

Watchpoint
Do not cook the prawns too long or on heat that is too high – they toughen quite easily.

SERVES 6

SZECHUAN FISH

The piquant spiciness of Szechuan pepper is quite different from that of black or white pepper. Beware, though, too much can numb the mouth temporarily!

450g/1lb whitefish fillets
Pinch salt and pepper
1 egg
75g/5 tbsps flour
90ml/6 tbsps white wine
Oil for frying
60g/2oz cooked ham, cut in small dice
2.5cm/1 inch piece fresh ginger, finely diced
½-1 red or green chilli pepper, cored, seeded and finely
    diced
6 water chestnuts, finely diced
4 spring onions, finely chopped
45ml/3 tbsps light soy sauce
5ml/1 tsp cider vinegar or rice wine vinegar
2.5ml/½ tsp ground Szechuan pepper (optional)
280ml/½ pint light stock
15ml/1 tbsp cornflour dissolved with 30ml/2 tbsps water
10ml/2 tsps sugar

1. To prepare the garnish, choose unblemished chilli peppers with the stems on. Using a small, sharp knife, cut the peppers in strips, starting from the pointed end.

2. Cut down to within 1.25cm/½ inch of the stem end. Rinse out the seeds under cold running water and place the peppers in iced water.

3. Leave the peppers to soak for at least 4 hours or overnight until they open up like flowers.

4. Cut the fish fillets into 5cm/2 inch pieces and season with salt and pepper. Beat the egg well and add flour and wine to make a batter. Dredge the fish lightly with flour and then dip into the batter. Mix the fish well.

5. Heat a wok and when hot, add enough oil to deep-fry the fish. When the oil is hot, fry a few pieces of fish at a time, until golden brown. Drain and proceed until all the fish is cooked.

6. Remove all but 15ml/1 tbsp of oil from the wok and add the ham, ginger, diced chilli pepper, water chestnuts and spring onions. Cook for about 1 minute and add the soy sauce and vinegar. If using Szechuan pepper, add at this point. Stir well and cook for a further 1 minute. Remove the vegetables from the pan and set them aside.

7. Add the stock to the wok and bring to the boil. When boiling, add 1 spoonful of the hot stock to the cornflour mixture. Add the mixture back to the stock and reboil, stirring constantly until thickened.

8. Stir in the sugar and return the fish and vegetables to the sauce. Heat through for 30 seconds and serve at once.

Step 1 Cut the tip of each chilli pepper into strips.

Step 3 Allow to soak 4 hours or overnight to open up.

Cook's Notes

 Time
Preparation takes about 30 minutes. Chilli pepper garnish takes at least 4 hours to soak. Cooking takes about 10 minutes.

 Serving Ideas
Serve with plain or fried rice. Do not eat the chilli pepper garnish.

Buying Guide
Szechuan peppercorns are available in Chinese supermarkets or delicatessens. If not available, substitute extra chilli pepper.

SERVES 6

KUNG PAO PRAWNS WITH CASHEW NUTS

It is said that Kung Pao invented this dish,
but to this day no one knows who he was!

2.5ml/½ tsp chopped fresh ginger
5ml/1 tsp chopped garlic
25g/1½ tbsps cornflour
1.25ml/¼ tsp bicarbonate of soda
Salt and pepper
1.25ml/¼ tsp sugar
450g/1lb uncooked prawns
60ml/4 tbsps oil
1 small onion, cut into dice
1 large or 2 small courgettes, cut into 1.25cm/½ inch
    cubes
1 small red pepper, cut into 1.25cm/½ inch cubes
60g/2oz cashew nuts

Sauce

180ml/6 fl oz chicken stock
15g/1 tbsp cornflour
10ml/2 tsps chilli sauce
10ml/2 tsps bean paste (optional)
10ml/2 tsps sesame oil
15ml/1 tbsp dry sherry or rice wine

1. Mix together the ginger, garlic, 25g/1½ tbsps cornflour, bicarbonate of soda, salt, pepper and sugar.

2. If the prawns are unpeeled, remove the peels and the dark vein running along the rounded side. If large, cut in half, Place in the dry ingredients and leave to stand for 20 minutes.

3. Heat the oil in a wok and when hot add the prawns. Cook, stirring over high heat for about 20 seconds, or just until the prawns change colour. Transfer to a plate.

4. Add the onion to the same oil in the wok and cook for about 1 minute. Add the courgettes and red pepper and cook about 30 seconds.

5. Mix the sauce ingredients together and add to the wok. Cook, stirring constantly, until the sauce is slightly thickened. Add the prawns and the cashew nuts and heat through completely.

Step 4 To dice the courgettes quickly, top and tail and cut into 1.25cm/½ inch strips.

Step 4 Cut the strips across with a large sharp knife into 1.25cm/½ inch pieces.

Cook's Notes

Time
Preparation takes about 20 minutes, cooking takes about 3 minutes.

Variation
If using cooked prawns, add with the vegetables. Vary amount of chilli sauce to suit your taste.

Serving Ideas
Serve with plain or fried rice.

SERVES 8

PEKING BEEF

In China, meat is often simmered in large earthenware casseroles placed on asbestos mats. A wok is a convenient substitute and the stand does the work of the traditional mat.

900g/2lb joint of beef
430ml/¾ pint white wine
570ml/1 pint water
2 whole spring onions, roots trimmed
2.5cm/1 inch piece fresh ginger
3 star anise
10ml/2 tsps sugar
140ml/¼ pint soy sauce
1 carrot, peeled
2 sticks celery
½ mooli (daikon) radish, peeled

Step 3 Cut the celery into three strips and then into thin strips.

1. Place the beef in a wok and add the white wine, water, spring onions, ginger and anise. Cover and simmer for about 1 hour.

2. Add the soy sauce and sugar, stir and simmer for 30 minutes longer, or until the beef is tender. Allow to cool in the liquid.

3. Shred all the vegetables finely. Blanch them all, except the spring onion, in boiling water for about 1 minute. Rinse under cold water, drain and leave to dry.

4. When the meat is cold, remove it from the liquid and cut into thin slices. Arrange on a serving plate and strain the liquid over it. Scatter over the shredded vegetables and serve cold.

Step 3 Cut the vegetables into 7.5cm/3 inch lengths. To shred carrots, cut each length into thin slices, stack the slices 3-4 at a time and cut through into thin strips with a sharp knife.

Cook's Notes

Time
Preparation takes about 25 minutes if shredding the vegetables by hand. This can also be done with the fine shredding blade of a food processor. Cooking takes about 1½ hours.

Economy
Because of the long cooking time, less expensive cuts of meat may be used for this dish.

Cook's Tip
If using a rolled roast, remove as much of the fat from the outside as possible. Skim off any fat that rises to the surface of the liquid as it cools, before pouring over the meat to serve.

SERVES 6

BEEF WITH TOMATO & PEPPER IN BLACK BEAN SAUCE

Black beans are a speciality of Cantonese cooking
and give a pungent, salty taste to stir-fried dishes.

30ml/2 tbsps salted black beans
30ml/2 tbsps water
2 large tomatoes
60ml/4 tbsps dark soy sauce
15g/1 tbsp cornflour
15ml/1 tbsp dry sherry
5ml/1 tsp sugar
450g/1lb rump steak, cut into thin strips
60ml/4 tbsps oil
1 small green pepper, seeded and cored
180ml/6 fl oz beef stock
Pinch pepper

1. Core tomatoes and cut them into 16 wedges. Crush the black beans, add the water and set aside.

2. Combine soy sauce, cornflour, sherry, sugar and meat in a bowl and set aside.

3. Cut pepper into 1.25cm/½ inch diagonal pieces. Heat the wok and add the oil. When hot, stir-fry the green pepper pieces for about 1 minute and remove.

4. Add the meat and the soy sauce mixture to the wok and stir-fry for about 2 minutes. Add the soaked black beans and the stock. Bring to the boil and allow to thicken slightly. Return the peppers to the wok and add the tomatoes and pepper. Heat through for 1 minute and serve immediately.

Step 1 Remove cores from the tomatoes with a sharp knife. Cut into even-sized wedges.

Step 4 Add the beef mixture to the hot wok and stir-fry until liquid ingredients glaze the meat.

Cook's Notes

Time
Preparation takes about 25 minutes, cooking takes about 5 minutes.

Serving Ideas
Serve with plain boiled rice.

Watchpoint
Do not add the tomatoes too early or stir the mixture too vigorously once they are added or they will fall apart easily.

Variation
Substitute mangetout for the green peppers in the recipe. Mushrooms may also be added and cooked with the peppers or mangetout.

SERVES 2-3

BEEF WITH BROCCOLI

The traditional Chinese method of cutting meat
for stir-frying used in this recipe ensures that
the meat will be tender and will cook quickly.

450g/1lb rump steak, partially frozen
60ml/4 tbsps dark soy sauce
15g/1 tbsp cornflour
15ml/1 tbsp dry sherry
5ml/1 tsp sugar
225g/8oz fresh broccoli
90ml/6 tbsps oil
2.5cm/1 inch piece ginger, peeled and shredded
Salt and pepper

1. Trim any fat from the meat and cut into very thin strips across the grain. Strips should be about 7.5cm/3 inches long.

2. Combine the meat with the soy sauce, cornflour, sherry and sugar. Stir well and leave long enough for the meat to completely defrost.

3. Trim the florets from the stalks of the broccoli and cut them into even- sized pieces. Peel the stalks of the broccoli and cut into thin, diagonal slices.

4. Slice the ginger into shreds. Heat a wok and add 30ml/2 tbsps of the oil to it. Add the broccoli and sprinkle with salt. Stir-fry, turning constantly, until the broccoli is dark green. Do not cook for longer than 2 minutes. Remove from the wok and set aside.

5. Place the remaining oil in the wok and add the ginger and beef. Stir-fry, turning constantly, for about 2 minutes. Return the broccoli to the pan and mix well. Heat through for 30 seconds and serve immediately.

Step 1 Use partially frozen meat and slice it thinly across the grain.

Step 3 Cut the broccoli stalks in thin diagonal slices.

Step 4 To shred ginger quickly, cut into thin slices, stack up the slices and cut into thin strips.

Cook's Notes

 Time
Preparation takes about 25 minutes and cooking takes about 4 minutes.

Preparation
Using meat that is partially frozen makes it easier to get very thin slices.

 Cook's Tip
If more sauce is desired, double the quantities of soy sauce, cornflour, dry sherry and sugar.

SERVES 2-4

SWEET & SOUR PORK

This really needs no introduction because of its popularity. The dish originated in Canton, but is reproduced in most of the world's Chinese restaurants.

120g/4oz plain flour
60g/4 tbsps cornflour
7.5ml/1½ tsps baking powder
Pinch salt
15ml/1 tbsp oil
Water
225g/8oz pork fillet, cut into 1.25cm/½ inch cubes

Sweet and Sour Sauce

30g/2 tbsps cornflour
120g/4oz light brown sugar
Pinch salt
120ml/4 fl oz cider vinegar or rice vinegar
1 clove garlic, crushed
5ml/1 tsp fresh ginger, grated
90ml/6 tbsps tomato ketchup
90ml/6 tbsps reserved pineapple juice

1 onion, sliced
1 green pepper, seeded, cored and sliced
1 small can pineapple chunks, juice reserved
Oil for frying

1. To prepare the batter, sift the flour, cornflour, baking powder and salt into a bowl. Make a well in the centre and add the oil and enough water to make a thick, smooth batter. Using a wooden spoon, stir the ingredients in the well, gradually incorporating flour from the outside, and beat until smooth.

2. Heat enough oil in a wok to deep-fry the pork. Dip the pork cubes one at a time into the batter and drop into the hot oil. Fry 4-5 pieces of pork at a time and remove them with a draining spoon to paper towels. Continue until all the pork is fried.

3. Pour off most of the oil from the wok and add the sliced onion, pepper and pineapple. Cook over high heat for 1-2 minutes. Remove and set aside.

4. Mix all the sauce ingredients together and pour into the wok. Bring slowly to the boil, stirring continuously until thickened. Allow to simmer for about 1-2 minutes or until completely clear.

5. Add the vegetables, pineapple and pork cubes to the sauce and stir to coat completely. Reheat for 1-2 minutes and serve immediately.

Step 2 Dip the pork cubes into the batter and then drop into the hot oil. Chopsticks are ideal to use for this.

Step 3 Place the onion half flat on a chopping board and use a large, sharp knife to cut across to thick or thin slices as desired. Separate these into individual strips.

Cook's Notes

 Time
Preparation takes about 15 minutes, cooking takes about 15 minutes.

 **Variation**
Use beef or chicken instead of the pork. Uncooked, peeled prawns may be used as can whitefish, cut into 2.5cm/1 inch pieces.

 Cook's Tip
If pork is prepared ahead of time, this will have to be refried before serving to crisp up.

SERVES 4

CHICKEN LIVERS WITH CHINESE LEAVES & ALMONDS

Chicken livers need quick cooking, so they are
a perfect choice for the Chinese stir-frying method.

225g/8oz chicken livers
45ml/3 tbsps oil
60g/2oz split blanched almonds
1 clove garlic, peeled
60g/2oz mangetout
8-10 Chinese leaves
10g/2 tsps cornflour mixed with 15ml/1 tbsp cold water
30ml/2 tbsps soy sauce
140ml/¼ pint chicken stock

Step 2 Cook the almonds slowly in the oil to brown evenly, stirring often.

Step 1 Cut off any yellowish or greenish portions from the livers and divide them into even-sized pieces.

Step 3 Quickly stir-fry the livers until lightly browned on the outside. May be served slightly pink in the middle.

1. Pick over the chicken livers and remove any dis-coloured areas or bits of fat. Cut the chicken livers into even-sized pieces.

2. Heat a wok and pour in the oil. When the oil is hot, turn the heat down and add the almonds. Cook, stirring continuously, over gentle heat until the almonds are a nice golden brown. Remove and drain on paper towels.

3. Add the garlic, cook for 1-2 minutes to flavour the oil and remove. Add the chicken livers and cook for about 2-3 minutes, stirring frequently. Remove the chicken livers and set them aside. Add the mangetout to the wok and stir-fry for 1 minute. Shred the Chinese leaves finely, add to the wok and cook for 1 minute. Remove the vegetables and set them aside.

4. Mix together the cornflour and water with the soy sauce and stock. Pour into the wok and bring to the boil. Cook until thickened and clear. Return all the other ingredients to the sauce and reheat for 30 seconds. Serve immediately.

Cook's Notes

Time
Preparation takes about 25 minutes, cooking takes about 4-5 minutes.

Preparation
Remove any discoloured portions from the livers as these can cause a bitter taste. Livers may be served slightly pink in the middle.

Serving Ideas
Serve with plain or fried rice. Chinese noodles also make a good accompaniment.

SERVES 4

CHICKEN WITH WALNUTS & CELERY

Oyster sauce lends a subtle, slightly
salty taste to this Cantonese dish.

225g/8oz boned chicken, cut into 2.5cm/1 inch pieces
10ml/2 tsps soy sauce
10ml/2 tsps brandy
5ml/1 tsp cornflour
Salt and pepper
30ml/2 tbsps oil
1 clove garlic
120g/4oz walnut halves
3 sticks celery, cut in diagonal slices
140ml/¼ pint water or chicken stock
10ml/2 tsps oyster sauce

Step 3 Add the walnuts to the wok and cook until they are crisp.

Step 4 Use a large, sharp knife to cut the celery on the diagonal into thin slices.

Step 3 Cook the chicken until done but not brown.

1. Combine the chicken with the soy sauce, brandy, cornflour, salt and pepper.

2. Heat a wok and add the oil and garlic. Cook for about 1 minute to flavour the oil.

3. Remove the garlic and add the chicken in two batches.

Stir-fry quickly without allowing the chicken to brown. Remove the chicken and add the walnuts to the wok. Cook for about 2 minutes until the walnuts are slightly brown and crisp.

4. Slice the celery, add to the wok and cook for about 1 minute. Add the oyster sauce and water and bring to the boil. When boiling, return the chicken to the pan and stir to coat all the ingredients well. Serve immediately.

Cook's Notes

Time
Preparation takes about 20 minutes, cooking takes about 8 minutes.

Watchpoint
Nuts can burn very easily. Stir them constantly for even browning.

Variation
Almonds or cashew nuts may be used instead of the walnuts. If the cashew nuts are already toasted, add them along with the celery.

Serving Ideas
Serve with boiled or fried rice.

Buying Guide
Oyster sauce, made from oysters and soy sauce, is available from Chinese supermarkets.

SERVES 6

CHICKEN WITH CLOUD EARS

Cloud ears is the delightful name
for an edible tree fungus which is
mushroom-like in taste and texture.

---

12 cloud ears, wood ears or other dried Chinese
  mushrooms, soaked in boiling water for 5 minutes
450g/1lb chicken breasts, boned and thinly sliced
1 egg white
10ml/2 tsps cornflour
10ml/2 tsps white wine
10ml/2 tsps sesame oil
2.5cm/1 inch piece fresh ginger, left whole
1 clove garlic
280ml/½ pint oil
280ml/½ pint chicken stock
15g/1 tbsp cornflour
45ml/3 tbsps light soy sauce
Pinch salt and pepper

---

1. Soak the mushrooms until they soften and swell. Remove all the skin and bone from the chicken and cut it into thin slices. Mix the chicken with the egg white, cornflour, wine and sesame oil.

2. Heat the wok for a few minutes and pour in the oil. Add the whole piece of ginger and whole garlic clove to the oil and cook for about 1 minute. Take them out and reduce the heat.

3. Add about a quarter of the chicken at a time and stir-fry for about 1 minute. Remove and continue cooking until all the chicken is fried. Remove all but about 30ml/2 tbsps of the oil from the wok.

4. Drain the mushrooms and squeeze them to extract all the liquid. If using mushrooms with stems, remove the stems before slicing thinly. Cut cloud ears or wood ears into smaller pieces. Add to the wok and cook for about 1 minute. Add the stock and allow it to come almost to the boil. Mix together the cornflour and soy sauce and add a spoonful of the hot stock. Add the mixture to the wok, stirring constantly, and bring to the boil. Allow to boil 1-2 minutes or until thickened. The sauce will clear when the cornflour has cooked sufficiently.

5. Return the chicken to the wok and add salt and pepper. Stir thoroughly for about 1 minute and serve immediately.

Step 1 Soak the cloud ears or mushrooms in boiling water for five minutes, they will swell in size.

Step 3 Stir-fry the chicken in small batches, placing in the oil with chopsticks.

Cook's Notes

Time
Preparation takes about 25 minutes, cooking takes about 5 minutes.

Preparation
If desired, the chicken may be cut into 2.5cm/1 inch cubes. If slicing, cut across the grain as this helps the chicken to cook more evenly.

Variation
Flat, cup or button mushrooms may be used instead of the dried mushrooms. Eliminate the soaking and slice them thickly. Cook as for the dried variety. 10ml/2 tsps bottled oyster sauce may be added with the stock.

Buying Guide
Cloud ears or wood ears are a type of edible Chinese tree fungus. They are both available from Chinese supermarkets and some delicatessens. Chinese mushrooms are more readily available. Both keep a long time in their dried state. Chinese ingredients are becoming more readily available. Check supermarket shelves for bottled sauces like Oyster Sauce.

SERVES 4

Spun Fruits

Often called toffee fruits, this sweet
consists of fruit fried in batter and
coated with a thin, crisp caramel glaze.

Batter
120g/4oz plain flour, sifted
Pinch salt
1 egg
140ml/¼ pint water and milk mixed half and half
Oil for deep frying

Caramel Syrup
225g/8oz sugar
45ml/3 tbsps water
15ml/1 tbsp oil
1 large apple, peeled, cored and cut into 5cm/2 inch
    chunks
1 banana, peeled and cut into 2.5cm/1 inch pieces
Ice water

1. To prepare the batter, combine all the ingredients, except the oil for deep frying, in a liquidizer or food processor and process to blend. Pour into a bowl and dip in the prepared fruit.

2. In a heavy-based saucepan, combine the sugar with the water and oil and cook over very low heat until the sugar dissolves. Bring to the boil and allow to cook rapidly until a pale caramel colour.

3. While the sugar is dissolving, heat the oil in a wok and fry the batter-dipped fruit, a few pieces at a time.

4. While the fruit is still hot and crisp, use chopsticks or a pair of tongs to dip the fruit into the hot caramel syrup. Stir each piece around to coat evenly.

5. Dip immediately into ice water to harden the syrup and place each piece on a greased dish. Continue cooking all the fruit in the same way.

6. Once the caramel has hardened and the fruit has cooled, transfer to a clean serving plate.

Step 2 Cook the syrup until the sugar dissolves and is a pale golden brown.

Step 4 Using tongs or chopsticks, immediately dip the fried fruit into the hot syrup, swirling to coat evenly.

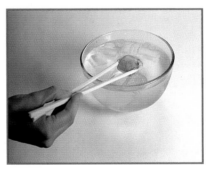

Step 5 Dip the caramel coated fruit into ice water to harden. Place on a greased dish to cool.

Cook's Notes

Time
Preparation takes about 25 minutes, cooking takes from 10-15 minutes.

Variation
Lychees may be used either fresh or canned. Organisation is very important for the success of this dish. Have the batter ready, syrup prepared, fruit sliced and ice water on hand before beginning.

Watchpoint
Watch the syrup carefully and do not allow it to become too brown. This will give a bitter taste to the dish.

MAKES 30 COOKIES

ALMOND COOKIES

In China these biscuits are often eaten as a between-meal snack. In Western style cuisine, they make a good accompaniment to fruit or sorbet.

120g/4oz butter or margarine
60g/4 tbsps caster sugar
30g/2 tbsps light brown sugar
1 egg, beaten
Almond essence
120g/4oz plain flour
5ml/1 tsp baking powder
Pinch salt
30g/1oz ground almonds, blanched or unblanched
30ml/2 tbsps water
30 whole blanched almonds

Step 2 Add egg and flavouring and beat until smooth.

Step 1 Cream the butter and sugars until light and fluffy.

Step 3 Shape into small balls with floured hands on a floured surface. Place well apart on baking sheets.

1. Cream the butter or margarine together with the two sugars until light and fluffy.

2. Divide the beaten egg in half and add half to the sugar mixture with a few drops of the almond essence and beat until smooth. Reserve the remaining egg for later use. Sift the flour, baking powder and salt into the egg mixture and add the ground almonds. Stir well by hand.

3. Shape the mixture into small balls and place well apart on a lightly greased baking sheet. Flatten slightly and press an almond on to the top of each one.

4. Mix the reserved egg with the water and brush each cookie before baking.

5. Place in a preheated 180°C/350°F/Gas Mark 4 oven and bake for 12-15 minutes. Cookies will be a pale golden colour when done.

Cook's Notes

 Time
Preparation takes about 10 minutes. If the dough becomes too soft, refrigerate for 10 minutes before shaping. Cooking takes about 12-15 minutes per batch.

 **Cook's Tip**
Roll the mixture on a floured surface with floured hands to prevent sticking.

 Watchpoint
Do not over beat once the almonds are added. They will begin to oil and the mixture will become too soft and sticky to shape.

 Serving Ideas
Serve with fruit, ice cream or sorbet. Do not reserve just for Chinese meals.

 Freezing
Cookies may be frozen baked or unbaked. Defrost uncooked dough completely at room temperature before baking. Baked cookies may be re-crisped by heating in the oven for about 2 minutes and then allowed to cool before serving.

SERVES 6

Sweet Bean Wontons

Wonton snacks, either sweet or savoury, are another popular
tea house treat. Made from prepared wonton wrappers and
ready-made bean paste, these couldn't be more simple.

15 wonton wrappers
225g/8oz sweet red bean paste
15g/1 tbsp cornflour
60ml/4 tbsps cold water
Oil for deep frying
Honey

1. Take a wonton wrapper in the palm of your hand and
place a little of the red bean paste slightly above the centre.

2. Mix together the cornflour and water and moisten the
edge around the filling.

3. Fold over, slightly off centre.

4. Pull the sides together, using the cornflour and water
paste to stick the two together.

5. Turn inside out by gently pushing the filled centre.

6. Heat enough oil in a wok for deep-fat frying and when
hot, put in 4 of the filled wontons at a time. Cook until crisp
and golden and remove to paper towels to drain. Repeat
with the remaining filled wontons. Serve drizzled with honey.

Step 4 Bring the
two sides together
and stick with
cornflour and
water paste.

Step 5 Push the
filled portion
gently through the
middle to turn
inside out.

Cook's Notes

Variation
Add a small amount of grated
ginger to the red bean paste
for a slight change in flavour. Wontons
may also be sprinkled with sugar
instead of honey.

Buying Guide
Wontons, wonton wrappers
and red bean paste are
available in Chinese supermarkets.

SERVES 6-8

ALMOND FLOAT WITH FRUIT

Sweet dishes are not often served in the course
of a Chinese meal. Banquets are the exception, and
this elegant fruit salad is certainly special enough.

1 envelope unflavoured gelatine
90ml/6 tbsps cold water
90g/3oz sugar
280ml/½ pint milk
5ml/1 tsp almond essence
Few drops red or yellow food colouring (optional)

Almond Sugar Syrup

90g/3oz sugar
570ml/1 pint water
2.5ml/½ tsp almond essence

Fresh fruit such as kiwi, mango, pineapple, bananas,
    lychees, oranges or satsumas, peaches, berries,
    cherries, grapes or starfruit
Fresh mint for garnish

1. Allow the gelatine to soften in the cold water for about 10 minutes or until spongy. Put in a large mixing bowl.

2. Bring 180ml/6 fl oz water to the boil and stir in the sugar. Pour into the gelatine and water mixture and stir until gelatine and sugar dissolves.

3. Add milk, flavouring and food colouring if using. Mix well and pour into a 20cm/8 inch square pan. Chill in the refrigerator until set.

4. Mix the sugar and water for the syrup together in a heavy-based pan. Cook over gentle heat until the sugar dissolves. Bring to the boil and allow to boil for about 2 minutes, or until the syrup thickens slightly. Add the almond essence and allow to cool at room temperature. Chill in the refrigerator until ready to use.

5. Prepare the fruit and place in attractive serving dish. Pour over the chilled syrup and mix well.

6. Cut the set almond float into 2.5cm/1 inch diamond shapes or cubes. Use a spatula to remove them from the pan and stir them gently into the fruit mixture. Decorate with sprigs of fresh mint to serve.

Step 2 Add boiling water and sugar, and stir until the mixture is clear and not grainy.

Step 6 Cut the set almond float mixture into cubes and remove from the pan with a palette knife.

Cook's Notes

Time
Preparation takes about 25 minutes. The almond float will need about 2 hours to set.

Preparation
To prepare kiwi fruit, peel with a swivel vegetable peeler and cut into thin rounds. To prepare lychees, peel off the rough outer skin. Cut around the stone or leave it in. To prepare mangoes, peel and cut into thin slices around the large stone. To prepare starfruit, wash and cut crosswise into thin slices. The shape of the slices will resemble a star.

Buying Guide
Use whatever fruits are in season at the moment, or use good quality canned fruit. Exotic fruits are available in most large supermarkets and some greengrocers. Allow about 900g/2lbs of fruit for 6-8 people.

MEXICAN COOKING

INTRODUCTION

In Mexico, as in most countries of the world that enjoy warm climates, the food is spicy. The addition of spices to food cooked in these climates has a two-fold purpose: they act as a preservative while also stimulating appetites flagging in the heat. But just because food is spicy, it need not be very hot. Cumin, coriander and cinnamon are favourite choices in Mexico and lend their fragrance and flavour without bringing tears to the eyes! For those who like things hot, fresh or dried chilli peppers or cayenne pepper will add fire to any dish. Green chillies and Jalapeno peppers, another variety, are also available canned.

If any one ingredient really symbolises Mexican cooking, it is the tortilla. In Mexico, tortillas in one form or another appear at every meal. Even if they are not an integral part of a recipe they are served warm as an accompaniment, even with eggs at breakfast. There are two types of tortilla, each made with different flours. Corn tortillas are made with Masa Harina, a fine corn flour that is not always easy to find. These corn tortillas are also slightly more difficult to make and to work with even though they are the more popular choice in Mexico. However, in the northern part of the country more wheat is grown, so tortillas are more often made with wheat flour. These are easy to make and more pliable, so they are easier to use in recipes and many people prefer them to the corn variety. Our recipe for flour tortillas can be used interchangeably with corn tortillas and you can even cut the tortillas into triangles or rounds and deep-fry them to make your own tortilla chips.

The use of cocoa powder in savoury dishes may seem a startling idea, but don't be put off. It gives a depth of colour and flavour to meat dishes without making them taste of chocolate. Spanish settlers in Mexico first used the plentiful cocoa bean in their cooking, adapting it to both sweet and savoury dishes. While the Spanish also introduced sugar and milk into the cuisine, sweets have not become overly popular in Mexico.

Over the past few years more and more prepared ingredients for Mexican cooking have appeared on the market. Corn tortillas come ready made and even shaped exactly right for tacos, making the cook's job easy. But, there is fun to be had in cooking this colourful and exciting cuisine in the traditional way, too.

MAKES ½ PINT

Taco Sauce

This basic recipe has many uses in Mexican cooking — sauce, topping, dip or as an ingredient to give a dish extra flavour.

15ml/1 tbsp oil
1 onion, diced
1 green pepper, diced
½-1 red or green chilli pepper
2.5ml/½ tsp ground cumin
2.5ml/½ tsp ground coriander
½ clove garlic, crushed
Pinch salt, pepper and sugar
400g/14oz canned tomatoes
Tomato purée (optional)

Step 3 Add remaining ingredients and use a potato masher or fork to break up tomatoes.

Step 2 Cut the chilli in half, remove the seeds and chop flesh finely.

Step 4 Cook the sauce over moderate heat to reduce and thicken.

1. Heat the oil in a heavy-based saucepan and when hot, add the onion and pepper. Cook slowly to soften slightly.

2. Chop the chilli and add with the cumin, coriander, garlic and cook a further 2-3 minutes.

3. Add sugar, seasonings and tomatoes with their juice.

Break up the tomatoes with a fork or a potato masher.

4. Cook a further 5-6 minutes over moderate heat to reduce and thicken slighly. Add tomato purée for colour, if necessary. Adjust seasoning and use hot or cold according to your recipe.

Cook's Notes

Time
Preparation takes about 15-20 minutes, cooking takes about 8-10 minutes.

Serving Ideas
Use as a sauce or topping for fish, meat or poultry main dishes. Use in tacos, tostadas, nachos and as a dip for tortilla chips or vegetable crudites

Freezing
Fill rigid containers with sauce at room temperature. Label and freeze for up to 3 months. Defrost at room temperature, breaking the sauce up as it thaws.

MAKES 12

FLOUR TORTILLAS

Tortillas made with wheat instead of corn are
traditional in Northern Mexico. Flour tortillas
are easier to make and use than the corn variety.

450g/1lb plain or wholemeal flour
15g/1 tbsp salt
90g/6 tbsps lard
280ml/½ pint hot water

Step 2 Knead a ball of prepared dough until smooth and pliable.

1. Sift flour and salt into a mixing bowl and rub in the lard until the mixture resembles fine breadcrumbs. Mix in the water gradually to form a soft, pliable dough. Wholemeal flour may need more water.

2. Knead on a well-floured surface until smooth and no longer sticky. Cover with a damp tea towel.

3. Cut off about 45g/3 tbsps of dough at a time, keeping the rest covered. Knead into a ball.

4. Roll the ball of dough out into a very thin circle with a floured rolling pin. Cut into a neat round using a 25cm/10 inch plate as a guide. Continue until all the dough is used.

5. Stack the tortillas as you make them, flouring each well to prevent sticking. Cover with a clean tea towel.

6. Heat a heavy-based frying pan and carefully place in a tortilla. Cook for about 10 seconds per side. Stack and keep covered until all are cooked. Use according to chosen recipe.

Step 4 Roll out the ball of dough thinly and cut into a 25cm/10 inch circle.

Step 6 Cook for 10 seconds per side in a hot frying pan.

Cook's Notes

 Time
Preparation takes about 60 minutes to make the dough and roll out all the tortillas, cooking takes about 5 minutes.

Serving Ideas
Use with any recipe that calls for tortillas. Also, serve hot as an accompaniment to any Mexican dish.

 Freezing
Tortillas can be prepared and cooked in advance and frozen. Stack the tortillas between sheets of non-stick or wax paper. Place in plastic bags, seal, label and freeze for up to 2 months. Defrost at room temperature before using.

SERVES 8

GUACAMOLE

This is one of Mexico's most famous dishes.
It is delicious as a first course on its
own or as an ingredient in other recipes.

1 medium onion, finely chopped
1 clove garlic, crushed
Grated rind and juice of ½ lime
½ quantity Taco Sauce recipe
3 large avocados
15ml/1 tbsp chopped fresh coriander
Pinch salt
Coriander leaves to garnish
1 package tortilla chips

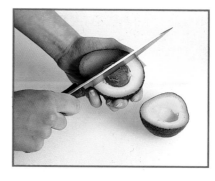

Step 3 Hit the stone with a large knife and twist to remove the stone.

Step 2 Cut avocados in half and twist the halves to separate.

Step 6 Use a potato masher to mash the avocado until nearly smooth.

1. Mix the onion, garlic, rind and juice of lime and the taco sauce together in a large mixing bowl.

2. Cut the avocados in half lengthways. Twist the halves gently in opposite directions to separate.

3. Hit the stone with a large, sharp knife and twist the knife to remove the stone.

4. Place the avocado halves cut side down on a chopping board. Lightly score the skin lengthwise and gently pull

back to peel. Alternatively, scoop out avocado flesh with a spoon, scraping the skin well.

5. Chop the avocado roughly and immediately place in the bowl with the onion and lime.

6. Use a potato masher to break up the avocado until almost smooth. Do not over-mash. Season with salt and stir in the chopped coriander. Spoon into a serving bowl and garnish with coriander leaves.

7. Surround the bowl with tortilla chips for dipping.

Cook's Notes

Time
Preparation takes about 25 minutes.

Preparation
Do not prepare too long in advance. The avocado will darken even with the addition of lime juice if left too long.

Cook's Tip
Try leaving the avocado stone in the mixture. This is said to retard discolouration.

SERVES 4

MOYETTES

While these sandwiches seem like lunch fare, they
are very popular for breakfast in Mexico.

4 crusty rolls
30g/2 tbsps butter or margarine
225g/8oz canned refried beans
2 spring onions, chopped
60g/4 tbsps grated Tilsit cheese

1. Cut the rolls in half and remove some of the inside.

Step 2 Spread both sides of each roll with softened butter or margarine, then fill the rolls with the refried beans.

Step 1 Remove some of the insides of each roll. Use a teaspoon to scrape out crumbs or cut out with a small knife.

2. Soften the butter and spread on both sides of the rolls.

3. Fill the rolls with the refried beans.

4. Sprinkle with the onion and top with the grated cheese.

5. Place the rolls on a baking sheet and cook in a pre-heated 160°C/325°F/Gas Mark 3 oven for 15-20 minutes, or until the cheese has melted and the beans are hot. Serve immediately.

Cook's Notes

Time
Preparation takes about 15 minutes and cooking takes about 15-20 minutes.

Cook's Tip
Sandwiches may be prepared in advance and heated through just before serving. Once heated, they do not reheat successfully.

Variation
Use red onion and Cheddar or Monterey Jack cheese, if available.

MAKES 12

TACOS

Packaged taco shells make this famous
Mexican snack easy to prepare, so spend
the extra time on imaginative fillings.

12 taco shells

Beef Filling

15ml/1 tbsp oil
450g/1lb minced beef
1 medium onion, chopped
10ml/2 tsps ground cumin
1 clove garlic, crushed
10ml/2 tsps chilli powder
Pinch paprika
Salt and pepper

Chicken Filling

45g/3 tbsps butter or margarine
1 medium onion, chopped
1 small red pepper, seeded and chopped
30g/2 tbsps flaked almonds
340g/12oz chicken breasts, skinned and finely chopped
Salt and pepper
1 piece fresh ginger, peeled and chopped
90ml/6 tbsps milk
10ml/2 tsps cornflour
140ml/¼ pint sour cream

Toppings

Shredded lettuce
Grated cheese
Tomatoes, seeded and chopped
Chopped spring onions
Avocado slices
Sour cream
Jalapeno peppers
Taco sauce

1. Heat oil for beef filling in a large frying pan and brown the beef and onions, breaking the meat up with a fork as it cooks. Add spices, garlic and seasoning and cook about

20 minutes. Set aside.

2. Melt the 30g/2 tbsps butter or margarine in a medium saucepan and add the onion. Cook slowly until softened.

3. Add the red pepper and almonds and cook slowly until the almonds are lightly browned. Stir often during cooking. Remove to a plate and set aside.

4. Melt the remaining butter in the same saucepan and cook the chicken for about 5 minutes, turning frequently. Season and return the onion mixture to the pan along with the chopped ginger.

5. Blend milk and cornflour and stir into the chicken mixture. Bring to the boil and stir until very thick. Mix in the sour cream and cook gently to heat through. Do not boil.

6. Heat the taco shells on a baking sheet in a preheated 180°C/350°F/Gas Mark 4 oven for 2-3 minutes. Place on the sheet with the open ends down.

7. To fill, hold the shell in one hand and spoon in about 15ml/1 tbsp of either beef or chicken filling.

8. Next, add a layer of shredded lettuce, followed by a layer of grated cheese.

9. Add choice of other toppings and finally spoon on some taco sauce.

Step 7 Hold taco shell in the palm of the hand and fill with about 15ml/1 tbsp filling.

Cook's Notes

Time
Preparation takes about 40 minutes. Cooking takes about 20 minutes for the beef filling, 15 minutes for the chicken filling and 2-3 minutes to heat the taco shells.

Cook's Tip
Placing the taco shells on their open ends when reheating keeps them from closing up and makes filling easier.

Serving Ideas
For a buffet, place all the ingredients out separately for guests to help themselves and create their own combinations.

SERVES 8-10

NACHOS

These make excellent cocktail savouries
and the variety of toppings and flavour
combinations is almost endless.

1 package round tortilla chips
1 can refried beans
1 can Jalapeno bean dip
Full quantity Taco Sauce recipe
8-10 cherry tomatoes, sliced
140ml/¼ pint sour cream or natural yogurt
Sliced black and stuffed green olives
Grated Cheddar cheese

Taco Filling

10ml/2 tsps oil
225g/8oz minced beef
10ml/2 tsps chilli powder
Pinch ground coriander
Pinch cayenne pepper
Salt and pepper

1. Prepare taco filling as for Tacos recipe. Top half of the tortilla chips with refried beans and half with beef taco filling.

2. Place a spoonful of taco sauce on the bean-topped chips and Jalapeno bean dip in the beef-topped chips.

3. Top the tortilla chips with tomatoes, sour cream or yogurt, olives or cheese in any desired combination, and serve.

Step 2 Spoon on taco sauce and Jalapeno bean dip on top of beans or beef.

Step 1 Use a teaspoon to top chips with beans and beef mixture. Spread out carefully with the bowl of the spoon.

Step 3 Top with chosen ingredients and serve. Heat through to melt cheese if desired.

Cook's Notes

Time
Preparation takes about 25 minutes.

Variation
If desired, heat through for 5 minutes in a moderate oven before topping with tomatoes, sour cream or olives. Cheese may be sprinkled on to melt before serving.

Cook's Tip
Tortilla chips will become slightly soggy if topped too soon before serving.

MAKES 12

TOSTADAS

These are popular all over Mexico and the toppings reflect the food available in each area. They are delicious, but difficult to eat!

10ml/2 tsps oil
450g/1lb minced beef or pork
10ml/2 tsps chilli powder
5ml/1 tsp ground cumin
5ml/1 tsp ground coriander
1 can refried beans
1 package tostada shells

Toppings

Shredded lettuce
Grated Cheddar cheese
Tomatoes, seeded and chopped
Sour Cream
Olives
Prawns
Spring onions, chopped
Taco sauce

Step 3 Spread refried beans carefully over each tostada shell.

1. Cook the meat in the oil in a medium frying pan. Sprinkle on the spices and cook quickly to brown.

Step 4 Spoon some of the meat mixture over the beans, pushing it down gently so that it sticks to the beans.

Step 5 Top with your choice of topping ingredients.

2. Reheat the beans and place the tostada shells on a baking sheet. Heat 2-3 minutes in a moderate oven.

3. Spread 15-30ml/1-2 tbsps of the beans on each tostada shell.

4. Top each shell with some of the beef mixture.

5. Add the topping ingredients in different combinations and serve immediately.

Cook's Notes

Time
Preparation takes about 40 minutes, cooking takes about 10-15 minutes.

Preparation
All the ingredients can be prepared ahead of time. The tostadas cannot be reheated once assembled.

Variation
Add chopped green or red peppers to the list of toppings along with chopped green chillies or Jalapeno peppers and guacamole.

FLAUTAS

Traditionally, these are long, thin rolls of tortillas with savoury fillings, topped with sour cream.

225g/8oz chicken, skinned, boned and minced or finely chopped
15ml/1 tbsp oil
1 small onion, finely chopped
½ green pepper, finely chopped
½-1 chilli pepper, seeded and finely chopped
90g/3oz frozen sweetcorn
6 black olives, pitted and chopped
120ml/4 fl oz double cream
Salt
12 prepared tortillas (see recipe for Flour Tortillas)
Taco sauce, guacamole and sour cream for toppings.

1. Use a food processor or meat mincer to prepare the chicken, or chop by hand.

2. Heat the oil in a medium frying pan and add the chicken, onion and green pepper. Cook over moderate heat, stirring frequently to break up the pieces of chicken.

3. When the chicken is cooked and the vegetables are softened, add the chilli, sweetcorn, olives, cream and salt. Bring to the boil over heat and boil rapidly, stirring continuously, to reduce and thicken the cream.

4. Place 2 tortillas on a clean work surface, overlapping them by about 5cm/2 inches. Spoon some of the chicken mixture onto the tortillas, roll up and secure with cocktail sticks.

5. Fry the flautas in about 1.25cm/½ inch oil in a large frying pan. Do not allow the tortillas to get very brown. Drain on paper towels.

6. Arrange flautas on serving plates and top with sour cream, guacamole and taco sauce.

Step 4 Place tortillas slightly overlapping on work surface and fill with chicken.

Step 4 Use cocktail sticks to secure tortillas.

Step 5 Fry slowly and turn carefully so the filling does not leak.

Cook's Notes

Time
Preparation takes about 1 hour for the tortillas and about 30 minutes to finish the dish.

Variation
Use pork or beef in place of the chicken. Green olives, may be substituted for black, and red peppers for green.

Serving Ideas
Flautas are often served with rice, refried beans and a salad.

SERVES 6

BURRITOS

The name means 'little donkeys' and the dish is
a very popular one. Beans are the traditional
filling, but meat may be used as well.

6 flour tortillas
1 onion, chopped
15ml/1 tbsp oil
450g/1lb canned refried beans
6 lettuce leaves, shredded
30ml/2 tbsps snipped chives
2 tomatoes, sliced
120g/4oz Cheddar cheese, grated
Full quantity Taco Sauce recipe
140ml/¼ pint sour cream
Chopped coriander leaves

Step 3 Use kitchen scissors to make snipping chives easy.

Step 3 Spoon some of the bean mixture down the centre of each tortilla.

Step 3 Fold the ends and sides of each tortilla around the filling to make rectangular parcels.

1. Wrap tortillas in foil and heat in a warm oven to soften.

2. Cook the onion in the oil until soft but not coloured. Add the beans and heat through.

3. Spoon the mixture down the centre of each tortilla. Top with lettuce, cheese, tomatoes and chives. Fold over the

sides to form long rectangular parcel. Make sure the filling is completely enclosed.

4. Place burritos in an ovenproof dish, cover and cook in a preheated 180°C/350°F/Gas Mark 4 oven for about 20 minutes.

5. Spoon over the taco sauce. Top with sour cream and sprinkle with chopped coriander to serve.

Cook's Notes

Time
Preparation takes about 25 minutes, not including making the tortillas. Cooking takes about 20 minutes.

Preparation
Heat just before serving. Burritos do not reheat well. Add extra chilli pepper to the taco sauce recipe if desired.

Serving Ideas
Serve with rice and guacamole.

SERVES 6

CHIMICHANGAS

A strange sounding name for a delicious snack
which is something like a deep-fried taco.

6 flour tortillas
Half quantity Chilli Con Carne recipe
6 lettuce leaves, shredded
6 spring onions, chopped
90g/3oz Cheddar cheese, grated
Oil for frying
Half quantity Guacamole recipe
140ml/¼ pint sour cream
1 tomato, seeded and chopped

Step 4 Lower the chimichangas carefully into hot oil in a large frying pan, folded side first.

Step 3 Fold the tortillas over the filling to enclose it completely and form a parcel.

Step 5 After about 3 minutes, turn chimichangas over with a draining spoon or fish slice to cook the other side.

1. Wrap the tortillas in foil and place in a warm oven for 5 minutes to make them pliable.

2. Heat the chilli briefly and spoon about 30ml/2 tbsps onto the centre of each tortilla. Top with lettuce, onions and cheese.

3. Fold in the sides to make a parcel, making sure all the filling is enclosed.

4. Heat about 2.5cm/1 inch of oil in a large frying pan and

when hot lower in the chimichangas, folded side down first. Cook 2-4 at a time depending on the size of the pan.

5. Cook for 3 minutes and carefully turn over. Cook a further 3 minutes and remove to paper towels and drain. Repeat with remaining chimichangas.

6. Spoon the guacamole over the top of each and drizzle over the sour cream. Sprinkle over the chopped tomato and serve immediately.

Cook's Notes

Time
Preparation takes about 30 minutes. This does not include time to prepare the tortillas or the chilli. Cooking time for the chimichangas is about 12-18 minutes.

Preparation
Tortillas and chilli can be made in advance and the chimichangas cooked just before serving. They do not reheat successfully.

Serving Idea
Serve with rice and refried beans.

SERVES 6

ENCHILADAS

Although fillings and sauces vary, enchiladas
are one of the tastiest Mexican dishes.

10 ripe tomatoes, peeled, seeded and chopped
1 small onion, chopped
1-2 green or red chillies, seeded and chopped
1 clove garlic, crushed
Salt
Pinch sugar
15-30ml/1-2 tbsps tomato purée
30g/2 tbsps butter or margarine
2 eggs
280ml/½ pint double cream
60g/4 tbsps grated cheese
340g/12oz minced pork
1 small red pepper, seeded and chopped
60g/4 tbsps raisins
60g/4 tbsps pine nuts
Salt and pepper
12 prepared tortillas (see recipe for Flour Tortillas)
Sliced spring onions to garnish

1. Place tomatoes, onion, chillies, garlic, salt and sugar in
a blender or food processor and purée until smooth.

2. Melt butter or margarine in a large saucepan. Add the
purée and simmer for 5 minutes.

3. Beat together the eggs and cream, mixing well. Add a
spoonful of the hot tomato purée to the cream and eggs
and mix quickly. Return mixture to the saucepan with the
rest of the tomato purée. Reserve cheese for topping.

4. Heat slowly, stirring constantly, until the mixture thickens. Do not boil.

5. While preparing the sauce, cook the pork and pepper
slowly in a large frying pan. Use a fork to break up the meat
as it cooks. Turn up the heat when the pork is nearly cooked
and fry briskly for a few minutes. Add the raisins, pine nuts
and seasoning.

6. Combine about ¼ of the sauce with the meat and divide
mixture evenly among all the tortillas. Spoon on the filling to
one side of the centre and roll up the tortilla around it,
leaving the ends open and some of the filling showing.

7. Place enchiladas seam side down in a baking dish and
pour over the remaining sauce, leaving the ends uncovered. Sprinkle over the cheese and bake in a preheated
180°C/350°F/Gas Mark 4 oven for 15-20 minutes, or until
the sauce begins to bubble. Sprinkle with the sliced onions
and serve immediately.

Step 3 Mix the eggs and cream with some of the hot sauce and then return it to the pan, stirring constantly.

Step 6 Spoon meat filling to one side of the tortillas and roll them up, leaving ends open.

Cook's Notes

Time
Preparation takes about 60
minutes to make the tortillas
and about 30 minutes more to finish the
dish.

Watchpoint
When preparing the sauce, do
not allow it to boil or it
will curdle.

Economy
Left-over meat or chicken can
be minced in a food processor
or finely chopped and used in place of
the freshly cooked meat.

SERVES 4

PRAWNS ACAPULCO

These make a stylish starter or a quickly
prepared snack. Make the bread slices
smaller to serve with cocktails.

4 slices bread, crusts removed
90g/6 tbsps softened butter
180g/6oz cooked and peeled prawns
2.5ml/½ tsp chilli powder
1.25ml/¼ tsp paprika
1.25ml/¼ tsp cumin
Salt and pepper
Watercress to garnish

1. Cut the bread slices in half and spread with 30g/2 tbsps butter. Butter both sides sparingly.

2. Place the bread on a baking sheet and cook in a preheated 180°C/350°F/Gas Mark 4 oven for 10-15 minutes until golden brown. Keep warm.

3. Melt the remaining butter in a small pan and add the prawns, spices and seasoning and stir well.

4. Heat through completely and spoon on top of the bread slices. Garnish with watercress and serve hot.

Step 2 Cook the bread on a baking sheet until golden brown and crisp.

Step 3 Cook the prawn and chilli mixture over gentle heat, stirring continuously.

Cook's Notes

Time
Preparation takes about 15 minutes. The bread will take 15-20 minutes to cook until golden, and the prawns take about 5 minutes to heat through.

Watchpoint
Do not heat the prawns too long or at too high a temperature; they toughen easily.

Cook's Tip
The bread may be prepared in advance and reheated 5 minutes in the oven. Do not reheat the prawns.

SERVES 4

CHILLI VEGETABLE SOUP

A simple-to-make and delicious soup
that makes a light first course.

15ml/1 tbsp oil
1 onion, chopped
120g/4oz canned whole green chillies, quartered
1 litre/2 pints chicken stock
1 large potato, peeled and cut into short strips
Full quantity Taco Sauce recipe
15ml/1 tbsp lime juice
Tortilla chips and lime slices to garnish
Salt

Step 1 Cook the onion slowly in the oil until translucent. Do not brown.

1. Heat the oil in a large saucepan and sauté the onion until translucent. Add the green chillies, stock, potato and taco sauce.

2. Cover the pan and simmer soup for 20 minutes. Stir in the lime juice and add salt.

3. Serve in individual bowls with tortilla chips.

4. Cut a thin slice of lime to float in each bowl of soup.

Step 1 Add the remaining ingredients and simmer for 20 minutes.

Cook's Notes

Time
Preparation takes about 20 minutes and cooking takes 20 minutes.

Variation
Use only half a can green chillies if desired, or cook green peppers with the onions instead.

Serving Ideas
For a more filling soup, add cooked rice.

SERVES 4

BEEF & BEAN SOUP

In Mexico, the day's main meal is
eaten at around 2.00 pm and this
soup is a popular starter.

1 large onion, peeled and finely chopped
2 sticks celery, chopped
1 red pepper, deseeded and finely chopped
30ml/2 tbsps oil
225g/8oz minced beef
6 tomatoes, peeled, seeded and chopped
420g/15oz canned refried beans
5ml/1 tsp ground cumin
5ml/1 tsp chilli powder
5ml/1 tsp garlic powder or purée
Pinch cinnamon and cayenne pepper
570ml/1 pint beef stock
Salt and pepper

spices, garlic and seasoning and mix well.

3. Stir in the stock and bring to the boil. Cover and simmer gently for 30 minutes, stirring occasionally.

4. Pour the soup into a blender or food processor and purée. The soup will be quite thick and not completely smooth.

5. Adjust the seasoning and serve with tortilla chips. Top with sour cream if desired.

Step 2 Cook the beef over medium heat until well browned.

Step 1 Cook the onion, celery and pepper in oil to soften. Stir frequently.

Step 4 Purée the soup in several batches until nearly smooth.

1. Fry the onion, pepper and celery in the oil in a large saucepan until softened.

2. Add the beef and fry over medium heat until well browned. Add the tomatoes and refried beans with the

Cook's Notes

Time
Preparation takes about 20 minutes and cooking takes about 50 minutes to soften vegetables, brown meat and simmer soup.

Watchpoint
Make sure the blender or food processor lid is closed securely before puréeing the hot soup. Purée in 2 or 3 small batches for safety.

Freezing
Allow the puréed soup to cool completely and skim any fat from the surface. Pour into freezer containers, label and freeze for up to 3 months.

SERVES 6

MEXICAN CHICKEN & PEPPER SALAD

This is the perfect lunch or light supper dish
during the summer, and it can be prepared in advance.

450g/1lb cooked chicken, cut in strips
140ml/¼ pint mayonnaise
140ml/¼ pint natural yogurt
5ml/1 tsp chilli powder
5ml/1 tsp paprika
Pinch cayenne pepper
2.5ml/½ tsp tomato purée
5ml/1 tsp onion purée
1 green pepper, seeded and finely sliced
1 red pepper, seeded and finely sliced
180g/6oz frozen sweetcorn, defrosted
180g/6oz long grain rice, cooked

1. Place the chicken strips in a large salad bowl.

2. Mix the mayonnaise, yogurt, spices, tomato and onion
purées together and leave to stand briefly for flavours to
blend. Fold dressing into the chicken.

3. Add the peppers and sweetcorn and mix gently until all
the ingredients are coated with dressing.

4. Place the rice on a serving dish and pile the salad into
the centre. Serve immediately.

Step 3 Fold all ingredients together gently so that they do not break up. Use a large spoon or rubber spatula.

Step 4 Arrange rice on a serving plate and spoon salad into the centre.

Cook's Notes

Time
Preparation takes about 30 minutes.

Buying Guide
Onion purée is available in tubes like tomato purée.

Preparation
Chicken salad may be prepared several hours in advance and kept covered in the refrigerator. Spoon onto rice just before serving.

Variation
Add sliced or diced green chillies or Jalapeno peppers for hotter flavour. Try chilli sauce or taco sauce as an alternative seasoning.

SERVES 6

CHILLI PRAWN QUICHE

Fresh chilli peppers give a Mexican flavour
to this quiche with its prawn filling.

Pastry

120g/4oz plain flour
Pinch salt
30g/2 tbsps butter or margarine
30g/2 tbsps white cooking fat
30-60ml/2-4 tbsps cold water

Filling

4 eggs
140ml/¼ pint milk
140ml/¼ pint single cream
½ clove garlic, crushed
120g/4oz Cheddar cheese, grated
3 spring onions, chopped
2 green chillies, seeded and chopped
225g/8oz cooked and peeled prawns
Salt
Cooked, unpeeled prawns and parsley sprigs for garnish

1. Sift the flour with a pinch of salt into a mixing bowl, or place in a food processor and mix once or twice.

2. Rub in the butter and fat until the mixture resembles fine breadcrumbs, or work in the food processor, being careful not to over-mix.

3. Mix in the liquid gradually, adding enough to bring the pastry together into a ball. In a food processor, add the liquid through the funnel while the machine is running.

4. Wrap the pastry well and chill for 20-30 minutes.

5. Roll out the pastry on a well-floured surface with a floured rolling pin.

6. Wrap the circle of pastry around the rolling pin to lift it into a 25cm/10 inch flan dish. Unroll the pastry over the dish.

7. Carefully press the pastry onto the bottom and up the sides of the dish, taking care not to stretch it.

8. Roll the rolling pin over the top of the dish to remove excess pastry, or cut off with a sharp knife.

9. Mix the eggs, milk, cream and garlic together. Sprinkle the cheese, onion, chillies and prawns onto the base of the pastry and pour over the egg mixture.

10. Bake in a preheated 200°C/400°F/Gas Mark 6 oven for 30-40 minutes until firm and golden brown. Peel the tail shells off the prawns and remove the legs and roe if present. Use to garnish the quiche along with the sprigs of parsley.

Step 6 Use the rolling pin to help lift the pastry into the flan dish.

Step 7 Carefully press the pastry into the dish to line the base and sides.

Cook's Notes

Time
Preparation takes about 40 minutes, which includes time for the pastry to chill. Cooking takes 30-40 minutes.

Variation
Add diced red or green peppers and chopped coriander leaves to the filling before baking.

Serving Ideas
Serve as a starter, cut in thin wedges or baked in individual dishes. Serve hot or cold with a salad for a snack or light meal.

SERVES 6

PRAWNS VERACRUZ

Veracruz is a port on the Gulf of Mexico
which lends its name to a variety
of colourful seafood dishes.

15ml/1 tbsp oil
1 onion, chopped
1 large green pepper, cut into 3.5cm/1½ inch strips.
2-3 green chillies, seeded and chopped
Double quantity Taco Sauce recipe
2 tomatoes, skinned and roughly chopped
12 pimento-stuffed olives, halved
10ml/2 tsps capers
1.25ml/¼ tsp ground cumin
Salt
450g/1lb prawns, uncooked
Juice of 1 lime

Refresh in cold water. The skins will now peel away easily.

Place the tomatoes in a pan of boiling water for a few seconds.

Step 2 Combine all the sauce ingredients in a heavy-based pan.

1. Heat the oil in a large frying pan and add the onion and green pepper. Cook until soft but not coloured.

2. Add chillies, taco sauce, tomatoes, olives, capers, cumin and salt. Bring to the boil and then lower the heat to simmer for 5 minutes.

3. Remove black veins, if present, from the rounded side of the prawns with a cocktail stick.

4. Add the prawns to the sauce and cook until they curl up and turn pink and opaque. Add the lime juice to taste and serve.

Cook's Notes

Time
Preparation takes about 25 minutes and cooking takes about 15 minutes.

Preparation
Sauce may be prepared in advance and reheated while cooking the prawns.

Variation
If using cooked prawns, reheat for about 5 minutes. Do not overcook.

SERVES 4

PLAICE WITH SPICY TOMATO SAUCE

This piquant fish dish is popular along
Mexico's Gulf coast.

90g/3oz cream cheese
5ml/1 tsp dried oregano
Pinch cayenne pepper
4 whole fillets of plaice
Lime slices and dill to garnish

Tomato Sauce

15ml/1 tbsp oil
1 small onion, chopped
1 stick celery, chopped
1 chilli pepper, seeded and chopped
1.25ml/¼ tsp each ground cumin, coriander and ginger
½ red and ½ green pepper, seeded and chopped
400g/14oz canned tomatoes
15ml/1 tbsp tomato purée
Salt, pepper and a pinch sugar

1. Heat the oil in a heavy-based pan and cook the onion, celery, chilli pepper and spices for about 5 minutes over very low heat.

2. Add red and green peppers and the remaining ingredients and bring to the boil. Reduce heat and simmer 15-20 minutes, stirring occasionally. Set aside while preparing the fish.

3. Mix the cream cheese, oregano and cayenne pepper together and set aside.

4. Skin the fillets using a filleting knife. Start at the tail end and hold the knife at a slight angle to the skin.

5. Push the knife along using a sawing motion, with the blade against the skin. Dip fingers in salt to make it easier to hold onto the fish skin. Gradually separate the fish from the skin.

6. Spread the cheese filling on all 4 fillets and roll each up. Secure with cocktail sticks.

7. Place the fillets in a lightly greased baking dish, cover and cook for 10 minutes in a preheated 180°C/350°F/Gas Mark 4 oven.

8. Pour over the tomato sauce and cook a further 10-15 minutes. Fish is cooked when it feels firm and looks opaque. Garnish with lime slices and dill.

Step 5 Using a filleting knife held at an angle, push the knife along, cutting against the fish skin. Use a sawing motion to separate flesh from skin.

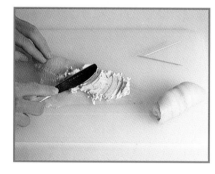

Step 6 Spread cheese filling on the fish and roll up each fillet.

Cook's Notes

 Time
Preparation takes about 30 minutes and cooking takes 20-25 minutes.

Serving Ideas
Add rice and an avocado salad.

 Special Occasions
Add prawns or crabmeat to the filling for a dinner party dish.

MAKES 6

EMPANADAS (SAVOURY TURNOVERS)

Fillings for these turnovers can also be sweet.
They are Spanish in origin and widely popular.

Triple quantity pastry recipe from Chilli Prawn Quiche
1 egg

Filling

1 onion, chopped
1 clove garlic, finely chopped
1 small green pepper, seeded and chopped
15ml/1 tbsp oil
225g/8oz minced beef
5ml/1 tsp cocoa powder
15g/1 tbsp flour
2.5ml/½ tsp ground cumin
2.5ml/½ tsp paprika
2.5ml/½ tsp dried oregano, crushed
Salt and pepper
1-2 chillies, seeded and chopped
30ml/2 tbsps tomato purée
45ml/3 tbsps water
30g/2 tbsps flaked almonds
30g/2 tbsps raisins

1. Prepare the pastry according to the recipe for Chilli Prawn Quiche, or use packaged shortcrust pastry.

2. Cook the onion, garlic and green pepper in the oil until soft but not coloured. Add the meat and fry quickly until well browned. Add the cocoa, flour, spices, oregano, and seasonings, stir well and cook briefly before adding the chillies, tomato purée and water. Cook slowly for 10-15 minutes. Add nuts and raisins and allow to cool.

3. Roll out the pastry on a floured surface and cut out 6 rounds using a 15cm/6 inch plate or saucepan lid as a guide.

4. Place the cooled filling on one side of the rounds of pastry and dampen the edges with water.

5. Fold over and press to seal the edges. Crimp the edges if desired.

6. Place on baking sheets and brush with a mixture of beaten egg and salt. Make sure the egg glaze is brushed on evenly. Prick once or twice with a fork and bake at 220°C/425°F/Gas Mark 7 for about 15 minutes, or until golden brown.

Step 5 Fold over and press the edges to seal firmly. Crimp if desired.

Step 6 Brush the surface of each turnover with beaten egg and prick the tops with a fork to let out steam.

Cook's Notes

Time
Preparation takes about 30 minutes. Dough should chill for about 30 minutes before rolling out. Filling takes about 20 minutes to cook and turnovers take about 15 minutes to bake.

Preparation
Turnovers may be baked in advance and reheated for about 5 minutes in a hot oven before serving. They may also be served cold.

Serving Ideas
Serve hot or cold as a snack or light meal accompanied with a salad. Perfect for picnics.

SERVES 4

CHILLI CON CARNE

Although this dish is Mexican in
origin, the version everyone knows
best is really more American.

15ml/1 tbsp oil
450g/1lb minced beef
10ml/2 tsps ground cumin
10ml/2 tsps mild or hot chilli powder
Pinch oregano
Salt, pepper and pinch sugar
1.25ml/¼ tsp garlic granules
30ml/2 tbsps flour
450g/1lb canned tomatoes
450g/1lb canned red kidney beans

1. Heat the oil in a large saucepan and brown the meat,
breaking it up with a fork as it cooks. Sprinkle on the cumin,
chilli powder, oregano, salt, pepper, sugar, garlic and flour.
Cook, stirring frequently, over medium heat for about 3
minutes.

2. Add the tomatoes and their liquid and simmer 25-30
minutes.

3. Drain the kidney beans and add just before serving.
Heat through about 5 minutes.

Step 1 Sprinkle
on the spice
mixture and stir it
into the meat.
Skim off any fat
that forms on the
surface.

Step 2 Add the
tomatoes and
their liquid. Use a
large spoon or
potato masher to
break up the
tomatoes.

Cook's Notes

Time
Preparation takes about 15
minutes. Cooking takes about
10 minutes to brown the meat and
15-30 minutes to cook after the
tomatoes are added.

Serving Ideas
Spoon the chilli on top of
boiled rice to serve. Top with
sour cream, chopped onion, grated
cheese, diced avocado or a
combination of the four ingredients.

Freezing
Allow the chilli to cool
completely and place in rigid
containers, seal, label and freeze for up
to 3 months. Thaw before reheating.

SERVES 4

MEXICAN BEEF PATTIES

Refried beans added to the meat mixture
make moist and flavoursome beefburgers
that are slightly out of the ordinary.

1 onion, finely chopped
15ml/1 tbsp oil
340g/12oz minced beef
225g/8oz canned refried beans
60g/4 tbsps breadcrumbs
2.5ml/½ tsp cumin
5ml/1 tsp chilli powder
1 clove garlic, crushed
Salt and pepper
1 egg, beaten
Flour to coat
Oil for frying
Watercress to garnish

1. Cook the onion in the oil until soft but not browned. Mix in the beef, beans, breadcrumbs, spices, garlic and seasoning and gradually add the egg until the mixture holds together well.

2. Turn the mixture out onto a well-floured surface and divide into 8 pieces.

3. Shape into even-sized patties with well-floured hands. Knead the pieces before shaping, if necessary, to make sure mixture holds together with no cracks.

4. Coat lightly with flour and refrigerate until firm.

5. Pour enough oil into a large frying pan to completely cover the patties. Fry 2 at a time until golden brown on all sides and completely cooked through.

6. Remove from the oil and drain on paper towels. Arrange on a serving plate and garnish with watercress.

Step 3 Shape meat mixture into firm, even-sized patties with well-floured hands.

Step 4 Coat lightly with flour on all sides and place on a plate or baking sheet to refrigerate until firm.

Step 5 Fry 2 patties at a time in hot oil. Make sure they are completely submerged.

Cook's Notes

 Time
Preparation takes about 20 minutes. The patties will take at least 1 hour to firm up sufficiently in the refrigerator.

 Preparation
If mixture is too soft to shape, add 30g/2 tbsps flour.

 Serving Ideas
Serve with sour cream or taco sauce and an avocado and tomato salad. Accompany with warm flour tortillas.

 Freezing
Meat patties can be made up ahead of time and frozen on baking sheets until firm. Place in rigid containers with non-stick paper or wax paper between each patty. Defrost in the refrigerator before cooking. Do not use minced beef that has been previously frozen or defrosted.

SERVES 4

ALBONDIGAS
(MEATBALLS)

A simple-to-make taco sauce makes plain meatballs
a lot less ordinary and a lot more fun to eat.

225g/8oz minced veal
225g/8oz minced beef
1 clove garlic, crushed
30g/2 tbsps dry breadcrumbs
½ chilli pepper, seeded and finely chopped
2.5ml/½ tsp ground cumin
Salt and pepper
1 egg, beaten
Oil for frying
Full quantity Taco Sauce recipe
2 spring onions, chopped

1. Mix together the veal, beef, garlic, breadcrumbs, chilli pepper, cumin, salt and egg until well blended. Add the egg gradually.

2. Turn the mixture out onto a floured surface and divide into 16 equal pieces.

3. With floured hands, shape the mixture into balls.

4. Pour about 45ml/3 tbsps of oil into a large frying pan and place over high heat.

5. When the oil is hot, place in the meatballs and fry for 5-10 minutes until brown on all sides. Turn frequently during cooking.

6. Remove the browned meatballs and drain well on paper towels. Place in an ovenproof dish and pour over the taco sauce.

7. Heat through in a preheated 170°C/350°F/Gas Mark 3 oven for 10 minutes. Sprinkle with chopped onions to serve.

Step 2 Divide the meat mixture into 16 equal pieces. Work on a floured surface.

Step 3 Flour hands well and roll each piece into a ball.

Step 5 Brown the meatballs on all sides in hot oil until a good colour.

Cook's Notes

Time
Preparation takes about 25 minutes and cooking time about 20 minutes.

Serving Ideas
Serve with rice, refried beans or guacamole. Drizzle with sour cream if desired.

Freezing
Prepare and cook the meatballs and allow to cool completely. Place meatballs on baking sheets and place in the freezer until firm. Transfer to freezer containers, label and store for up to 3 months. Defrost in the refrigerator and reheat according to the recipe.

SERVES 4

MEXICAN KEBABS

Kebabs are a favourite barbecue food
almost everywhere. The spice mixture and
sauce give these their Mexican flavour.

450g/1lb pork or lamb, cut into 5cm/2 inch pieces
120g/4oz large button mushrooms, left whole
2 medium onions, quartered
8 bay leaves
5ml/1 tsp cocoa powder
10ml/2 tsps chilli powder
1.25ml/¼ tsp garlic powder
2.5ml/½ tsp dried marjoram
Salt and pepper
90ml/6 tbsps oil
180g/6oz cooked rice
½ quantity Taco Sauce recipe

Step 3 Thread the meat and mushrooms onto skewers, alternating with onions and bay leaves.

Step 4 Place the kebabs on a lightly oiled rack and grill until meat is tender and onions are cooked. Baste frequently, using a small brush.

Step 1 Place meat and mushrooms in a deep bowl with the marinade ingredients and stir to coat thoroughly.

1. Place meat and mushrooms in a bowl. Add the bay leaves, cocoa, chilli powder, garlic powder, marjoram and seasoning to the oil and stir to coat all the ingredients with the marinade.

2. Cover the bowl and leave to marinate at least 6 hours, preferably overnight.

3. Remove meat, mushrooms and bay leaves from the marinade and reserve it. Thread onto skewers, alternating meat, onions, mushrooms and bay leaves.

4. Place under a preheated grill for 15-20 minutes, turning frequently until cooked to desired doneness. If using pork, the meat must be thoroughly cooked and not served pink. Baste with reserved marinade.

5. Mix hot rice with taco sauce and spoon onto a warm serving dish. Place the kebabs on top of the rice to serve.

Cook's Notes

Time
Preparation takes about 15 minutes, with at least 6 hours to marinate meat and mushrooms. Cooking time for the rice is about 12 minutes and 15-20 minutes for the meat.

Preparation
The kebabs may be cooked on an outdoor barbecue grill, if desired.

Variation
Add pieces of red or green pepper, cherry tomatoes or sliced courgettes to the kebabs and cut meat into slightly smaller pieces so everything cooks in the same length of time.

SERVES 4

Spare Ribs in Chilli & Cream Sauce

Unsweetened cocoa lends colour and depth to a sauce for ribs that's slightly more sophisticated than the usual barbecue sauce.

1kg/2¼lbs spare ribs
5ml/1 tsp cocoa powder
15g/1 tbsp flour
2.5ml/½ tsp cumin
2.5ml/½ tsp paprika
2.5ml/½ tsp dried oregano, crushed
Salt and pepper
280ml/½ pint warm water
30ml/2 tbsps thin honey
30ml/2 tbsps double cream
Lime wedges and watercress for garnish

Step 2 Cook the ribs until the meat is tender to the point of a knife and the sauce is reduced.

Step 3 Place ribs on a chopping board and cut into pieces.

Step 1 Cook the ribs until well browned. Remove from the roasting pan and pour off the fat.

1. Leave the ribs in whole slabs and roast at 200°C/400°F/Gas Mark 6 for 20-25 minutes, or until well browned. Drain off all the excess fat.

2. Blend together the cocoa, flour, cumin, paprika, oregano, seasoning, water and honey and pour over the ribs. Lower the temperature to 180°C/350°F/Gas Mark 4

and cook ribs for a further 30 minutes, until the sauce has reduced and the ribs are tender.

3. Cut the ribs into pieces and arrange on a serving dish.

4. Pour the cream into the sauce in the roasting pan and place over moderate heat. Bring to the boil and pour over the ribs.

5. Garnish with lime wedges and serve.

Cook's Notes

Time
Preparation takes about 20 minutes, cooking takes 50-55 minutes.

Preparation
Ribs may be cooked for the last 30 minutes on an outdoor barbecue grill.

Serving Ideas
Serve with rice and an avocado or tomato salad.

SERVES 6

MINUTE STEAKS WITH TACO SAUCE

A quick meal needn't be ordinary. Prepare taco sauce ahead
and keep it on hand to add last-minute spice to a meal.

Full quantity Taco Sauce recipe
30g/1oz butter or margarine
30ml/2 tbsps oil
6 minute steaks
Salt and pepper
120g/4oz button mushrooms, left whole
Chopped parsley or coriander leaves

1. Prepare taco sauce according to the recipe directions.
Heat the butter or margarine and oil together in a large
frying or sauté pan. Season the steaks with salt and pepper
and fry 2 or 3 at a time for 2-3 minutes on each side, or to
desired doneness.

2. Remove the steaks to a warm serving dish and add the
mushrooms to the pan. Sauté over high heat to brown
lightly, remove and keep warm.

3. Drain most of the fat from the pan and pour in the taco
sauce. Place over low heat until just bubbling. Spoon over
the steaks.

4. Top the steaks with the sautéed mushrooms and
sprinkle over parsley or coriander before serving.

Step 1 Cook
steaks over high
heat until done to
desired degree.
To check, make a
small cut in the
centre.

Step 2 Add
mushrooms to the
pan and cook
briskly until lightly
browned.

Cook's Notes

Time
Preparation takes about 15
minutes. Cooking time takes
6-9 minutes per batch of steaks and
about 10 minutes more to finish off the
dish.

Variation
Substitute turkey escalopes
for the steaks, if desired, and
cook until juices run clear.

Serving Ideas
Serve with rice or flour tortillas.

SERVES 4

LEG OF LAMB WITH CHILLI SAUCE

Give Sunday roast lamb a completely
different taste with a spicy orange sauce.

1kg/2¼lb leg of lamb

Marinade

5ml/1 tsp cocoa powder
1.25ml/¼ tsp cayenne pepper
2.5ml/½ tsp ground cumin
2.5ml/½ tsp paprika
2.5ml/½ tsp ground oregano
140ml/¼ pint water
140ml/¼ pint orange juice
140ml/¼ pint red wine
1 clove of garlic, crushed
30g/2 tbsps brown sugar
15ml/1 tbsp cornflour
Pinch salt
Orange slices and coriander to garnish

1. If the lamb has a lot of surface fat, trim slightly with a sharp knife. If possible, remove the paper-thin skin on the outside of the lamb. Place lamb in a shallow dish.

2. Mix together the marinade ingredients, except cornflour, and pour over the lamb, turning it well to coat completely. Cover and refrigerate for 12-24 hours, turning occasionally.

3. Drain the lamb, reserving the marinade, and place in a roasting pan. Cook in a preheated 180°C/350°F/Gas Mark 4 oven for about 2 hours until meat is cooked according to taste.

4. Baste occasionally with the marinade and pan juices.

5. Remove lamb to a serving dish and keep warm. Skim the fat from the top of the roasting pan with a large spoon and discard.

6. Pour remaining marinade into the pan juices in the roasting pan and bring to the boil, stirring to loosen the sediment. Mix cornflour with a small amount of water and add some of the liquid from the roasting pan. Gradually stir cornflour mixture into the pan and bring back to the boil.

7. Cook, stirring constantly, until thickened and clear. Add more orange juice, wine or water as necessary.

8. Garnish the lamb with orange slices and sprigs of coriander. Pour over some of the sauce and serve the rest separately.

Step 6 Pour the marinade into the roasting pan and bring to the boil. Scrape to remove browned juices.

Step 7 Cook, stirring constantly, until thickened and clear. Add more orange juice, wine or water as necessary.

Cook's Notes

 Time
Preparation takes about 15 minutes, with 12-24 hours for the lamb to marinate. Cooking takes about 2 hours for the lamb and 20 minutes to finish the sauce.

Cook's Tip
The marinade ingredients can also be used with beef or poultry.

 Serving Ideas
Serve with rice or boiled potatoes and vegetables.

SERVES 6

MANGO FOOL

To cool the palate after a spicy
Mexican meal, the taste of mango,
lime, ginger and cream is perfect.

2 ripe mangoes
1 small piece fresh ginger, peeled and shredded
120g/4oz sifted icing sugar
Juice of ½ a lime
280ml/½ pint double cream

Step 1 Cut the mango in half, slicing around the stone. Scoop out pulp.

1. Cut the mangoes in half, cutting around the stone. Scoop out the pulp into a bowl, blender or food processor. Reserve two slices.

2. Add the ginger, icing sugar and lime juice and purée in the blender or food processor until smooth. Use a hand blender or electric mixer in the bowl, pushing mixture through a sieve afterwards, if necessary.

3. Whip the cream until soft peaks form and fold into the

Step 3 Whisk the cream to soft peaks.

Step 3 Fold the cream into the mango purée using a large spoon or rubber spatula.

mango purée.

4. Divide the mixture between 6 glass serving dishes and leave in the refrigerator for 1 hour before serving.

5. Cut the reserved mango slices into 6 smaller slices or pieces and garnish the fool.

Cook's Notes

Time
Preparation takes about 20 minutes. Fool should be refrigerated 1 hour before serving.

Serving Ideas
Accompany with biscuits.

Watchpoint
When whipping cream, refrigerate it for at least 2 hours before use. Overwhisked cream turns to butter, so whisk slowly and watch carefully.

SERVES 6

TROPICAL FRUIT SALAD

A refreshing mixture of exotic fruits is the
most popular sweet in Mexico. Add tequila or
triple sec to the syrup for a special occasion.

½ cantaloup or honeydew melon, cubed or made into
   balls
½ small fresh pineapple, peeled, cored and cubed or
   sliced
120g/4oz fresh strawberries, hulled and halved (leave
   whole, if small)
1 mango, peeled and sliced or cubed
225g/8oz watermelon, seeded and cubed
120g/4oz guava or papaya, peeled and cubed
2 oranges, peeled and segmented
1 prickly pear, peeled and sliced (optional)
120g/4oz sugar
140ml/¼ pint water
Grated rind and juice of 1 lemon
30g/2 tbsps chopped pecans to garnish (optional)

1. To make melon balls, cut melons in half and scoop out
seeds and discard them. To use a melon baller, press
cutting edge firmly into the melon flesh and twist around to
scoop out round pieces.

2. It is easy to core the pineapple if it is first cut into quarters.
Use a serrated fruit knife to cut the point off the quarter,
removing the core. Slice off the peel. Cut into slices or cubes
and mix with the other fruit.

3. Dissolve the sugar in the water over gentle heat and
when the mixture is no longer grainy, leave it to cool
completely.

4. Add lemon rind and juice to the sugar syrup and pour
over the prepared fruit. Refrigerate well before serving.
Sprinkle with chopped nuts, if desired.

Step 1 Cut melon
in half and scoop
out seeds.

Step 1 Twist
melon baller
around to scoop
out round shaped
pieces.

Step 2 Cut out
pineapple core
with a serrated
fruit knife.

Cook's Notes

Time
Preparation takes about 45
minutes. The syrup will take
about 5-7 minutes to make.

Preparation
Allow the syrup to cool
completely before adding any
fruit. Hot syrup will cook the fruit and
draw out the juices.

Variation
Use other varieties of fruit,
choosing whatever is in
season.

SERVES 4

MEXICAN CHOCOLATE FLAN

Flan in Mexico is a moulded custard with
a caramel sauce. Chocolate and cinnamon
is a favourite flavour combination.

120g/4oz sugar
30ml/2 tbsps water
Juice of ½ a lemon
280ml/½ pint milk
60g/2oz plain chocolate
1 cinnamon stick
2 whole eggs
2 egg yolks
60g/4 tbsps sugar

1. Combine the first amount of sugar with the water and lemon juice in a small, heavy-based saucepan.

2. Cook over gentle heat until the sugar starts to dissolve. Swirl the pan from time to time, but don't stir.

3. Once the sugar liquifies, bring the syrup to the boil and cook until golden brown.

4. While preparing the syrup, heat 4 ramekin dishes in a 180°C/350°F/Gas Mark 4 oven. When the syrup is ready, pour into the dishes and swirl to coat the sides and base evenly. Leave to cool at room temperature.

5. Chop the chocolate into small pieces and heat with the milk and cinnamon, stirring occasionally to help chocolate dissolve.

6. Whisk the whole eggs and the yolks together with the remaining sugar until slightly frothy. Gradually whisk in the chocolate milk. Remove cinnamon.

7. Pour the chocolate custard carefully into the ramekin dishes and place them in a roasting pan of hand-hot water.

8. Place the roasting pan in the oven and bake the custards until just slightly wobbly in the centre, about 20-30 minutes. Cool at room temperature and refrigerate for several hours or overnight before serving. Loosen custards carefully from the sides of the dishes and invert into serving plates. Shake to allow custard to drop out.

Step 3 Boil sugar syrup rapidly until golden brown.

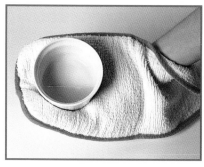

Step 4 Pour caramel into warmed dishes and swirl to coat base and sides.

 *Cook's Notes*

 Time
Preparation takes about 30 minutes, cooking takes about 35-40 minutes.

 Variation
Leave out chocolate, if desired, for cinnamon flan.

! **Watchpoint**
Do not allow custard to over-cook or it will form a tough skin on top. If the oven temperature is too high, it will cause the custard to boil and spoil the texture.

 Serving Ideas
Garnish with pecans or chocolate curls. Also good with fruit such as raspberries or bananas with chocolate; peaches or strawberries with cinnamon.

SERVES 4

TEQUILA SUNRISE

120ml/4 fl oz tequila
430ml/¾ pint orange juice
60ml/4 tbsp Cointreau or Grand Marnier
Ice
60ml/4 tbsps Grenadine syrup

1. Crush ice and place in a blender with the tequila, orange juice and orange liqueur and mix thoroughly.

2. Chill 4 tall glasses in the refrigerator and when cold, pour in the cocktail mixture.

3. Hold each glass at a tilt and carefully pour 15ml/1 tbsp

Hold glass at a tilt and carefully pour grenadine down the side for the tequila sunrise.

Grenadine syrup down one side. Syrup will sink to the bottom giving the drink its sunrise effect.

SERVES 2

MARGARITA

1 lime
Coarse salt
120ml/4 fl oz tequila
30ml/2 tbsps triple sec
4 ice cubes

1. Squeeze the lime and moisten the rim of two cocktail

Rub rims of cocktail glasses with half a lime to moisten for the margarita.

glasses with a small amount of juice.

2. Pour salt onto a plate and dip in the moistened rims of the glasses, turning to coat evenly. Refrigerate to chill thoroughly.

3. Crush 4 ice cubes and place in a blender with the tequila and triple sec. Process until well blended and slushy. Pour into the chilled glasses and serve immediately.

Pour salt onto a plate and dip in the moistened rims of the glasses.